OBAMA'S TIME

Obama's Time

. . .

A HISTORY

Morton Keller

UNIVERSITY PRESS

OXFORD
UNIVERSITY PRESS

Oxford University Press is a department of the University of Oxford.
It furthers the University's objective of excellence in research, scholarship,
and education by publishing worldwide.

Oxford New York
Auckland Cape Town Dar es Salaam Hong Kong Karachi
Kuala Lumpur Madrid Melbourne Mexico City Nairobi
New Delhi Shanghai Taipei Toronto

With offices in
Argentina Austria Brazil Chile Czech Republic France Greece
Guatemala Hungary Italy Japan Poland Portugal Singapore
South Korea Switzerland Thailand Turkey Ukraine Vietnam

Published in the United States of America by
Oxford University Press
198 Madison Avenue, New York, NY 10016

Library of Congress Cataloging-in-Publication Data
Keller, Morton.
Obama's time : a history / Morton Keller.
p. cm.
Summary: "A pioneering historical assessment of the Obama presidency"—
Provided by publisher.
Includes bibliographical references.
ISBN 978-0-19-938337-5 (hardback : acid-free paper) 1. United States—Politics
and government—2009- 2. Obama, Barack—Political and social views. I. Title.
E907.K44 2014
973.932—dc23

2014006780

1 3 5 7 9 8 6 4 2

Printed in the United States of America on acid-free paper

In memory of James Q. Wilson

Contents

. . .

Preface

...

OBAMA'S FIRST TERM is history; his second term is a work in progress. Is it too early for a historian to unfold his telescope, reverse it, and take a longer-perspective view of a still-evolving event?

This book rests on the assumption that it is possible to write history while the subject is very much around; still, so to speak, warm. Admittedly, the argument against trying to do so is compelling. What good is history without the perspective of lapsed time? Asked his view of the French Revolution, Zhou-en-Lai famously responded: "It is too early to tell." (Though he may well have thought he was being asked about the events of Paris 1968, not Paris 1789.)

I hold that he was wrong in two senses. It is *never* too early for a first stab at telling; it is *always* too early to tell once and for all.

This is a preliminary shot at a story that will be recounted from innumerable perspectives in years to come. Let me offer two justifications for doing it. The first is that, in a culture where most writing about politics is tediously one-sided, there is something to be said for the historian's ideal of trying to understand and explain without being driven primarily by prejudices and predilections: in other words, to be more like a judge than a prosecuting attorney.

Of course I have my own beliefs. But when I think and write as a historian, I try to put those beliefs aside or at least (being human) to hold them in check. My goal is not to score points but to seek a historical perspective, which, however hobbled by its temporal closeness to its subject, may have some lasting value in part because it is of the time that it examines.

I have sought to rely on what my best friend and severest critic has called my propensity to be pathologically fair-minded. If Obama's supporters find this book to be overly critical of his administration, I shall be content. My content will only grow if his opponents find it to be too favorable.

Then there is my second apologia: the sheer joy of trying something that is not conventionally approved. I retired from being a professor of history more than a decade ago. Since then, against the normal expectation of what advanced age is supposed to do to you, I have found it liberating to write not with my academic peers in mind but that much more challenging and amorphous target, the general reader.

Academic historians, like the rest of the professoriate, are for the most part confined to the tenets of discourse and perception defined by their discipline. That is a pity. It is clear that there is a hunger (or at least an appetite) for history that both tells a story and explains the world.

Analysis and historical comparison, not storytelling, are my stock in trade. But anyone who lays claim to being a historian has, I think, a responsibility to aim for clarity and readability to the limits of his talent. That I have sought to do.

Enough high-flying; now for the nitty-gritty. This is an early attempt to tell the story of Obama's presidency up to now and to speculate on the likely course of what remains of his second term. I didn't—I couldn't—rely on that standard historian's source, the archives of participants. They're still not available or exist as e-mails in the Internet cloud.

Nor have I tried to emulate the good journalist's tool of extensive interviewing, as Ronald Sussman, Robert Woodward, and others have so ably done. Instead I have gathered, day by day, the on-the-scene, as-it-is-happening reports and analyses by journalists and pundits of the unfolding story of Obama's presidency: what has been called the first rough draft of history. Relying on this raw material and on my understanding of the American political system, I have sought to write a history of Obama's presidency and the political world in which it moves: in short, of Obama's time.

The Internet, with its attendant army of journalists and bloggers, has made this way of doing things possible on a scale inconceivable in the pre-Internet Dark Ages. So all thanks to that intrusive, vulgar, unreliable, indispensable artifact of the modern world.

Thanks as well to that archaic survivor, the readiness of friends, colleagues, and strangers who helped out by responding to my questions and reading my prose, among them, historian Stephan Thernstrom, political scientists Sidney Milkis and Mo Fiorina, Oxford Press editor David McBride, and Phyllis Keller, the last not only, as already noted, my best friend and severest critic, but also my severest friend and best critic.

Introduction

. . .

> Continuity with the past is not a duty, it is only a necessity.
>
> —Oliver Wendell Holmes

> I wisht I was a German, an' believed in machinery.
>
> — Mr. Dooley

WHAT DO I have to impart in this book? Historians generally don't put their conclusions up front; otherwise, how could they live up to their professional obligation to lessen the interest and attention of their readers? But as I said, age and retirement have liberated me from lots of conventions, including that one.

Oliver Wendell Holmes's aphorism conveys the essence of my first theme. Even so once-born a president as Barack Obama, with notable communication skills, remarkably few ties to the mainstream politics of his time, and a messianic desire to strike out in new directions, has been circumscribed by old devils: the institutional surround of the presidency and party politics, a polarized political culture, the entangling web of economic and ideological interests, and the constant intrusion of unexpected developments.

The second major theme is captured in Mr. Dooley's comment. The core belief of the Obama administration is in the power of the national government—of "machinery"—to do social good. Adhering to and indeed expanding this goal has been Job One of the Obama presidency. But it has had to make its way against a strong countercurrent of opposition. Here, too, the weight of the past and the contingencies of the present have set the tone of Obama's time.

THE PRESIDENT

Obama: What in his personality, experience, and ideology makes him tick? How has he conducted his presidency? Where does it fit in the larger historical context of the office? How has he identified with and been influenced by his predecessors?

Obama's presidential self-image is very much that of an academic: a teacher with a message to impart and a mission to lead the national student body. To a lesser degree he has been influenced by his relatively radical and notably limited political past. He raised large hopes that he had the brains and skills to sell his message and convert it into policy.

The fact that Obama is the nation's first African-American president is of great though as yet difficult to measure import. To what degree has this shaped his presidency? A number of Obama's closest confidants—Valerie Jarrett, Eric Holder, and not least his wife, Michelle—share that identity. He has had an impact on the political participation of blacks comparable to that of Al Smith and John F. Kennedy on the nation's Catholics. Yet his signature policies—the Stimulus, Obamacare, and Dodd-Frank—speak to national rather than racial or ethnic concerns. His rhetoric has dwelt on "the middle class" rather than on the poor, black or otherwise.

Like his closest presidential analogue Woodrow Wilson, Obama won a second term with a vote (though a diminished one) of public approval. His youth, fluency, and Now persona continue to have wide appeal. As Wagner (so Mark Twain observed) was better than he sounds, Obama is more popular than his policies. But his place in history depends on more than this. Will his early claim to a New Foundation resonate as has FDR's New Dealer LBJ's Great Society? The record thus far suggests not.

GOVERNMENT

How has American government fared during Obama's presidency? What is new and what is familiar in his relations with Congress, his cabinet and his staff, the bureaucracy, and the courts? How has American federalism functioned in a time of substantial growth in the goals and resources of the national government?

Whatever his transformative aspirations, Obama quickly found that governing is encased in a cake of practice and precedent that long preceded him, obtrusively coexists with him, and is sure to outlast him.

Obama's approach to policy and governance is steeped in the verities of the twentieth-century Democratic reform tradition. His pole star is the large, active welfare state. And for all his populist rhetoric, big government, big unions, big business, and big media are prominent players in the Obama presidency.

The Republican opposition has been heavily buffeted by the winds of economic and cultural change. The Tea Party perspective has given new vigor to a hostility to government that is visceral but often detached from the demands of contemporary American life. If Obama's liberalism appears to be locked into the worldview of the large, activist, centralized twentieth-century state, Republican–Tea Party conservatism shows a comparable devotion to the precepts of nineteenth-century laissez-faire.

It is in the states and cities, afflicted by a severe fiscal crisis, over-heavy commitments and under-heavy revenue, that a new style of government less committed to the big-state assumptions of the past century has begun to make itself heard. How far this will go is anyone's guess.

Governing is intimately linked to legislation: the creation of policy, domestic and foreign. What is Obama's record here, and (again) how does it compare with his predecessors? Is it best seen as building on the FDR–New Deal legacy, perpetuated by Truman, Kennedy, and Johnson? Or has he deviated from that legacy, as Carter and Clinton did before him?

Obama came into office determined to do big things, from universal health care and cap and trade to immigration and education reform. But he was immediately plunged into a banking-financial-mortgage-jobs crisis that was not of his doing but quickly became his responsibility.

Whether the Stimulus was the job-creating, economy jump-starting, technology-transforming elixir that its supporters claim is arguable. But it resonates with FDR's relief programs, just as Obama's health-care reform and Dodd-Frank financial regulation act summon up memories of and comparisons with the New Deal's Social Security Act and its banking and financial reforms.

The difficulty of implementing these ambitious projects reminds us that modern bureaucracy is prone to systemic problems of implementation and to the iron law of unexpected consequences. Note, for instance, the sudden rise of fracking and abundant domestic shale gas and oil as challenges to Obama's clean/renewable energy vision. Or the travails of Obamacare's implementation and the uncertainties surrounding Dodd-Frank.

As the reality of the Great Recession altered the domestic policy of Obama's first term, so have the ever-changing facts of international life shaped the course of his foreign policy. Here, too, the dictates of the world as it is clash with his messianic impulses.

Is it appropriate to speak of an Obama Doctrine governing our relations abroad, as it was to speak of the Truman-Eisenhower-Kennedy-Johnson-Nixon-Carter-Reagan responses to the Cold War? Is Obama's foreign policy more notable for its deviations from or its adherence to that of his predecessor George W. Bush?

The dark Bush days saw the War on Terror, Guantanamo Bay, targeted assassinations of Islamic terrorists, domestic wiretapping, and touchy relationships with the Arab world, Russia, and China. The hopeful Obama succession has seen the War on Terror, Guantanamo Bay, targeted assassinations of Islamic terrorists, domestic wiretapping, and touchy relationships. . . .

POLITICS

Finally there is the realm of politics. Have elections in the Obama years followed established modern patterns? If not, how have they differed? What has been the impact of the media, of advocacy groups, of campaign organization, of money? What may we expect to happen next?

I don't approach these questions from the view that Obama's presidency is a resplendent event, as do Jonathan Alter in *The Promise* and *The Center Holds*, or Michael Grunwald in *The New New Deal.* Nor do I see it as the devil's spawn, as do Edward Klein in *The Amateur* or Dinesh D'Souza in *Obama's America.* I don't think the GOP is beyond the pale, as Thomas Mann and Norman Ornstein do in *It's Even Worse Than It Looks*, or that the Democrats are something similar, as Jay Cost does in *Spoiled Rotten.*

Surely there is room for a more analytical way of looking at politics in the Obama years. I argued in a previous book, *America's Three Regimes*, that since the New Deal and World War II we have moved from a party-dominated to a populist politics. By this I mean that in the past, bosses and party machines called the turn over who ran for office, what the issues were, and how elections were run and paid for. Today autonomous candidates and outside players (the media, advocacy groups, monied ideological political action committees) are more prone to influence these things.

Party conventions have given way to primaries as the way to choose the candidates. Candidate-run money-raising has replaced party-run patronage and funding. Campaign foot soldiers are less likely to be party hacks and servitors and more likely to be special-cause hacks and servitors. Third parties are no longer necessary, because the more single-mindedly ideological major parties meet the need. Has this evolution ebbed, or is it likely to by the end of Obama's time? No, and possibly.

The most common cliché of our political age is that politics are uniquely polarized. This may be true of the presidency, Congress, state governments, and the parties. But is it true of the voters?

The electorate's ideological and party inclinations have been measured by decades of polling, and a few patterns are clear. There has been a slow but steady rise in the number of voters who identify as Independents. More Americans consider themselves Democrats than Republicans, yet more Americans consider themselves conservative than liberal. On issues such as abortion and the role of government, most voters occupy a middle-ground position.

Then why are our parties so polarized? Why don't they seize the day and set out to woo the moderate center, instead of endlessly catering to their presumably secure ideological tails?

One answer is the decline of the old party-dominated political culture. The media, advocacy groups, and big sources of money have little interest in fostering compromise or moderation by the parties and candidates that they support. Their numerical and financial clout lies in their ability to appeal to their ideological brethren, not to a broader, more diverse constituency. This is true of Fox News and the *New York Times*, of the National Rifle Association and the Sierra Club, of the Koch brothers and George Soros.

The electoral consequence of these developments is evident. Obama's 2008 victory was not a party or policy triumph. It was the product of his appeal to voting groups defined by ethnicity, age, and cultural predisposition; to big players in the popular culture (the mainstream media, Hollywood, TV); to an unpopular incumbent president and a less than compelling opponent; and perhaps most of all to a financial collapse with timing that made it seem like the direct interposition of God into human affairs.

The 2010 off-year election underlined the fact that Obama brought no profound change to the prevailing reality of declining party identity and a more populist politics. If the fresh persona and post-partisan message of Obama was the most notable element in 2008, the Tea Party reaction against his policies played that role in 2010.

Obama's 2012 reelection confirms this view of the American political present and its likely near future. Money, get-out-the-vote organization, the opposition's ineptitude, and Obama's personal and cultural appeal carried the day.

There is little evidence of larger shifts in political or social ideology, of the sort that accompanied the Democratic age of Andrew Jackson, the Republican age of Abraham Lincoln, or the Democratic age of FDR. Obama's time as president is winding down. But there is good cause to doubt if it will come to be known as Obama's Age.

CHAPTER ONE

. . .

Obama

WE BEGIN WITH the president: his persona, his agenda.

Extraordinarily high expectations attended Barack Obama's January 2009 inauguration. It came at a time of economic crisis that, however less devastating, evoked memories of the Great Depression. Popular dissatisfaction with Obama's predecessor George W. Bush echoed—but again, not at the same level—that enjoyed (or not enjoyed) by Herbert Hoover in 1932. Special, too, was the widespread national pride over the ascension of the first African-American president.

By any measure, Obama was an unusual public figure. The media and the educated classes in particular had a strong belief in his unique talents and the prospect of an epochal presidency. (So, apparently, did Obama. Early on he asked a group of historians what it took to be a transformative president.) His staff had even higher expectations. With minimal irony, they referred to him as Black Jesus.[1]

Family and friends, too, were worshipful. According to *New York Times* reporter Jodi Kantor, "Michelle told Oprah Winfrey before the 2008 election: 'The question isn't whether Barack Obama is ready to be president. The question is whether *we're* ready.'" His closest confidante, Valerie Jarrett, thought that Obama was "bored to death his whole life. He's just too talented to do what ordinary people do."[2]

National Endowment for the Arts chair Rocco Landesman observed that as a memoirist Obama was "the most powerful writer since Julius Caesar." More widely noted was TV commentator Chris Matthews's confession that when Obama spoke, he "felt this thrill going up my leg." *The New Yorker*'s Ryan Lizza concluded that Obama's "post-post-partisan Presidency," based on "working the system, not changing it," made his first two years "one of the most successful legislative periods in modern history. Among other achievements, he has saved the economy from depression, passed universal health care, and reformed Wall Street."[3]

There were times when Obama committed all-too-human gaffes, as when he said that the Union had 57 states, that Austria's language was Austrian, and that there was a president of Canada. But the media was not disposed to make much of these solecisms. After all, it was not as if they had come from George W. Bush.[4]

Hype aside, Obama did project a compelling presidential persona of intelligence, eloquence, and confidence. He would maintain a place in public confidence and esteem that consistently outstripped the popularity of his policies.

Books on Obama and his presidency generally reflect the prevailing adulatory tone, with occasional critiques that dismiss him in comparably over-the-top language. At one end of the spectrum is Harvard historian James Kloppenberg's elevation of Obama as the product of a philosophical liberalism that drew on Alexis de Tocqueville, William James, John Dewey, John Rawls, Reinhold Niebuhr, and (to add a dash of radical spice) Saul Alinsky and Jurgen Habermas. At the other is conservative Dinesh d'Souza's portrayal of "a made-to-order front man for contemporary, upscale, shy-about-itself, *nouveau* socialism": the product of an anticolonialist radical left tradition embodied in the writings of Frantz Fanon and Edward Said and the actions and words of 1960s' Weatherman William Ayers and the Reverend Jeremiah Wright.[5]

In between but strongly sympathetic are David Remnick's *The Bridge: The Life and Rise of Barack Obama* (2010) and David Maraniss's *Barack Obama: The Story* (2012), the most substantial biographies to date. Remnick grounds Obama in the civil rights movement (Obama: "it's *my* story"), drawing his title from John Lewis's observation that "Barack Obama is what comes at the end of that bridge in Selma," where blacks seeking freedom memorably confronted white police seeking to deprive them of it.

The flood of books on Obama sorts out in other ways as well. Like the Kloppenberg intellectual biography, the first tranche of psychobiographies tended to the eulogistic. One of them spoke of Obama's "obsessive bipartisan disorder" as contrasted with the "us/them psychology" of the Bush presidency.[6]

Obama may have come into office with more radical instincts than his predecessors or more than he let on to the public. But he was soon constrained by the realities of the presidency and American politics, which bridled change and imposed continuity—a theme that emerged in books dealing more with his presidency than his persona.

Most of these studies are quite favorable. But a note of dissatisfaction, even disappointment, intruded early. With the passage of time, more critical works emerged, dwelling as much on his inexperience and remove as on his radicalism (or lack of it).[7]

Beyond special pleading for or against, and the limits of journalism, is there a broader basis for evaluation and analysis? One of these, surely, is the character of the incumbent. Why has he performed as he did? The other theme to be explored is his conduct of his presidency and its relation to the political tradition to which he supposedly belongs.

I. THE CONTENT OF HIS CHARACTER

Over the course of his presidency, the most striking change in the political class's perception of Obama has been the attention paid to his remove from the normal give-and-take of American politics. Early on, Washington was "thick with stories about Obama's insularity and distance." One senator, asked if he could name someone who really knew Obama, said he could not.

This is not to say that Obama was indifferent to politics. He played the game as intensely and as well as anyone. But he did so on his own terms, with little regard for the political tradition of the Democratic party. In this he was distant indeed from his Democratic predecessors FDR, Truman, JFK, and LBJ and closer to Carter and Clinton. He reinforces the view that a more autonomous, populist political culture has replaced the previous strongly party-defined one.[8]

Acerbic *New York Times* columnist Maureen Dowd noted a disconnect between Obama's persona and his performance. In January 2012, three years on in his first term, she found him still "cool, joyous, funny, connected." But he also was a deeply divisive president (a May 2012 Gallup poll would confirm that), unable "to read America's panic and its thirst for a strong leader." Sympathetic journalist Ron Suskind concluded that Obama's problem in dealing with the recession was "in guiding the analysis toward what a president is paid, and elected, to do: make tough decisions."[9]

Every century or so we have what might be called an intellectuals' president: Thomas Jefferson in the early 1800s, Theodore Roosevelt and Woodrow Wilson in the early 1900s, Barack Obama in the early 2000s. Only Wilson was a professor. But Jefferson thought that founding the University of Virginia was an act on a par with his Virginia Statute for Religious Freedom and the Declaration of Independence. Obama's approach to his presidency often has had a profoundly academic cast.[10]

He has an unusually broad, removed view of his office, seeing it as the abode of a philosopher king and not just a rent-seeking politician. His Hope and Change campaign slogan, his New Foundation program label, were more than rodomontade. They were how he defined his presidency.

This should not be surprising. After all, much of Obama's adult life was spent not in politics or business but in higher education, as a student and law school lecturer. He flourished in those venues because of his intelligence, his way with words, his self-confidence. He received a steady stream of recognition from an affirmative action–saturated academy, hungry to bestow its laurels on someone who was a person of talent as well as a person of color. Nor did it do his self-esteem any harm to move from the Illinois state legislature to the presidency in four years, as if guided by a special Providence.

Evidence of Obama's academic bent abounds. He has kept as far away as he could from that intensely political and not easily controllable exercise, the presidential press conference. The communications-challenged George W. Bush ventured into that realm 11 times in his first three years in office; the far more well-spoken Obama did so a modest 17 times. For seven weeks and more in the election summer of 2012, he took no substantive question from the White House press corps. In contrast, FDR had 337 press conferences in his first term, a third of the thousand that he conducted in the course of his presidency.

Obama prefers one-on-one interviews with journalists—office hours, so to speak, where he is in firm control. He had 408 of them by the end of February 2012, more than Clinton and George W. Bush combined.[11]

Reporter Ron Suskind observes that Obama's favorite venue is "the prepared speech, meticulously crafted and delivered": the political equivalent of a classroom lecture. Liberal columnist Robert Kuttner called his campaign address on the financial crisis "Roosevelt quality: the president as teacher-in-chief."[12]

After the 2010 election—in a sense Obama's midterm exam (and indeed it was often referred to as "the midterm")—he sat down with Suskind to meditate on the lessons to be learned from that "shellacking." His response was very much that of a professor, secure in his command of his subject matter, ruminating on his students' inability to absorb what they had been taught.

His failure, he said, "was less on the policy front and more on the communications front." He had been elected "because I told a story to the American people . . . People felt I had connected our current predicaments with the broader arc of American history." The demands of day-to-day problem-solving frayed that narrative. Now the necessity remained "to tell a story to the American people about where we are and where we are going."

Several years later, Obama was asked in a TV interview what he considered to be his biggest misstep. "The mistake of my first term," he replied, "was thinking that this job was just about getting the policy right. . . . But the nature of this office is also to tell a story to the American people that gives them a sense of unity and purpose and optimism, especially during tough times."[13]

I can't prove that Obama identifies more with past presidents than his predecessors did. But I believe that he has a special need for validation from previous authorities, as academics are prone to have. He frequently summons up the shades of transformational chief executives. This "channeling" (dictionary definition: "The act or practice of serving as a medium through which a spirit guide purportedly communicates with living persons") is the product of a complex mix of self-regard, initial inexperience, Republican obduracy, and the institutional weight of the presidency.

From 2007, when he announced his candidacy in Lincoln's Springfield, to 2013, when he took his second oath of office on Lincoln's Bible, the Great Emancipator was on Obama's mind. When he came into office, he closely identified with FDR's 100 Days as a model of crisis management. He took note of how FDR let all know he was in charge, put people first, restored confidence. He aimed to set a progressive agenda for the new century, as FDR had for the previous one. He was not alone in this. *The New York Times* and the *Washington Post* conjoined "Obama" and "100 Days" almost 900 times in the first six months of 2009.

Obama has sought for and found meaning in "his peer group, his competitors": FDR, "much of whose New Deal did not work, but who restored the confidence of the American people; or John F. Kennedy, whose economic policies are forgotten but not his Peace Corps." In a *60 Minutes* interview in December 2011, he declared: "I would put my legislative and foreign policy accomplishments of my first two years against any president with the possible exceptions of Johnson, FDR, and Lincoln"—a self-judgment prudently edited out of the broadcast version.[14]

As difficulties mounted, and the 2010 election setback occurred, less majestic analogues came to mind. He admitted to sharing with Jimmy Carter and Clinton "the disease of being policy wonks." But "a larger and ostensibly more effective model of leadership would be a star to guide him in the years ahead."[15]

Obama identified briefly with Theodore Roosevelt's New Nationalism of 1911–1912, and more frequently with, of all people, Ronald Reagan. During their primary battle, Hillary Clinton accused him of the sin of "admiring Ronald Reagan." He envied Reagan for being "very comfortable in playing the role of president." His predecessor took pride in "not engaging in a lot of symbolic gestures, but rather thinking practically." Obama thought that his own "symbols and gestures mattered as much as what my ideas were," and he believed that "leadership in this office is a matter of helping the American people feel confident," as FDR and Reagan did before him.[16]

Obama's political trajectory has been much like Woodrow Wilson's (although he has been loath to identify with that closest of predecessors). Each won an initial victory that was in good part the result of external events: the TR-Taft split in 1912, the financial collapse of 2008. Each took credit for a substantial body of legislation in his first two years in office. Each ran into big trouble in the ensuing bye-election: The GOP gained 62 seats in 1914, 63 in 2010. Each won a second term, with reduced support, against a pallid Republican opponent, and each faced a rising sea of troubles as his second term unfolded.[17]

Critics could reasonably observe that Obama, as Clemenceau said of Wilson, talks like Jesus Christ and acts like Lloyd George. But that combination should not be taken lightly. In the hands of a master—FDR enacting Social Security, or Reagan dealing with tax policy—it can produce policy results of a high order, suggesting that a statesman can be a live politician and not necessarily a dead one. Obama's equivalent task is to see to it that his health-care reform is successful. That is likely to be his greatest challenge as he serves out his presidential time.

In the wake of Obama's 2010 loss of Congress, two other past presidential records took on new significance: Harry Truman's in 1946–1948, and Bill Clinton's in 1994–1996. For all their similarities—a bad off-year defeat followed by victory in the succeeding presidential election—Truman and Clinton adopted very different models of response. Truman in 1948 ran against a Republican Congress and managed to revive enough of the FDR–New Deal coalition to win. Clinton distanced himself from the New Deal–Great Society tradition of his party—and won.

Did Obama, facing a similar political situation, repeat his 2008 message of a presidency that transcended partisanship? Or did he try to double down, Truman-style, on his liberal base? As the 2012 campaign unfolded, his choice was clear: to adopt the Truman model of strong, ideological identification and a presidential persona that outclassed his opponent: Thomas E. Dewey then, Mitt Romney now.[18]

The intensity of GOP congressional opposition provided some justification for taking a Trumanesque line. But Obama's 2010–2012 was not Truman's 1946–1948. Then the New Deal and World War II, the glue that held the Roosevelt coalition together, were still vivid memories. Nor was it Clinton's 1994–1996. Clinton's support for NAFTA, welfare and tax reform, and modest engagement overseas was a new politics for a new America, caught up in the challenges of a postindustrial economy and a post–Cold War world.

Obama's 2012 reelection has been credited with a comparable affinity to a demographically and culturally changing country. The validity of this view, confirmed (though not overwhelmingly so) by his 2012 victory, would be another test of his second term.

2. THE ORBIT OF HIS PRESIDENCY

Obama's response to the challenges of his presidency not surprisingly reflected the strengths and limitations of his persona. He ran an eminently successful 2008 campaign, though certainly it benefited from the perfect storm of Bush's unpopularity, McCain's limitations, and the financial crisis. He also enacted much of his ambitious legislative program. If the scale of what he has done does not match FDR's New Deal or LBJ's Great Society, it outdid the first terms of his Democratic predecessors Carter and Clinton.

Supporters found in Obama's early legislative victories confirmation that his was indeed a transformative presidency. So too was a substantial recasting of government: the bureaucracy, federal agencies, and their powers and responsibilities. Here was evidence that a remarkable leader was accomplishing unprecedented things. Along with his intellectual and oratorical gifts, Obama's youth and mixed racial background made him for many an unusually attractive candidate and an excitingly fresh occupant of the White House.

But he soon was confronted by the unbearable heaviness of governing. That condition, faced by every president, is the antithesis of the theme of Milan Kundera's great novel *The Unbearable Lightness of Being.* Kundera's protagonists struggle with the reality that their life—their being—is self-contained, isolated, without a mission: "light." Presidents live in a quite different world, a "heavy" one, in which the weight of past precedents, institutional surround, vested interests, and the ever-contingent course of events prevails.

Early on, the normal vicissitudes of the presidency kicked in. Legislation had to be modified or abandoned; best-laid plans of governance went awry. Obama's initial high popularity eroded; interparty rigidity rose; he relied increasingly on the power of the executive branch to circumvent legislative stalemate.

Obama may have underestimated how difficult it would be to largely alter the prevailing political environment. And while there was a substantial public desire for change, it is less clear that there was a desire to see change effected through more active and more costly government.[19]

The first benchmark in the demystification process was Obama's early decision to forego bipartisan support for his major legislative achievements: the Stimulus, Obamacare, and Dodd-Frank. This was forced on him by Republican bloody-mindedness, say his supporters; he took this course because he was a deeply ideological president, say his opponents.

The next moment of truth was the severe swing to the Republicans in the 2010 elections, widely read as the result of high unemployment, high debt, and a sluggish economy but also as a rebuke to Obama's Stimulus and health-care reform.

How did Obama respond to these challenges in the second half of his first term? He proposed no major new legislative program: no Second New Deal, no Great Society. In halfhearted homage to the Clinton precedent, he made some attempt to strike a deal with the Republican House leadership.

But he did not adopt Clinton's post-1996 election conclusion that "the era of big government is over." Instead he sought to merge a desire for more effective government with the commitment to keep it large and active. He dwelt on the need to make the American economy more competitive, to simplify the tax code, reduce the deficit, expand trade, improve the schools, and streamline government. He emphasized the development of high-speed rail, clean renewable energy, universal access to the Internet: "a New Foundation for a post-crisis economy, á la the New Deal."[20]

In short, Obama doubled down on his commitment to economic stimulus through substantial deficit spending, a search for new revenue and a reluctance to cut existing entitlement programs, forceful regulation, and subsidies for renewable energy. He may well have felt that he had no alternative, given the obduracy of an increasingly antigovernment GOP. But it reflected as well his deepest beliefs.

Obama sought to give his approach political legs by seeking to move public attention away from trillion-dollar annual deficits and an escalating national debt. Instead, he focused on the unequal distribution of wealth in the society and the need to secure more tax revenue from the rich. His tax-the-rich / protect-the-middle-class strategy had obvious political potential and stood him in good stead in the election of 2012.

It had costs as well. One was Obama's failure to meaningfully support the recommendations of his own Bowles-Simpson committee for a mix of spending cuts and revenue increases. The other was a long and ultimately fruitless attempt to carve out a compromise with the House Republicans on taxes, spending, and debt. Whoever was to blame for this, the net effect was to erode some of Obama's primary sources of public appeal: his commitment to a less polarized politics, his responsiveness to the public desire for hope and change, his ability to get things done.[21]

The charismatic campaigner of 2008 turned out as president to lack a professional politician's practiced ease with people. He was manifestly uncomfortable with the small talk, backslapping, and often faux conviviality of the political world. In this Obama was very unlike FDR, Reagan, and Clinton and more like those more buttoned-down templates Wilson, Hoover, Nixon, and Carter.

The stresses of his presidency hardly made him a more engaged leader. Observers spoke of Obama becoming a "loner president," of entering into a "self-imposed exile" with his family and his closest and oldest Chicago associates. Journalist Jodi Kantor thought that he and his wife Michelle felt "overassaulted and underappreciated."[22]

This mindset had strong psychological roots. But it also derived naturally from the parabola of Obama's career, particularly his dizzying ascent to the presidency. While he had ties (some of them questionable) to the very political world of Chicago's Democratic pols, his academic–community organizer persona set him apart. So did the rapidity of his rise, which catapulted him from one level to another before he fully assimilated to it.

Most of all, Obama is distinctive for being the first African-American president. The place of that fact—and indeed of the larger American dilemma of race—in the Obama presidency will take a long time to unravel.

The kind of African-American he is—half white, half African, brought up in Indonesia and Hawaii—sets him apart from the great majority of American blacks. Nor has he made the core issues of the black underclass a central theme of his presidency: his "middle-class" mantra hardly speaks to them or their condition.

Yet Obama has been impelled by circumstance—the black community's stake in his ascent, the satisfaction that so many whites derive from an African-American president—to pursue the dual demands of the nation that he leads and the social watershed that he represents.[23]

There is a noticeable duality as well in Obama's approach to his presidency. On the one hand he has presided over a demi-revolution in running campaigns and pushing his agenda. Organizing for America, his primary instrument for campaign fundraising and agenda support-building, was a personal rather than a party device.

Obama has appeared to turn inward over the course of his presidency: to family, to old and close associates, to familiar political themes and comfortable modes of communicating. At night he frequently holes up with his family, books, and an Internet browser.

He did make sporadic attempts to play the political game the traditional way: some cocktail parties for congressmen from the two parties; the occasional invitation to watch a Sunday football game on TV; hospitality to big donors. But by most accounts these outreaches were awkward, and over time he abandoned them. With far more enthusiasm he has used those favored instruments of contemporary mass culture talk shows and the social networks, much as FDR did radio and JFK TV.

Obama's is not an easy, casual self-assurance but a tense, Nixon-like one. He explained to House Majority Whip Eric Cantor in a discussion over the size of the 2009 stimulus bill: "I won." He reportedly waved aside a Blue Dog Democrat's concerns over a 2010 congressional defeat similar to Clinton in 1994: "the big difference here and in '94 was you've got me."[24]

As the 2012 election approached, it turned out that Obama's political position was by no means as parlous as 2010's results implied. It was not that his policies won him increased popularity, as happened with FDR after 1934 and Clinton after 1994. But his inequality theme struck a popular chord; Republican obstructionism continued to reap public disapproval; and the unattractive GOP presidential primary follies and less than compelling Romney candidacy added to Obama's appeal.

So did his effective balancing act of verbally stroking his liberal-left core constituency while compromising on policy issues. One critic observed, "The President falls between stools. He is a man of half measures." He never shows bravery, complained *The Economist.* He flip-flops, tacks and weaves, says one thing and does another, is better at governing than leading, his critics noted. This may have disappointed hope-and-change votaries. But Obama's more flexible and varied self-presentation served him in good political stead.[25]

Obama's early foreign policy record also buttressed his standing. A prudent withdrawal from his original pledge to close the Guantanamo Bay prison, the elimination of bin Laden, the successful removal of Ghaddafi, and the growing use of drones to kill terrorists without American troops at risk won greater popular approval than his more contentious domestic policies. Potential overseas problems—China's increasing military assertiveness, Putin's Stalinist-lite obstructionism, no decrease in Arab-Islamic anti-Americanism, the ongoing problem of Iran's quest for a nuke, the Syrian civil war—have not yet become significant political or policy flash points.[26]

In the course of the 2012 election, Obama appeared to regain much of his earlier élan. The heady whirl of campaigning—lecturing, as it were—had an appeal that the hard slog of governing may not have provided. Much was made of his supposedly lackadaisical performance in the first presidential debate; but he quickly regained his form.

On the eve of the election, journalist Matt Bai speculated on the curious lacunae in the performance of this highly gifted, charismatic politician. His was a well-worn question: Why had Obama failed to put his achievements (impressive, whether regarded favorably or unfavorably) in some larger narrative context, to which the public might relate? Put another way: Why was there so little talk of Obama's New Foundation as an appropriate successor to the New Deal or the Great Society?

Bai had a number of answers. Less speechifying and more governing seemed appropriate after the emotive campaign of 2008 gave way to the crisis-ridden condition of 2009 America. Obama was more interested in the prose than the poetry of governing and had no taste for "political theatrics and mindless repetition." (This is disputable.) Perhaps most decisively, the solidity of his 2008 victory led him and his advisers to push their program through without worrying overmuch about its coherence.[27]

During the interregnum between the election and his inauguration, and during the budget-debt crisis in the fall of 2013, Obama displayed a seasoned ability to hold the political spotlight and portray the Republican congressional opposition as rigidly obstructionist. He was substantially assisted in this by the Republicans themselves.

At the same time, his rhetorical stance reinforced the fear of his critics (and the hope of his supporters) that he would regain the transformative vigor of his early presidential days. But as overambitious second terms (FDR's, Wilson's, Bush II's) suggest, this carries heavy risks. The unfolding saga of Obamacare has the potential to, in effect, end his presidency, as it once had the potential of enshrining it.

How might he yet fulfill the promise that he stirred in so many breasts? First and foremost there is Obama himself, who remains in possession of a unique public persona: the first African-American president; unusual rhetorical gifts; a kinship with younger, hip, ethnically diverse Americans not seen since Kennedy.

The support of Obama by the chattering classes—the media, professionals, academia—also has not had a parallel since Kennedy. Like Kennedy, Obama's substantive domestic record is elusive. His foreign policy successes, like Kennedy's, consist more of crises avoided than challenges mastered. While nothing Obama has faced matches the Cuban missile crisis, he has surpassed Kennedy in meeting the public desire to downscale foreign entanglements. His Iraq–Afghanistan–Arab Spring–Syria–Iran distancing may be more successful than Kennedy's entanglement in Vietnam. It may also turn out to entail long-term costs in stability and security.

Kennedy's record was truncated by the sudden, tragic end to his presidency. Obama still has much of his second term to serve. Whether it will burnish his reputation, as in the cases of Lincoln and Clinton, or diminish it, as in the cases of Wilson, Eisenhower, and (spectacularly) Nixon and Johnson, has yet to be seen. The same may be said of Obamacare, his signature domestic achievement.

There was little in the election of 2012, or in developments since, to portend a new birth of leadership. The currents of cultural and social change, the condition of domestic and foreign affairs, are more continuous than not.

And Obama himself? Perhaps more than most presidents, his persona remains difficult to fathom. Some advocates see him as a president who in his first term was not sufficiently confrontational with an obdurate GOP opposition, a "pragmatic liberal" who by moving to the left could have an "extraordinary" second term.

Opponents see things differently. Their Obama is self-obsessed, unable or unwilling to engage in the deal-making of normal politics, fixedly set on adhering to a left-wing agenda. In his own, very different way, Obama is as polarizing as his predecessor—with the difference that George W. Bush attracted more hatred from his detractors than admiration from his supporters; in Obama's case, the reverse.

There is little reason to think that this disparity will disappear. Obama remains, and is likely to remain, a mix of high aspiration and preternatural political self-awareness, embodied in his post-election declaration that "I'm more than familiar with all the literature about presidential overreach in second terms. We are very cautious about that."[28]

There is a continuing tension between Obama's messianic/transformative view of his presidency (and perhaps of himself) and the unbearable heaviness of governing. Obama resists this more than most. He has spoken privately of "going Bulworth," a reference to the 1998 movie that told the story of a politician with radical beliefs driven to the brink (and over) by the need to adopt a moderate guise. The tension between what Obama wants to be and what American political reality forces him to be is likely to be present, and unresolved, right up to January 2017.[29]

As the glow of the 2012 victory gave way to a rising sea of second-term troubles, evaluations of Obama took a new turn. Conservative critics continued to strike by now familiar themes: that this was a president whose left-wing beliefs put him outside the American political mainstream (precisely the argument that many liberals direct at the GOP); that his treatment of the Republicans as The Enemy, always present behind his facade of bipartisan rhetoric, was outsized. Another—contradictory—conservative meme is that at least in foreign affairs Obama follows deliciously in the footsteps of his despised predecessor George W. Bush.[30]

Closely allied is the view—now expressed ever more openly not only by opponents but by some supporters—that he isn't using his presidency effectively; that he doesn't seem to know how to govern.[31]

The spring 2013 Fester Parade of the IRS/Tea Party, Justice/Associated Press, and NSA/e-mail-telephone revelations was followed by the deeply flawed rollout of Obamacare in the fall, the festering Syria and Iran situations, and the Putin *défi* in Crimea. The gap between "the second term that he had hoped for" and "the second term that he actually has" became stark, lending new fuel to the theme of presidential passivity and remove. Those more favorably inclined to him joined his critics in this view, though they dwelt more on the tension between his messianic impulse to bend things to his will and his high awareness of the inherent limits of his office.[32]

The Economist offered advice on "How to Save Obama's Second Term": continue to seek deals with the GOP on immigration, push for cost reductions for pensions and health care, and simplify the tax code. But this was to propose a *volte-face* that appeared to be quite out of character.[33]

As his problems mounted, two explanatory themes found favor. The first was that all presidents faced growing frustrations in governing and increasing pressure to change course. Examples are Nixon and China, Reagan and the size of government, Bush I and taxes, Clinton and triangulation, Bush II and Iraq. The second was that Obama's problems were heightened by his inability to govern as successfully as he politicked. The likely judgment of history? Both of these are true and have substantially diminished the probability that Obama's will be the transformative presidency that his supporters expected and his opponents feared.[34]

There is another, larger perspective from which to view Obama's time. That is the long-term ascendancy of the regulatory-welfare-warfare state. Since the 1930s Democratic presidents (except Clinton) have sought to expand it, Republican presidents (except Nixon) to contract it. But there are signs that the active state may be running out of steam. Obama's drawback of American military involvement overseas promises to be the most popular achievement of his presidency. His expansion of social welfare through Obamacare may well turn out to be its least popular achievement. If this evolution in public sentiment persists, Obama's time may have both arrived, and passed.

CHAPTER TWO

. . .

Governance: The Obama Administration

The MOST CONSPICUOUS tension in Obama's presidency has been between his messianic ambitions and the constraints of past precedent, present pressures, vested interests, and the American constitutional system.

In this he is hardly unique. Every modern president has had to deal with this challenge. It explains why there has been such a disconnect between the game-changing rhetoric with which Obama gained office and the all-too-familiar difficulty of turning rhetoric into reality.[1]

I. THE OBAMA STYLE

Well before Arthur Schlesinger called Nixon's presidency Imperial, the label was applicable to American chief executives. Obama is no exception. His administration has come under fire for circumventing Congress, applying environmental and labor policy by regulatory fiat; for deciding not to enforce the Defense of Marriage Act or restrictions on illegal immigrants; for making new foreign policy without legislative approval; for delaying the implementation of several Obamacare mandates; and for failing to fulfill its promise of being the most open administration ever. A clutch of scandals, characterized by familiar faults of political exigency and bureaucratic overreach, further links Obama's time in office to recurring patterns of the modern American presidency.[2]

It is widely agreed that Obama's governing style reflects his desire to be a transformative chief executive. FDR-like, he came into office facing an economic crisis. FDR- and LBJ-like, he sought to enact large domestic policies. Nixon-like, he inherited and sought to close down unpopular wars.

But Obama has not explicitly sought to ground his presidency in the Democratic reform tradition of the twentieth century. His preferred role models have been chief executives who thought and acted in a large way: Republicans Lincoln, Theodore Roosevelt, and Reagan, and Democrats FDR, JFK, and LBJ. Nor, for all his opponents' accusations that he seeks to impose socialism or European social democracy, does he identify with those traditions.

Early on, Obama spoke of laying down a New Foundation. His aspiration was as ambitious as FDR's New Deal and LBJ's Great Society; its implementation, less sweeping. Obama's vision was more resonant with Theodore Roosevelt's New Nationalism and Woodrow Wilson's New Freedom in 1912: grandiose in conception, vague in objectives, and limited in particulars.

Obama's policies reflect his and his supporters' belief that interventionist, centralized government is the primary way to confront the nation's needs and problems. His defining legislation—first the Stimulus, then Affordable Health Care, and then the Dodd-Frank reform of the financial system—reflects this view.

Not coincidentally, Obama's first term contributed significantly to the century-long growth of federal regulation and bureaucracy.

The administration's enactments are enormously detailed—more like codes of law than policy guideposts—but also give great discretion to regulatory agencies. Critics warned that the traditional fear of agencies being captured by the powerful interests that they supervised was now in danger of being replaced by the fear that regulators would run roughshod over the regulated.[3]

One of them calls this "suicidal government," in the sense that the regulatory agencies run the risk of exceeding their capacity. But it is sustained by a sea change in Americans' relationship to the federal government. Almost half of them receive at least one federal benefit: Social Security, Medicare or Medicaid, food stamps, veterans' benefits, or housing subsidies. Tax breaks bring the beneficiary total to three quarters.[4]

This was hardly Obama's creation. The accretion of government has been going on since the New Deal and under Republican as well as Democratic presidents. The New Foundation rested its legitimacy not on force majeure but on what Obama and his supporters believed to be a democratic process of policy responses by elected officials to popular needs and desires. It was sustained by a supportive structure of "policy intellectuals"—think tanks, universities, pundits and experts, the media, an ever-growing bureaucracy—who have conceived, justified, built, and staffed the modern American welfare-warfare-regulatory state.[5]

The central problem—the one that Obama, like his predecessors, has had to wrestle with—is how to square commitment to an active state with a political culture often uneasy with that reality. This is conspicuously, though not solely, an American dilemma. Challenges to big government have risen in Europe as in the United States, and they come from the Left as well as the Right.[6]

A July 2011 poll found that 62 percent of American voters—76 percent of Republicans, 68 percent of Independents, and 48 percent of Democrats—did not trust government. A Gallup poll more fully explored American attitudes toward the state in September 2011. Eighty-one percent of respondents were dissatisfied with the way that the United States was being governed: 65 percent of Democrats and 92 percent of Republicans. While only 28 percent of Democrats thought that the government threatened popular rights and freedom, 61 percent of Republicans and 47 percent of Independents did. A mere 11 percent of voters identified themselves as liberals, while 44 percent said that they were conservatives and 40 percent called themselves moderates.

If these questions had been asked during the Bush years, the party percentages might have been reversed. But the bottom line would have been the same. It may well be asked what the prospects were of the transformative presidency that Obama sought.[7]

2. PRESIDENT AND CONGRESS

The clash between Obama's ambitions and the realities of American public life was most evident in the mosh pit of Congress. Not surprisingly, the president's popularity far outstripped that of the legislature. But if Obama was popular, many of his policies were not. Similarly, while Congress as an institution was widely unpopular, voters thought better of their own representatives.[8]

The 111th Congress (2009–2011), which came in with Obama, was solidly Democratic, though not overwhelmingly so. The party's Senate strength only briefly reached the magic 60 mark that allowed it to invoke cloture, end a filibuster, and force a vote. The inability, or disinclination, of Obama and the Democratic leadership to troll for GOP votes meant that the signature laws of the early Obama administration—the Stimulus, Obamacare, the Dodd-Frank financial reform act—were essentially one-party measures. Given their scale and significance, this raised problems of implementation and popular acceptance.

The 2010 GOP capture of the House and gap-narrowing in the Senate did not boost Congress's popularity or its effectiveness. The 112th Congress (2011–2013) was the first since 1985–1987 to be divided between the parties from its inception. The Senate lived up to its deadlock potential by passing only 80 bills in its first session, the lowest since 1947. (Most of these were housekeeping items such as naming post offices or extending existing laws.) It broke new nonperformance ground in time spent in debate, the number of conference reports produced, and votes on the Senate floor.

The House racked up a similar record: it was the tenth-least-productive in that chamber's history. By its end in January 2013, the 112th Congress had reached new levels in the number of bills introduced by members without benefit of committee review, the paucity of bills considered or passed, the dearth of formal House-Senate negotiations, and the lack of public approval (as low as 10 percent). During the first six months of 2013, the 113th Congress lived up to the new normal. It passed 15 bills that became law: a record low. The fall 2013 gridlock and shutdown only added to its reputation for dysfunction.[9]

Polarization as measured by congressional voting has increased substantially over the past half century. The culture of contemporary American politics—the outsized influence of the media, blogosphere, advocacy groups, and political action committees rarely interested in compromise—has made Congress, like all public arenas, a more contentious place.[10]

Most political scientists and the mainstream media find Republicans more to blame for this than Democrats. If true, that may be attributable in part to the GOP being out of power (and thus out of sorts) more frequently than its Democratic opponents. But this is at best an impression, much subject to partisan inclination.

Are Democratic leaders Nancy Pelosi and Harry Reid more or less polarizing than their GOP counterparts John Boehner and Mitch McConnell? Are the 52 nonblack members of the House's Progressive Caucus and the 42 members of the Black Caucus more or less obdurately single-minded in their voting than the 50 or so members of the Tea Party Caucus? Definitive answers to these questions will not be found here nor (as yet) anywhere else.

While gridlock was the most conspicuous feature of the post-2010 Congress, there was in fact—there had to be—some degree of agreement. Much of it was pro forma and/or minor. But it occurred in substantive areas—expenditure, raising the debt limit, trade agreements—as well.[11]

The Constitution built in a degree of tension between the executive and legislative branches. In the past, relations between the president and his party's congressional leaders have often been strained. But less so in recent times: testimony to each party's growing ideological homogeneity. Obama's dealings with Democratic congressional leaders Harry Reid and Nancy Pelosi appear to be relatively unruffled. They differ little over policy. Presumably it has helped that his pre-presidential political career was exclusively legislative (in Illinois, in Washington); that he chose to run with old-pro Senator Joe Biden; and that many top administration posts went to former congressional staffers.

Obama has been content to lay out the broad outline of a policy and let the congressional leadership tend to the noisome details. Only intermittently has he sought to directly influence congressional activity: it would seem less than FDR, LBJ, and Ronald Reagan did.

As for interparty relationships, getting along by going along has been superseded by getting along by going it alone. It took Obama 18 months to invite his 2008 opponent John McCain to the White House for a talk. Senate Minority Leader Mitch McConnell didn't get a private meeting with the president until August 2010, after former GOP Senator Trent Lott told former Democratic Senator Tom Daschle that Obama needed to consult top Senate Republicans if he wanted to get his nuclear arms treaty with Russia ratified. When Obama gathered with the congressional leadership of both parties at the end of February 2012, it was his first meeting in seven months with House Speaker Boehner or Senate Minority Leader McConnell.[12]

Yet Obama made much of a post-partisan approach to his presidency in the 2008 campaign. *The Economist* in December 2008 identified 23 centrist Senators, Republicans and Democrats, susceptible to cross-party suasion. In his first State of the Union message, Obama called for monthly meetings with both parties' congressional leadership. There were in fact five such gatherings (including a TV-staged Blair House discussion on the health-reform bill) in the nine months following.

Republican opposition to the Stimulus and health-care and financial reform was all but unanimous. The contrast between the polarization of recent years and the preceding seven-plus decades is stark:[13]

Votes on Major Legislation, 1935–2010

	House		Senate	
Legislation	For	Against	For	Against
Social Security (1935)				
Dem	284	15	60	1
Rep	81	15	16	5
Civil Rights (1964)				
Dem	153	91	46	21
Rep	136	35	27	6

continued

Votes on Major Legislation, 1935–2010 (cont.)

	House		Senate	
Legislation	For	Against	For	Against
Voting Rights (1965)				
Dem	221	61	47	17
Rep	112	24	30	2
Medicare (1965)				
Dem	137	48	57	7
Rep	70	68	13	17
NAFTA (1993)				
Dem	102	156	27	27
Rep	132	47	34	10
Welfare Reform (1996)				
Dem	98	97	25	21
Rep	230	2	53	0
No Child Left Behind (2001)				
Dem	197	10	41	6
Rep	186	34	46	3
Medicare D (2003)				
Dem	16	189	11	35
Rep	204	25	42	9
Tax Cuts (2004)				
Dem	10	198	12	31
Rep	224	0	46	2
Stimulus (2009)				
Dem	244	11	61	0
Rep	0	176	3	37
Health Care (2010)				
Dem	219	34	60	0
Rep	0	178	0	39
Financial Reform (2010)				
Dem	223	0	57	1
Rep	0	176	3	38

Did Obama turn to partisanship Pelosi-Reid style because of his own inclinations and pressure from his base? Or did Republican obduracy, reflecting the pressure from *their* base, reject Obama's policies? The answer to these questions is: yes.

The more germane issue is why Obama chose to pursue the legislative strategy that he did: the Stimulus, followed quickly by health-care and financial reform. In August 2010 John Podesta of the liberal Center for American Progress noted that Obama thought that his primary presidential responsibility in meeting the nation's needs was to pass large-scale legislation. His obvious models were the New Deal and the Great Society.

This appears to have led him to push for the Stimulus, and especially his health-care bill, before building popular support. He justified this strategy by the scale of the recession, the likelihood of rapid recovery under the Stimulus, and the manifest desirability and predictable popularity of health-care reform, cap and trade, and financial reform.

But recovery stalled, cap and trade failed, his health-care bill did not become popular, and financial reform was not high on a jobs-focused public agenda. Obama's larger strategy, in a highly polarized political environment, may have dictated setting aside the campaign trope of bipartisanship in favor of the take-no-prisoners approach of his legislative, media, and advocacy-group base. But inevitably that incurred political costs.[14]

Obama had a strong transformative impulse, but he was not alone in this. The same facts of modern American political culture that shaped Obama's policy strategy defined the Republican response. The theme of change was in the political air, as the Tea Party reaction to Obamacare in the summer of 2010 showed.

GOP leaders Boehner in the House and McConnell in the Senate faced a dilemma not unlike the one that faced Obama: the tension between the kind of responsible post-partisan leadership most voters said they wanted and the no-holds-barred partisanship that their core supporters sought. Even after the 2010 election, the problem was not eased. Congress remained a deeply unpopular institution, and the Republicans were less well-regarded (or more ill-regarded) than the Democrats.

If San Franciscan Nancy Pelosi spoke for the urban liberal core of the Obama Democrats, John Boehner of southwestern Ohio embodied Midwestern Republicanism. Pelosi paid little attention to the more moderate Blue Dog Democrats, and indeed about half of them fell victim to the 2010 Republican juggernaut. Boehner had his own fractious coalition: a flock of newly elected Tea Party sympathizers, concentrated in the Sun Belt, with uncompromising positions on spending (cut it) and taxes (don't raise them).

He sought to keep their support while staying within the broader parameters of policymaking that the speakership demanded. No Newt Gingrichian Contract with America for Boehner; instead, one leg in the Tea Party camp, the other in the let's-make-a-deal tradition of congressional leadership. Boehner did not, after all, have predecessor Pelosi's luxury of party control over both Houses. Nor did he have the ambition-stoking presidential aspirations of predecessor Newt Gingrich.[15]

In the wake of his 2010 defeat, Obama made the requisite noises about renewing his quest for a more bipartisan Washington environment. His new Chief of Staff Bill Daley was widely, and rightly, seen as a means to that end.

At times the centripetal pull of the need to compromise for mutually beneficial ends worked against the centrifugal pull of political and ideological polarization. There were more instances of this dynamic in the dealings of Senate Majority Leader Harry Reid and Minority Leader Mitch McConnell and in the interventions of Vice President Joe Biden, a Senate veteran, than of their House counterparts Pelosi and Boehner, The Senate had a more clubby tradition, and representing a state involved more diverse interests than representing a district.[16]

But the deep divergence of the parties' views on spending, taxation, and debt, fueled by media support and money from advocacy groups with little interest in compromise, made agreement on big issues all but impossible. Congress and the president could summon up only a patchwork compromise to a debt-ceiling deadlock, and they failed to produce a Grand Bargain on spending and taxation. On the eve of the 2012 election, the only tangible result was a looming January 1, 2013 precipice of tax increases and spending cuts that no one wanted.[17]

Polarization and the split in Congress turned out to be a potent formula for gridlock. The Republican commitment to cutting expenditure but no new taxes clashed irreconcilably with the Democrats' commitment to "revenue enhancement" and preserving entitlements and other big-spending programs. The ensuing deadlock had political, ideological, programmatic, and systemic sources: formidable indeed.

In 2012, over 50 members of Congress and 10 senators (10 percent or more of their respective bodies) chose not to run for reelection. This was the largest number of retirements in 20 years. Census-based redistricting in 2010, which left 24 incumbents to run against one another, was one factor. Another was that most redistricting was in the hands of GOP-run states, which added to the drawback of being an office-seeking Democrat.[18]

Could the 2012 election have significant consequences not only for the presidency and national policy, but for the relationship of president and Congress, and Congress and the bureaucracy, or the ability of Congress to function with some effectiveness? That depended in large part on significant change in the party makeup of the two chambers. This was not to be.

3. CABINET AND STAFF

One of the most venerable themes in the history of government is the interplay between the leader (monarch, prince, president) and those who serve him or her: prime minister, cabinet, chief of staff, aides. This was true of American government. The relations between the president's men (and now women) and the character of the presidency have been important since its beginnings.

Obama's initial cabinet appointments drew heavily on ex-Clintonites, not least Hillary Clinton as Secretary of State, and Secretary of the Treasury Timothy Geithner, who was close to sometime–Clinton Secretary of the Treasury Larry Summers. The Attorney General customarily had important political ties to the new president, but Eric Holder had been Clinton's Deputy Attorney General. One commentator thought that it "looked like the third Clinton administration." This was understandable: Obama had little experience or acquaintanceship in his public (or private) past on which to draw.[19]

Obama's cabinet (15 members, plus 8 Cabinet-level appointees) reflected his campaign. Bush's Secretary of Defense Robert Gates broke with tradition by staying on, underlining the felt need for continuity in what the GOP persisted in calling the War on Terror and Obama renamed Overseas Contingency Operations.

Three African Americans were appointed—Attorney General Holder, UN Ambassador Susan Rice, and Environmental Protection Agency Administrator Lisa Jackson—as were two Asian Americans: Steven Chu in Energy and Eric Shinseki in Veterans Affairs. Six cabinet members were women: Hillary Clinton in State, Hilda Solis in Labor, Kathleen Sibelius in Health and Human Services, and Janet Napolitano in Homeland Security, as well as Rice and Jackson.

There were only three cabinet and cabinet-level replacements in Obama's first term, the same as with Bush, which was testimony to the ideological cohesion of each party and the loose management styles of the incumbents. (The more hands-on Bill Clinton racked up eight substitutions in his first term.) The only significant changes were former Democratic congressman Leon Panetta, who replaced Gates in Defense after his predecessor's relatively noncontentious retirement, and the similarly unruffled transition in State from Hillary Clinton to John Kerry.

The calm may also reflect the reduced importance of the cabinet. One of the defining characteristics of the modern presidency has been the rise of the White House staff in defining policy. So in important foreign policy and national security matters, the national security adviser and the director of national intelligence and their staffs are co-equal (and sometimes more than that) with State and Defense. Deputy Chief of Staff Nancy-Ann DeParle played a pivotal role in the formulation of Obamacare. In the ongoing response to debt, taxation, and spending levels, Treasury was at most primus inter pares with Federal Reserve chair Bernanke and the president's stable of economic advisers, Lawrence Summers in particular.

The longevity of Attorney General Holder is testimony not only to his close personal tie to Obama but also to the special relationship between modern presidents and their chief legal officers in those sensitive areas where law and politics come together. Holder fit readily into this tradition.[20]

As is customary, key cabinet members—Clinton of State, Geithner of Treasury, Panetta of Defense—announced their intention to depart at the end of the first term. Here again, the precedents—and the pressures—of the executive branch prevailed. Their designated successors—former GOP senator Chuck Hagel in Defense (in homage to the Republican Gates's tenure), Senator John Kerry in State, White House Chief of Staff Jack Lew for Treasury—signified, if anything, the greater authority and self-confidence of the reelected president. They were, more fully than their predecessors, the president's men.[21]

Have there been Obama administration counterparts to key aides such as FDR's Raymond Moley and Harry Hopkins; Nixon's John Ehrlichman and H. R. Haldeman, Carter's troika of Hamilton Jordan, Bert Lance, and Jody Powell; Ronald Reagan's James Baker; or George W. Bush's Dick Cheney and Karl Rove? (There were no comparably powerful figures in the administrations of master politicians LBJ and Clinton.)

Obama, like his predecessors, initially relied on people who were from his home turf and had been close to him before or during his election campaign. Just as Nixon drew on southern Californians and Carter on a Georgia "mafia," Obama brought with him a Chicago troika of campaign strategist David Axelrod, enforcer Rahm Emanuel, and consigliere Valerie Jarrett.

The major addition to the new administration, dictated by the financial/jobs crisis, was a team of economic advisers. It was in this consequential and politically fraught realm that the most visible policy disputes broke out (though well within the prevailing Democratic worldview).

What happened was much like the centrist Raymond Moley–leftist Rexford Tugwell clash in the early New Deal. "Team A," including former Federal Reserve chairman Paul Volcker, Council of Economic Advisers chair Christine Romer, and Council of Economic Advisers member Austen Goolsbee, sought more stimulus spending and a sharper break with the past. "Team B," led by Emanuel, Geithner, and National Economic Council head Larry Summers, wanted a more restrained policy.

But they had a shared commitment to a Keynesian approach to economic and fiscal policy, which Summers equated with science—in his world, social science: "We've gone from a moment when we've never had a *less* social science–oriented group [the Bush administration] to a moment when we've never had a *more* social science–oriented group. So . . . we'll see what happens."[22]

FDR finally ditched Moley and went with the more committed New Dealers: it was, after all, the time of the Great Depression. Obama, reflecting his belief that the Recession was easing, cast his lot with Team B.[23]

There is another point of comparison with the New Deal: inter-adviser infighting replete with accusations of incompetence and misjudgments, the unavoidable static of a hyperactive administration. "It was chaos," said one participant. By the summer of 2010 tension was building between Axelrod, who wanted a "movement presidency," and Emanuel, who allied himself with the more cautious Summers, Geithner, and Office of Management and Budget director Peter Orszag.

Though Obama agreed more than disagreed with him on policy, Summers supposedly groused to Orszag that they were the only adults, "home alone," and that Clinton "would never have made these mistakes." A (possibly planted) *Washington Post* article claimed that Emanuel was "the only person keeping Obama from becoming Jimmy Carter."[24]

The first tranche of close associates rarely survives the first term or even the first half of the first term. (The contrast with the stability of the cabinet may reflect the lesser power of that body.) There began what Press Secretary Robert Gibbs called "a natural churning of personnel." James Jones, Obama's national security adviser, and two of the original Chicago triad, Chief of Staff Emanuel and senior adviser Axelrod, departed after the 2010 election. So did economic advisers Summers, Goolsbee, Romer, and Orszag, leaving Treasury Secretary Geithner to run the ship (or pick up the pieces).[25]

Did this signal a shift of policy or ideological gears, as did FDR's changes and Bush II's Rumsfeld-Gates switch in Defense after his

2006 election setback? Emanuel was eventually replaced by Chicago mayor Richard Daley's brother Bill, whose JPMorgan Chase background and emollient style were seen as a response to the 2010 election fire bell. GOP guru Karl Rove thought that Daley's arrival signaled a turn away from the administration's class warfare rhetoric. Daley played a key role in getting the administration to back long-pending free trade bills with Panama and Colombia. He reached out to Boehner, seeking a grand deal on taxes and spending.

But that attempt soon collapsed. Senate leader Harry Reid was furious over Daley's suggestion that congressional Democrats shared the blame with Republicans in making it difficult for Obama "to be anything like a chief executive." Daley was shunted aside in early 2012, as the Obama team geared up for the fall election, supposedly declaring, "I'm going back to Chicago where they stab you in the front."[26]

Rumor had it that Michelle Obama and Valerie Jarrett were instrumental in Daley's departure. Certainly it was the case that in the final year of his first term Obama appeared to be increasingly reliant on Jarrett and other members of his chicago coterie. It looked as if he was returning to his roots, personal as well as ideological.[27]

The Obama style of governing evoked not only predictable ground-pawing by the Republican opposition but also growing dissatisfaction from the Left. What the surviving key advisers—most notably, Jarrett, Geithner (like Obama, raised abroad)—and Attorney General Holder, the only major cabinet member to stay on into the second term—had in common was not so much ideology as close personal relationships with Obama.

Some thought that the most influential of these was Jarrett. On paper she headed the Orwellian-sounding Office of Public Engagement (old name: Office of Public Liaison). In practice she was a general fixer in the Harry Hopkins mode. Jarrett was a conspicuous member of the rising Chicago black upper-bourgeoisie, of which the Obamas were very much a part, an identity that ultimately prevailed over white Jewish fellow-Chicagoans Emanuel and Axelrod, Irish pols like Daley, and academicians Summers, Rohmer, and company.[28]

4. THE BUREAUCRACY

The world of the cabinet and the staff is an intensely political one. The president hires and fires them; his political agenda is forefront, despite their ever-larger administrative duties.

The bureaucracy is, or is supposed to be, something else. There is in principle a built-in tension between those political beings—the president, the cabinet, and the White House staff—and the civil servants who march to the different drummers of their lifetime careers.

But since the New Deal and the rise of the welfare-warfare state, the relationship between these groups has become more complex and nuanced. Under Ronald Reagan and more conspicuously under George W. Bush, tales circulated of the bureaucracy resisting or subverting administration policies. Presumably that relationship changed when Obama came into office. Here was a symbiosis of policy and purpose: both bureaucrats and Obamacrats wanted bigger, more active government.

Ironically (or, in current parlance, systemically), the most notable instance of bureaucratic growth began under George W. Bush. In the wake of 9/11, he created the Department of Homeland Security. Its remit was to consolidate and direct the government's response to terrorism, manmade accidents, and natural disasters. With this sweeping mandate, the department absorbed the Immigration and Naturalization Service, the Federal Emergency Management Agency, the Coast Guard, and the Secret Service: it was the largest reorganization in the federal government since the creation of the Department of Defense in 1952. By 2012 the department had a budget of around $57 billion and some 240,000 employees.

The federal workforce in 2008 was a 9/11-enhanced 1.875 million. During the next two years it rose to 2.128 million (including a temporary 2010 Census bump): a growth rate of 13.5 percent. The Office of Management and Budget thought this to be the largest expansion since LBJ's presidency.

Government employees earning $150,000 a year or more doubled under Obama. They were estimated to make twice as much as their private counterparts. After the wake-up call of the 2010 election, Obama found it necessary to impose a pay freeze on federal workers, ending it only in March 2013, comfortably after the 2012 contest.[29]

The most conspicuous expression of expanding government was the growing lushness of the District of Columbia. Washington had the largest population inflow and the healthiest economy of any big American city. Its unemployment rate in mid-2012 was 5.7 percent, compared to New York's 10.3 percent and Chicago's 9.6 percent. House prices in the area went up when elsewhere they languished.

The District's *embonpoint* stemmed in part from the expansion of the regulatory departments and agencies responsible for environment and energy, health care, and financial regulation. Their budgets increased by 16 percent ($54 billion), and federal agencies' remits kept expanding. Defenders of Obama's Internal Revenue Service (IRS) dwell on the larger demands made on it after the Supreme Court's *Citizens United* decision by groups seeking tax-exempt status. (This would bear the unattractive fruit of apparent IRS harassment of Tea Party groups.) The Veterans' Administration has been swamped not only by the return of Iraq and Afghanistan veterans but by a vast increase in the number of claims stoked by an ever-expanding definition of disability. Obamacare promises to bring large new accretions of responsibility (and prospects of bureaucratic overreach) to the IRS and Health and Human Services.[30]

Along with the growth of the bureaucracy has come a barnacle-like accretion of lobbyists, consultants, contractors, and nongovernmental associations clustered in the city and its surrounding counties: a Stimulus–renewable energy complex that echoes the military-industrial complex of the Second World War and the Cold War.

More Stimulus money per capita was spent in the District and its surround than in any state. As in the Cold War years, a quid pro quo of contributions and political support in return for legislative and administrative favors flourished. Bureaucracy, lobbying, and greenery did not come cheaply. By 2012, seven of the ten American counties with the highest household incomes were in the Washington area. Adding spice to the fevered atmosphere was a metastasized media, who with lobbyists and young staffers gave the District a Hollywood Tinseltown tone.[31]

Conservatives responded to this new configuration much as their predecessors did to the New Deal. Critics spoke of supra-Constitutional authoritarianism, as FDR's adversaries did of his arrogation of executive power. The diktats and ukases of the Environmental Protection Agency's Lisa Jackson, Kathleen Sibelius of Health and Human Services, Janet Napolitano of Homeland Security, and Eric Holder in Justice provided grist for GOP mills as FDR's New Dealers had three quarters of a century before.[32]

Perhaps the closest analogue to that earlier time was the rise (and fall) of "czars": White House appointees not subject to congressional approval or oversight, charged to coordinate activity that cut across traditional department-agency borders. Similar figures were prominent in previous crisis times: World Wars I and II and the Great Depression. A dozen or so (though confirmed by the Senate) were appointed by George Bush.

There were more than twenty czars in the early stage of Obama's presidency. Lawrence Summers more or less oversaw economic policy, as Nancy-Ann DeParle did health-care reform. Violence against women, drugs, border security, urban affairs, Stimulus accountability, Iran, the Middle East, the auto industry, and cyber security: each was grist for a new czar's mill.

The shady Van Jones (sometime avowed Communist and advocate of the Truther theme that Bush and company were behind 9/11) was made special adviser for green jobs, enterprise, and innovation. At the other end of the spectrum, the work of auto czar Steven Rattner in overseeing the bailing out of the car companies and of Kenneth Feinberg in tackling executive compensation was widely praised.

The summer 2010 recess appointment of Dr. Donald Berwick to head the Centers for Medicare and Medicaid Services suggested the power potential of the office. His departure in November 2011, encased in controversy, revealed its fragility.[33]

In July 2011 Obama quietly scrapped some of the more controversial czardoms. But like his predecessors, he at times found it necessary to use recess appointments to circumvent partisan opposition in Congress. He had done so with Berwick and again in early 2012 with two members of the National Labor Relations Board and the head of the Consumer Financial Protection Bureau. A squall arose over whether the Senate was indeed in recess at the time. An interparty deal in the summer of 2013 led to the appointees' departure, not least because the federal courts were hostile to the manner of their appointment. The Supreme Court was expected to void them in the spring of 2014.[34]

In a May 2011 report, the Business Council, a long-established group that advised on business-government relations, rated Obama's appointees lower than their predecessors in expertise, in having an anti-institutional bent, and for poor communication with career bureaucrats. If so, this may have been part of the cost of the administration's vigorous effort to go outside traditional recruitment areas and bring more women and minorities into the bureaucracy.[35]

Just as Republican administrations made appointments more notable for their ideological acceptability than their political acumen, so was this the case in the Obama years. Some instances:

Rajiv Shah, a 36-year-old physician from the Gates Foundation, was made head of the Agency for International Development, the government's chief dispenser of foreign aid. Five days into his job he was confronted with the task of overseeing the American response to the devastating January 2010 Haiti earthquake. A *Washington Post* article extravagantly extolled his leadership qualities and his "limitless future" in setting the course of foreign aid.

No one could live up to this billing. Six months later the Haitian aid effort was mired in sloth and inadequacy, and Shah's attempt to gain more independence for his agency was checkmated by the more politically muscled Secretary of State Hillary Clinton. In May, House Republicans called the American aid program to Haiti as "pathetic." Shah went into the black hole of media oblivion.[36]

Sherry A. Glied, assistant secretary of Health for planning and evaluation, was a health policy management economist from the Columbia School of Public Health. With a B.A. from Yale and an economics Ph.D. from Harvard, she was the very model of a modern academic-in-government.

Political smarts was another matter. She came up with the idea of a survey by a team of "mystery shoppers" posing as patients, who would call more than 4,000 doctors in nine states.

Each would be phoned twice: once by a caller pretending to be a holder of private insurance and once by someone supposedly dependent on Medicare or Medicaid. A sample of the sample would be called yet a third time, by a team member adopting the persona of a Health and Human Services representative, who would ask if the physician would accept both sorts of patients. The object of the experiment was to see if the lower reimbursements of Medicare and especially Medicaid induced doctors to turn the "patient" away.

A contract was signed with Chicago's National Opinion Research Center to conduct the inquiry. The scheme came under GOP criticism, and two days later it was halted. "We have determined that now is not the time to move forward with this research project," a Health and Human Services spokesperson explained. The public was assured that "politics did not play a role in the decision."[37]

In 2012 the Food and Drug Administration undertook widespread surveillance of its own scientists' e-mails, supposedly to stop the leaking of proprietary information. What stopped instead was the surveillance.[38]

In 1999 the Clinton administration committed to compensation of $50,000 to each of thousands of black farmers with plausible claims to injury from bias by federal loan officers. Hispanics and women began to make similar claims. The Supreme Court finally struck down all but a few of these suits. But Obama's Justice and Agriculture departments pledged $1.3 billion to compensate thousands of female and Hispanic farmers who had not claimed bias. This was the work of the White House and political appointees in the departments, against the opposition of career lawyers and bureaucrats. Politically interested lawmakers and fee-interested law firms were behind the deal, which expanded to over 90,000 claims, costing $4.4 billion. Advocates for Native American farmers secured an additional kitty of $760 million; actual claims totaled only $300 million; the residue went to Native American farmer advocacy groups. Accusations of fraud multiplied, as did rip-offs and skimming by middlemen.[39]

Episodes such as these were hardly unique to the Obama administration. Biting off more than you can chew and mishandling authority are integral parts of all modern bureaucracies. This is a style of abuse common in the modern, active, policy-driven American state: not so much self-enrichment as self-aggrandizement, legitimated by the political beliefs of the participants.[40]

5. POLITICS AND PRINCIPLE

The Obama campaign committed itself to a new order of ethics in the relationship between public officials and private interests. Lobbyists were no longer to be part of the governing process; public service would be detached from private gain; openness would be the defining characteristic of the administration. But human nature, an active state, ideology, and politics inexorably eroded these lofty sentiments: not exceptionally so but customarily so.

In March 2011 Obama got an award from open government advocates—in an event closed to the press. It was in an old tradition (not least in the Department of Commerce) when it emerged that Secretary John Dyson had a large stake in the solar-powered electric car industry that his department was flogging. Equally familiar was Peter Orszag's migration from White House budget director to vice chairman and senior economic adviser of Citibank, a financial institution that needed all the well-connected representation it could get.[41]

Politics inevitably reared its head in the sensitive realm of the disposal of nuclear waste. The proposed Yucca Mountain site in

Nevada made sense to many Nuclear Regulatory Commission scientists but not to the Obama administration or Nevada senator Harry Reid. Nuclear Regulatory Commission head Gregory Jaczko had his scientists' report modified to remove its Yucca findings, and Congress ended funding for the project.[42]

Attorneys general had a long tradition of serving their presidents as something like mafia consigliores. It emerged that Eric Holder and his department controversially spied on Associated Press reporters and toyed with legal action against a Fox News journalist.[43]

Lobbyists were anathema to the incoming Obama administration: political contributions from them were banned. But the flood of new spending ensured that the traditional ways of doing business with the government went on. Washington lawyer-insider Antoinette C. Bush, friend of Obama, cousin of Valerie Jarrett, spokeswoman for Viacom, Sony, and News Corporation, was noteworthy only for being so typical of the breed.

No less customary was the correlation between the largesse of campaign contributors and White House visits (though the Clinton gift of sleepovers in the Lincoln bedroom was not revived). Some 20 percent of $30,000-or-less donors had that privilege, compared to 75 percent who gave $100,000 or more.

The Obama administration followed a familiar trail as well in bestowing ambassadorships on generous supporters. (Nixon with typical delicacy had said that a $250,000 contribution was the threshold.) Forty-four percent of the 185 most attractive posts (including Great Britain, France, Japan, Spain, and Australia) went to Obama donors rather than Foreign Service officers, substantially more than the numbers racked up by Clinton and Bush II.[44]

More serious, if no less customary, was the emergence of scandals that suggested corruption, politics, and/or incompetence. In its first term the Obama administration appeared to be no more prone to this than its predecessors; perhaps less so, though gentler media surveillance makes this hard to judge. The prime examples were the Solyndra, Fast and Furious, and Benghazi affairs.

Solar panel startup Solyndra was as close to the heart—and the budget—of the Obama team as Halliburton was to Bush's vice president Cheney. Major Obama fundraiser George Kaiser had a large stake in the company, which won an outsized half-a-billion-dollar-plus loan from the government. Solyndra closed up shop in the summer of 2011, leaving the taxpayers (but not Kaiser) to shoulder the loss.[45]

Fast and Furious was a program, conceived but not implemented under the Bush administration, to entrap Mexican drug cartels by letting their people buy guns in the United States and bring them back to Mexico. It appears that the Obama administration also hoped this would strengthen popular support for gun control. Disaster followed: the guns dropped out of sight until some of them were uncovered after a firefight in which an American federal agent was killed. House Oversight Committee chair Darrell Issa did his best to turn the episode into a major embarrassment for the administration. But a generally uncooperative media and the less-than-earth-shaking character of the episode worked against him.

Much the same was the case when on the eve of the 2012 election four Americans, including the ambassador to Libya, were killed in Benghazi on the anniversary of 9/11. GOP-friendly Fox News dwelt on the evidence of an administration cover-up; the mainstream media kept its curiosity in check. Secretary of State Hillary Clinton's exasperated response to congressional inquirers—"What difference does it make?"—added little to her compassion quotient and might cause her trouble if she runs for president in 2016. But she did seem to reflect the popular view. Benghazi has not won the attention and notoriety of Iran-Contra under Reagan, though it lingers like a mild fever.

Growing revelations of scandal are a recurring feature of second terms in the presidency. So it was with Harry Truman, when 166 IRS employees were fired or resigned because they took bribes, and Attorney General J. Howard McGrath was dismissed for summarily getting rid of a special prosecutor. So it was with Dwight Eisenhower and the mishandling of the U-2 spy plane scandal.

Nixon's Watergate is the poster child of the genre. Reagan bore the brunt of the Iran-Contra embarrassment. Clinton had to deal with the Monica Lewinsky episode and House impeachment for perjury and obstruction of justice. George W. Bush had the Valerie Plame incident, misbehavior in Abu Ghraib prison, terrorist waterboarding, and the response to Hurricane Katrina to contend with, along with the albatross of the Iraq war.

So it was hardly unprecedented when in the spring of 2013 a spate of revelations emerged regarding misuses of federal power, all but one with partisan political intent.

From 2010 on the IRS energetically targeted conservative political groups seeking 501 tax status, in contrast with its more benign attitude toward similar liberal aspirants. Eric Holder's Department of Justice turned out to have tapped Associated Press journalists' computers and telephones. Fox reporter James Rosen's e-mails also underwent scrutiny, and Holder signed off on a warrant to investigate (Holder's term) or prosecute (his critics' term) Rosen for complicity in a revelation regarding North Korea that embarrassed the administration. Then leaker Edward Snowden made public the National Security Agency's (NSA) broad oversight of the e-mails and social network chatter of Americans and foreigners.

The *New York Times*, which treated the Benghazi, IRS, and Justice revelations with its customary mix of indifference and equanimity toward administration misdeeds, stirred itself over the NSA disclosures. It gave Obama an unprecedented rap on the knuckles: "The Obama administration issued the same platitude it has offered every time President Obama has been caught overreaching in the use of his powers. . . . The administration has now lost all credibility on this issue. Mr. Obama is proving the truism that the executive branch will use any power it is given and very likely abuse it."[46]

In an otherwise unrelievedly partisan time, this was an issue that cut across the political spectrum. Critics from the fringes included Glenn Beck on the Right and Michael Moore on the Left; Democratic senators Harry Reid, Ron Wyden, Mark Udall, and Dick Durbin; and GOP House Speaker John Boehner. Barack Obama and John McCain joined in the NSA's defense.[47]

Misuse of public power is as old as politics—anybody's politics. In colonial America, when there wasn't all that much to steal, corruption took the form of British governors treating the colonies as founts of office and its emoluments. The new nation and the rise of mass parties and voting democratized the process. Pols and contractors fed from an ever-larger public trough.

In recent times a different sort of misbehavior has come to the fore, with a more political and often ideological face. Nobody enriched themselves in Watergate or the IRS or Justice incidents. Instead, functionaries responded to what they took to be nudge-nudge hints from their political overlords, using the power of government to block or clamp down on the opposition.[48]

Whether the 2013 revelations are in the Watergate class or are (as the administration and its supporters put it) "phony" has yet to be seen. The media reaction was notably low key, compared to Watergate or even the highly factitious Valerie Plame affair under George W. Bush. But an American Civil Liberties Union official thought that the IRS targeting was "about as constitutionally troubling as it gets." Strongly pro-Obama *Washington Post* columnist Eugene Robinson observed that "this heavy-handed business isn't chilling, it's just plain cold"—and possibly unconstitutional. A conservative critic held that the IRS episode was worse than

Watergate, which involved "elites using the machinery of government to spy on elites . . . It's something quite different when elites use the machinery of government against ordinary people."[49]

The context for both Watergate and the recent disclosures was an event second only to an execution in its mind-focusing power: a national election. It was a good measure of Nixon's paranoid inclinations that he countenanced these methods during that ultimate in slam-dunk contests, the 1972 campaign against the hapless George McGovern. The comparable stimulus for the Obama administration's embarrassments may have been its messianic strain, which led it to the view that the surging Tea Party in 2010 and the GOP in 2012 were not merely The Opposition but The Enemy—or, as the president put it, a "threat to democracy."[50]

Watergate's backstory was decades of Red Scare government abuses and the fears stirred by the countercultural revolution of the 1960s. The recent crop of misdeeds, bolstered mightily by the NSA disclosures, highlights the problem of potentially out-of-control big government: the "surveillance state."[51]

In early May 2013, on the cusp of the various revelations, Obama offered an impassioned defense of the active state and why it should be trusted. But law professor Jonathan Turley argued that the rise of the administrative state—"the fourth branch of government"—"represents perhaps the single greatest change in our system of government since the founding." State, the IRS, Justice, NSA, the VA: these are among the jewels in the government crown, and it is unsettling indeed if they are enmeshed in scandal.[52]

It is unlikely that President Obama is directly implicated, as was Nixon. His governing style is too hands-off for that. But fairly senior officials—Lois Lerner, head of the IRS's exempt organizations office, IRS general counsel William Wilkins, Attorney General Holder—appear to have been involved, and congressional Republicans soldier on with their inquiries.

Given the media's disinclination to make a federal case of these federal cases, the lack of large public outrage, and the Republicans' not very effective assaults, a Watergate-level firestorm is remote. The likely impact on Obama is not Nixonian disgrace or Reagan-scale Teflonlike invulnerability but a contribution to a more general and all-too-familiar phenomenon: the diminishing stature of a second-term president.

CHAPTER THREE

. . .

Governance: The American State

OBAMA'S ADMINISTRATION DID not spring full-grown from the womb of the 2008 election. It evolved within the dense and long-established structure of American government. That structure embraces broad realms: regulation, judicial review, and federalism.

I. THE REGULATORY STATE

Federal regulation in the twentieth century initially fell into two categories: economic oversight of big business (trust-busting and corporate and financial rules) and social control (the prohibition of liquor and quota-based immigration restriction). The resulting regulatory structure was hardly a simple case of people's tribunals overseeing vested interests. Xenophobia and ethnic tension were prime contributors to early-twentieth-century social policy. Large corporations frequently used economic regulation to improve their competitive position with lesser firms or with one another. Capture of the regulators by the regulated was more common than regulatory excess.[1]

A deregulatory backlash scored some victories in the late twentieth century, notably the end of the Interstate Commerce Commission and the Federal Aeronautic Administration. In addition, reduced federal regulation has won much political lip service and popular support. The idea of a universal sunset rule—that all regulations should expire after 10 or 15 years—attracts recurring attention. Nevertheless the long-term trend has been for an ever-larger regulatory state. From the New Deal on, the scale and scope of federal economic oversight vastly expanded, and the government intervened ever more actively in the causes of racial and gender equality.[2]

The interests playing on that state have changed over time. Organized economic, cultural, and social advocacy groups abound, as do think tanks, foundations, and public policy professionals, with their own often ideologically tinged predispositions and prescriptions. They vie for policy primacy with lobbyists and trade associations, public employee unions, government contractors, and money- and vote-seeking pols.

Today's regulatory state is distinctive in several respects besides its greatly enlarged agenda. It is more ideological, less visibly corrupt, and embedded in legal and economic professionalism. But it is also more subject to the pressures of a populist, polarized political culture.

After three years of the Obama administration, 194 major new regulatory rules, each with an estimated economic impact of $100 million or more, had been added to the *Federal Register*. One estimate was that the new regulations would take $6.6 billion to implement and cost the economy $10 billion a year. The Dodd-Frank financial regulation act and oversight by the Environmental Protection Agency (EPA) are major sources of that growth. *The Economist* spoke of an "over-regulated America."[3]

This was part of a trend that stretched back well before the Obama years. Federal regulatory agency expenditures grew from

$533 million under John F. Kennedy to a projected $57.3 billion by the end of 2012: more than a hundredfold. The observation of a defender of regulatory growth—that it is "driven much more by the events of the times that we live in than it is by the ideology of whoever's in the White House"—has the ring of truth.[4]

Obama is at times mindful of the problem. His 2011 State of the Union message called on all agencies to work on reducing the supervisory burden on business. He later reported that agencies responded with 580 proposals to lessen regulation—to no noticeable effect.[5]

Not all parts of the vast new American state are equal. Long-established departments—Defense, Commerce, Labor, Agriculture, Veterans' Affairs, Health and Human Services—have deeply embedded relationships with their government clients, Congress, contractors, and lobbyists. Newer agencies are less well entrenched, and their remit is still developing.

The departments of Housing and Urban Development, Energy, Education, and Homeland Security, and the Environmental Protection Agency (EPA) are especially prone to regulatory and bureaucratic mishaps. There is a recurring tension between their reliance on "scientific" studies that seek to correlate cause and effect and measure financial costs and benefits and the fact that they oversee highly interest-laden—and thus highly political—social and economic activities. The EPA was apt to get enmeshed in conflict-of-interest and conflict-of-jurisdiction issues. Protecting the environment has come to mean reducing pollution: a duty embodied in the Clean Air Act of 1970. But this responsibility brings the EPA into close and contentious contact with the extractors and producers (and often polluters) of an industrialized society.

Adding to the EPA's difficulties is its relationship to American federalism. The agency sets anti-pollution standards, but the states retain the power to decide how to enforce (or replace) them. The tropistic impulse of new regulatory agencies to expand and of established authorities to retain their powers is compounded by the states' financial crisis and feeds the potential for conflict.[6]

Certainly the regulators, new and old, are there because of felt national needs, translated into laws and legislation. Given the ever-larger list of problems that afflict the society and the tenor of the Obama approach to governance, it is difficult to imagine a different outcome.

But regulatory excess spawns the equivalent of urban legends. According to *The Economist*, a Florida law called for labels on vending machines urging the public to report if the label was not there. The Federal Railroad Administration required that every train engine have a painted "F"—for front—on (of course) its front. Bethesda, Maryland, authorities were reported to have shut down children's lemonade stands because they were unlicensed. After Obamacare goes into effect, mandated illness and injury claim categories were due to rise from 18,000 to 140,000, including nine codes covering injuries caused by parrots and three by burning water skis.[7]

In September 2009 a new czar was born: an anti-regulatory regulator. This was law professor Cass Sunstein, the liberal spokesman for a new generation of policy experts who occasionally met a regulation they didn't like. Sunstein headed a new Office of Information and Regulatory Affairs (a title that sounds like a spinoff of the BBC comedy *Yes, Minister*'s Ministry of Administrative Affairs). His charge was to review the ever-growing mass of government regulation and to use cost-benefit analysis for appropriate culling.

As the 2012 election approached, Sunstein showed sympathy for business complaints over some regulations as burdensome and/or unnecessary. But left-liberal groups groused that he was too acquiescent to these interests, and Obama himself was increasingly critical of them. Sunstein announced in early August 2012 that he was leaving his post.[8]

Inevitably the growth of the regulatory state, along with its necessary checks on economic and social harm, has led to misuse. Take, for example, licensing. Government authorization to pursue a trade or calling is as old as history. Licensing by its very nature generates an ever-growing number of requirements: training, certification, rules of conduct. The regulatory system necessary to implement and enforce the License Raj incurs economic costs through narrowed entry, restricted competition, and the unequal politics of diffuse opponents facing united, well-organized advocates. A century ago the practice was firmly embedded in the party-machine system. Special-interest-led legislatures enacted the rules of the game; licenses were commonly used to block entry by newcomers; the party system battened off license-granting bribes and fees.

This venerable device flourishes in the modern regulatory state. Politicians today, *The Economist* acidly observes, provide "freedom from unlicensed hair cutters, freedom from cowboy flower-arrangers and, most important of all, freedom from rogue interior designers." In the 1950s about 5 percent of working Americans needed licenses. Now, after decades of deregulation, almost 30 percent do. In addition, modern licensing has found a new source of sustenance: the widespread sense among the environmentally sensitive that there is no human activity, however mundane, that is without adverse consequences for plants or animals.[9]

2. THE JUDICIAL BATTLEGROUND

The interplay of the president and the judiciary is another recurring theme in American government. It waxes and wanes in intensity and scale. After the flareup between a conservative Supreme Court and the New Deal, controversy over the judiciary's role died down, and aside from civil liberties issues the Court adopted a hands-off policy toward the expanding American state. From 1937 until the late 1950s, as the Cole Porter song had it, "anything goes."

But then civil rights and abortion returned the Court to the epicenter of American politics. Its role in resolving the 2000 election controversy added fuel to the fire. That decision elicited a storm of liberal disapprobation comparable to (though less strident and widespread than) the conservative reaction to the *Roe v. Wade* abortion decision.

During the early Obama years the Court impinged on public awareness primarily because of the sharp divide between four liberal and four conservative judges, with the less readily defined Justice Anthony Kennedy in the balance. The 2010 *Citizens United* decision, which extended First Amendment protection to political contributions by corporations, advocacy groups, and labor unions, heated up the high potential for conflict between a conservative-leaning Court and a liberal president. Obama strongly condemned the decision in his January 2010 State of the Union address, with several justices in attendance.

While the Court's decisions do not necessarily follow the election returns, its makeup certainly follows the cultural returns. The conservative bloc (plus Kennedy) consists of four white and one black Catholic males. The liberal bloc, three of them women, is made up of three Jews and a Hispanic. White male Protestants are nonexistent, in tune with an African-American president and the 2012 GOP ticket of Mormon Romney and Catholic Ryan.

When it took up the constitutionality of Obama's health-care bill in the spring of 2012, the Court held center stage in American public life more so than at any time since the 2000 election crisis. Here, it was widely believed, would be an acid test of the conflict between an expansive and a limited view of federal power: a return in effect to the great days of the New Deal and the civil rights conflict.

Ultimately 28 Republican-led states, more than half, joined the constitutional challenge to Obamacare. The 2010 election, it appeared, had consequences, and popular unease with the health-care law was widespread. The rise of that challenge was as much a surprise to liberal America as the Tea Party and the GOP sweep of 2010. Nancy Pelosi's "Are you serious? Are you serious?" response to an opponent of health care's constitutionality was from the heart, not just from the Democratic playbook.

The focal point was the law's mandate for universal participation. To put this into effect required state exchanges, elaborate subsidies, and a bureaucratic infrastructure that set off all sorts of alarm bells. The progress of the challenge through the federal courts resembled the legislative process. Some district and appellate courts upheld the bill; others struck down parts or the whole. The Supreme Court agreed to take up the issue and, in recognition of its importance and the intensely political surround, allowed for an unprecedented five hours of oral argument.

As befitted so significant a case, the legal commentariat plunged in on a grand scale. Supporters of Obamacare mounted a two-stage constitutional defense. It was an acceptable regulation of interstate commerce; if not, then it was an acceptable use of the federal power to tax. Opponents cited the Tenth Amendment's restriction of federal power and the law's overstretch of the Commerce Clause.

But the political dimension of the argument was never far from anyone's mind. Liberal blogger Ezra Klein suggested that eliminating the mandate would smooth the way to a single-payer, government-run system. The administration's position strategically shifted from flatly denying that the mandate penalty was *not* a tax but a regulation of commerce to insisting that it was *not* a regulation of commerce but a tax.[10]

The contest came to involve constitutional law issues—interstate commerce, taxation, federalism, the police power—that had been relatively quiet for decades. *Washington Post* columnist Charles Lane saw it as a struggle between competing views on the limits of government and the character of American citizenship.[11]

In some respects the case echoed the *Schechter* decision of 1935, one of the Court's more politically resonant actions during the New Deal. The justices unanimously found that the National Recovery Administration, FDR's cornerstone instrument of industrial policy, was an unconstitutional extension of the commerce clause. Justice Brandeis supposedly instructed an FDR aide, "I want you to go back and tell the president that we're not going to let this government centralize everything."

That was then; *National Federation of Independent Businesses v. Sebelius* was now. Constitutional law experts widely agreed that Obama care was a legitimate application of the commerce power as it was perceived today. A more nuanced argument was that in comparably difficult cases in the past, the Court had to transcend textual interpretation or precedent and fall back on first principles: in effect, wait for public and political opinion to catch up. There was good reason to think that the public was not favorably disposed to the bill. A December 2010 Associated Press poll found that 29 percent of respondents supported it, while 49 percent did not. According to a Gallup poll in February 2012, over 75 percent thought it unconstitutional.[12]

But for most discussants the politics of Obamacare transcended the issue of its constitutionality. Opponents were flatly confident that its policy flaws and constitutional illegality were interchangeable. Defenders were convinced that to challenge it was beyond the Court's writ. *New York Times* Supreme Court savant Linda Greenhouse came out of retirement to equate those who questioned the constitutionality of Obamacare with doubters of evolution or climate change. She emerged from reading the case briefs with the conviction that "the question of constitutionality is simply wrong. . . . There's just no there there."

On the same far shore, a law professor called for the impeachment of those justices who voted to overturn "a clearly constitutional law": homage of sorts to the Impeach Warren defenders of racial segregation. Another old idea, FDR's Court-packing proposal, was revived: term limits on the justices. Like so much else, the debate over Obamacare fed the prevalent political polarization. One observer equated a close decision to strike down the measure with the convulsion over the Court's role in the 2000 presidential election.[13]

The prevailing view was that the administration came off poorly in the oral presentation and that Justice Kennedy, the Court's switch hitter, would join the anti-Obamacare conservative foursome rather than the pro-Obamacare liberal foursome.

In response, the legal establishment and the administration levied a full-court press against the all but unthinkable proposition that the Court would strike down the law. Senate Judiciary Committee chair Pat Leahy urged Chief Justice Roberts to recognize the deference that the Court owed to Congress. President Obama raised an eyebrow or two by warning that if the Court rejected Obamacare it would be an "unprecedented and extraordinary" action, in which "an unelected group of people would somehow overturn a duly constituted . . . law . . . passed by a strong majority of a democratically elected Congress." ("A strong majority of the Democrats elected to Congress" would have been a more accurate formulation.)

Conservatives attacked this assault as beyond the political pale. But former presidents—Lincoln, Theodore Roosevelt, and FDR among them—had not been above Court-bashing and decision-influencing. Precisely because the justices are nominated by the president, confirmed by the Senate, and tasked to pass on constitutional questions, the Court is an indelible part of the American political process.[14]

Chief Justice John Roberts's June 28 decision upheld most of the law, including the mandate. Along with the five liberals on the Court, he redefined the mandate as a tax rather than an extension of the commerce power. By a 7-to-2 margin the justices held that states opting out of the law's Medicaid expansion could not be denied aid from the federal government.

The decision seems likely to have some influence on issues that are very much part of contemporary American government. One of these is the relation between the federal government and the states; here the Court gave potentially significant support to the latter.

Another is the government's power to regulate interstate commerce. The decision did not overtly weaken that ability. But when it came to the relationship between regulating, and requiring, an activity in interstate commerce, the decision went against an expansive view of the commerce power. By defining the mandate as a tax rather than a regulation of commerce, it effectively moved contention over Obamacare from the amorphous realm of just what is interstate commerce to the far more politically sensitive realm of taxation. That may indeed have political and policy consequences.

Liberals celebrated the Court's retention of the mandate jewel in the Obamacare crown. Many conservatives denounced its upholding the act's constitutionality as a betrayal. Roberts's intentions remain unclear. Did he merely follow the legal path that his understanding of constitutional law dictated? Or did he craft an essentially political decision out of legal/constitutional clay, as John Marshall did with his lose-the-battle / win-the-war strategy in *Marbury v. Madison*?

The decision at least for the time buttressed the cause of judicial independence and returned Obamacare to its customary place in the realm of politics and public policy. In so doing, Roberts paid homage to Justice Oliver Wendell Holmes's dictum that, for the most part, government policymaking should be left to the legislative and executive branches.[15]

The Court ended its 2012–2013 term with a clutch of decisions—on gay marriage, the Voting Rights Act, and racial preference in college admissions—reinforcing the prevailing view that it was defined primarily by its 4–4 liberal-conservative balance, with Justice Anthony Kennedy the swing vote. But liberal analyst Linda Greenhouse thought that Chief Justice Roberts had emerged as the Gray Eminence (or the Prince of Darkness) presiding over a Court-led dismantling of the activist state. A more restrained estimate is that he was indeed committed to a long (conservative) judicial game, adeptly bringing along liberal colleagues through artfully compromised decisions. Only Justice Kennedy was more often in the majority. Roberts appears to be an increasingly influential chief justice, in the John Marshall–Charles Evans Hughes–Earl Warren mold.[16]

The sometimes fraught relationship between Court and President in Obama's time is hardly a new chapter in American history. The hoary ronde of power-juggling among the executive, legislative, and judicial branches is alive and well: another sign that Obama's commitment to change could not readily override the embedded culture of the American state.

3. FEDERALISM

The federal government has been a growing presence in American public life for more than a century. Today it spends about three times as much as state and local governments combined. Obama identifies himself with the big-spending welfare state as has no chief executive since Lyndon Johnson.

Paradoxically (or perhaps inevitably), during his first term there was an upsurge of state governors with a different view of things. Phoenix-like, the venerable theme of federalism—the independence of state from national government—survives (indeed, thrives) amid the consuming fires of centralization. It is worth noting that the presidency in recent times has had twice as many former governors (Carter, Reagan, Clinton, Bush II) as former bureaucrats or senators (Bush I, Obama).[17]

Jurisdictional conflict between the federal government and the states continues to have a lot of life, as disputes over the regulation of illegal immigrants and the financing and provision of Medicaid demonstrate. In Europe, too, regional and local government shows new signs of vitality. And after two centuries of nation-building, national governments are showing signs of senility.[18]

Progressivism

A systemic crisis of over-scale expenditure and under-scale income afflicts the governments of the United States, Japan, and most of Western Europe. This extends as well to a number of American states and cities. The political and policy consequences of their plight has instructive parallels and contrasts with their experience a century and more ago.

An iron triangle of state and city political bosses and machines, contractors and corporations, and corrupt governors, mayors, and legislators grew over the course of the nineteenth century in pace with industrialization, urbanization, and machine-party politics. At the turn of the twentieth century there arose in response a burst of media exposure ("muckraking"), a popular political reaction, and a substantial (if not transformational) body of reform: what historians call the Progressive movement.

The economic downturn of the 1890s and the new urban, middle-class society of the early twentieth century gave birth to that development. Today the Great Recession of the early twenty-first century and its impact on homeowners and taxpayers feed a changing state politics.[19]

There is, however, a major difference in goals. The Progressive movement heralded the rise of active government. Its core belief was that a more engaged state was necessary to secure the diverse reforms that Progressives sought. And diverse they were, as befitted a society deeply conflicted between its desire for government support and its fear of government power.

When it came to political reform, Progressives called on the state to encourage party primaries and discourage the use of corporate money in elections. They wanted women's suffrage so as to uplift the tone of politics. The same goal led many of them to support laws that made it harder for blacks and immigrants to vote.

Progressive economic regulation had comparable diversity. The antitrust movement sought to break up overly large corporations (too big to succeed?). Others saw the benefits of concentrated business and finance, but wanted stronger oversight. A third theme was to improve the lot of workers by regulating hours, wages, and working conditions.

A similar eclecticism—and reliance on more active government—characterized Progressive social reform. There were efforts to improve the housing and family life of the cities' heavily immigrant poor. Many reformers sought (often with the same social justification) to prohibit liquor and restrict the inflow of new immigrants.

In foreign policy the range of Progressive causes stretched from pacifism and the he-kept-us-out-of-war neutrality of Woodrow Wilson's first term to the war-to-end-war interventionism of his second. In the ultimate application of the Progressive mantra of more active government, Wilson sought after the war to create a League of Nations, an international public agency that could use force to preserve peace.[20]

The common denominator of these causes was to turn to government as the primary agent of change. This impulse would later come to fruition, on its darkest side, with European Fascism and Communism and the Second World War and, more beneficently, with the

New Deal, the Great Society, and the West's social welfare states. The twentieth was the century of the multipurpose national state: regulatory, welfare, warfare. Barack Obama's New Foundation (to mix metaphors) rested on a solid and extensive old one.[21]

Anti-Progressivism?

A century after the Progressive movement, a new and very different crisis in governance is stirring up a state politics of exposure, electoral reaction, and policy reform. Public employee unions and their leaders have a position that in some respects echoes the party bosses and immigrant voters of a century and more ago. They provide the money, manpower, and votes that elections require. Compliant legislators and governors make mutually beneficial deals with union leaders, as their counterparts more than a century ago did with contractors and corporations.

Public employees enjoy wage, health care, and pension advantages, as loyal voters in the past got jobs and help in time of need. The tide of immigrant workers and their votes reinforced boss-machine politics in the past. The substantial presence of public sector workers (civil servants, teachers, police, firefighters), the black urban poor, and Hispanic newcomers now plays a similar role.

In the Midwest and the South, there are comparable alliances between vested economic and social interests and compliant governors and legislatures. So far, however, the primary popular-political backlash has come in the unionized industrial states, as was the case in the early stages of the Progressive movement.

Political patronage was difficult (indeed, impossible) to distinguish from graft and corruption in the late nineteenth and early twentieth centuries. Today, aid to the needy has evolved from relief ("alleviation, ease, or deliverance through the removal of pain, distress, oppression") to welfare ("the provision of a minimal level of well-being and social support for all citizens"). Public employee wage, health, and pension provisions have evolved from fringe benefits to entitlements. These terms are freighted with political meaning: they reflect a sea change in the role of government.[22]

It is widely believed that the wages and especially the retirement and medical benefits of public employees are noticeably better than those of their private counterparts. Public employees are far more likely to have defined benefit than defined contribution pension plans. Public pensions often assume commitments and are based on expected returns on investment that far outstrip what they are likely to raise or to pay out.[23]

Will the governors who challenge the current system come to be seen as the forerunners of what might be called an anti-Progressive movement: one as concerned with limiting or even reducing government power and largesse as its prototype a century ago was determined to enhance it? The latter-day advocates of change and reform are as yet far from attaining so substantial a political presence, and indeed they may never do so. Nevertheless there are conspicuous parallels between the turn-of-the-twentieth, century Progressive movement and much state politics today.

The Progressive reaction to the party boss-machine system of the late nineteenth and early twentieth centuries began in the cities and states of the Midwest—most notably Ohio, Michigan, and Wisconsin—and then spread across the nation. With varying degrees of commitment, governors such as Robert La Follette in Wisconsin, Hiram Johnson in California, Theodore Roosevelt and Charles Evans Hughes in New York, and Woodrow Wilson in New Jersey were prominent figures in the Progressive movement. Four of them (La Follette, Roosevelt, Hughes, and Wilson) ran for president.

Today many of the same states have leaders embroiled in the issue of what to do about their large-scale spending and long-term entitlements. A Republican fivesome of Mitch Daniels in Indiana, Chris Christie in New Jersey, John Kasich in Ohio, Scott Walker in Wisconsin, and Rick Snyder in Michigan conspicuously confronted public unions and their members' entitlements.[24]

Daniels could claim the most substantial record, and until he decided not to run he was a prominent prospect for the 2012 GOP presidential nomination. Under him Indiana cut back on pension and health-care obligations to its public employees and ended their right to collective bargaining. The state's debt turned into a $1.5 billion surplus, and the Indiana economy withstood the recession better than most of its neighbors. More recently Chris Christie and Scott Walker have attracted comparable attention, amid much speculation as to their national political prospects.[25]

Just as the Progressive movement had *prominenti* from both parties, so does discomfort with the current state of affairs cross party lines. Most Democratic governors have sought to ease their states' fiscal pains by raising taxes rather than reducing entitlements. New York's governor Andrew Cuomo is the most visible Democrat challenging the public sector unions on pensions and other perks. Despite (or because of) this, Cuomo is a 2016 Democratic presidential possibility.[26]

Things are not working out well in Illinois, where taxes have been substantially raised and outlays have been minimally cut, yet debt and deficits remain unnervingly high. Democratic Maryland, Rhode Island, and Connecticut appear to be faring better. In any event, Brandeis's vision of the states as laboratories of democracy is alive and well.[27]

La Follette's Wisconsin was the poster child of the Progressive era. With Governor Walker and Congressman and 2012 GOP vice presidential candidate Paul Ryan, it has been comparably conspicuous in the current effort to roll back entitlement spending.[28]

Walker posed an especially contentious challenge to the state's public sector union–Democratic party alliance when he got the legislature to ban collective bargaining by state employees. He faced a recall election in 2012, which he won by a larger margin than in his initial election two years before. The new austerity, like the old Wisconsin progressivism, is far from coherent or fully defined. But like its predecessor, it strikes a popular chord.[29]

California was the great success story of post–World War II America. It has become a showcase for the effects of large-scale public spending and ample public employee entitlements. Its wealth and a strong tradition of active state government account in part for this preeminence. But what was special about California was the unusual importance of Progressive-era innovations in participatory government: the initiative and the referendum. These devices, originally intended to counter the power of party machines and corporations, turned out to be well suited to a populist political culture—and to the growth of entitlements.

California's public sector unions, who won the right to collective bargaining in 1978, became the most powerful political interest group. Meanwhile the old conservative centers of privilege—banking, railroads, and real estate—were supplanted by new, more liberal ones: Hollywood, Silicon Valley, the state college and university system. The major new arrivals in the late twentieth century were Mexican immigrants, quickly absorbed into the Democratic party. The GOP became a marginal political presence.[30]

The fiscal and policy cost of decades of growth in California's workforce and its perks became ever more evident. Highways and schools decayed; welfare costs and public worker benefits outstripped the revenue available to pay for them; business and income taxes rose steeply; and growing numbers of businesses and middle-class citizens departed.[31]

The state faced a budget gap of about $16 billion in 2012, a California-sized version of the problem facing other commonwealths. Governor Jerry Brown initially echoed New York's Cuomo in stressing the need to scale back spending and commitments. He vetoed 34 laws passed by the legislature, most of them fine-tuning the regulation of working conditions, as either unenforceable or detrimental to the state's shaky economy.

At the same time he backed Proposition 30, a referendum proposal that sought to ease California's stressed educational system by increasing state sales taxes for four years and adding a surcharge on incomes over $250,000 for seven years. The political, union, and business establishments supported Prop 30, which comfortably won. California's budget crunch eased in 2013. But, like Wisconsin, its long-term fiscal and economic prospects remain clouded.[32]

Is Wisconsin or California the signpost for what is to come? Almost certainly, both are. Just as the Progressive movement was shaped by the complex interplay of competing interests, so is that the case today. Private union members are not very sympathetic to public sector employees' efforts to improve their (often superior) perks: a fact of political life that the GOP has noticed. Nor do private sector taxpayers or currently employed state and city employees worry overmuch about meeting the pension costs of already retired public workers. Public school teachers, college professors, police officers and firefighters, and civil servants do not always have interests in common. The fact that the financial fiscal woes of Democratic blue states outweigh those of Republican red ones may have as yet unpredictable policy and political consequences.[33]

The Shame of the Cities

Lincoln Steffens, the most prominent of the muckraker journalists of the Progressive era, focused national attention on the political corruption of his time. His *The Struggle for Self-Government* (1906) described the boss-machine-business triad in six states. But his iconic work was *The Shame of the Cities* (1904), which informed its readers how a number of the largest American cities were (mis-) governed.

Like the states, many American cities now face out-of-control costs and commitments. Public employee pension plans (3,200 of them), health care, and salaries raise the same problems of taxation and debt. The unfunded liabilities of local pension plans were estimated at over $574 billion in 2012. Perhaps as a consequence, today's mayors include some of the more interesting and independent-minded figures in American politics, such as now-senator Cory Booker of Newark, Michael Nutter of Philadelphia, and Julián Castro of San Antonio.[34]

Los Angeles mayor Antonio Villaraigosa and his successor Eric Garcetti, Michael Bloomberg of New York, and Rahm Emanuel of Chicago echo state governors in wrestling with the inadequately funded pension and other costs of public unions (the teachers' in particular). New York City's contribution to its employees' pension plans rose from $1.5 billion to $8 billion in the twenty-first century's first decade. Three percent of the city's property tax revenues went for pension costs in 2001; a 34 percent slice is the estimate for 2015. This revenue source has been hard hit by the recession. But Bloomberg's successor Bill de Blasio hews to an unreconstructed pro-union, liberal-Left approach to the office, promising an interesting case study in the city as government laboratory.[35]

California's cities and towns have been poster children of the unsustainable liabilities issue. Vallejo went through a painful and widely publicized bankruptcy, though it has begun to recover unexpectedly well. Stockton, too, has been edging toward the bankruptcy cliff. To avoid that fate, the residents of San Diego and San Jose (on the same day that Wisconsin governor Walker retained his job) voted overwhelmingly to cut city worker pensions, current and future. More recently, Detroit has become the largest American city to enter into bankruptcy.[36]

When he was in the White House, presidential counselor Rahm Emanuel had to deal with obdurate Republican congressional opposition. As mayor of Chicago he has had to cope with a no less entrenched Democratic–public union political establishment. He went after ballooning pension costs, warning of their impact on education, public services, and real estate taxes. His attempt to rein in the Chicago teachers' union kicked off a strike in September 2012. Though the teachers' salaries were among the highest in the country and the union had over three times as many retired as working members, it retained public support. Its members' loyalty echoed that of the party machine faithful a century ago. Emanuel had to settle for much less saving than he thought necessary.[37]

With all this ferment, the state and local response to fiscal crisis at times poses a dramatic contrast to the gridlock and stasis of the federal government and the European community. The unimpeded flow of capital, labor, and entrepreneurship from less to more promising locales is a distinguishing feature of the American federal system. It fosters a political flexibility lacking on the national scene. But the larger problem of rising expectations and demands for what government can do in the face of diminished realities of economic growth and public revenue is felt at all levels of American government, as it is elsewhere in the world.[38]

The July 2012 report of a State Budget Task Force headed by financial gurus Paul Volcker and Richard Ravitch unsurprisingly concluded that this was a long-term crisis. It was the product of years of underfinanced pension commitments, unrealistic expectations for pension investment earnings, and seemingly insuperable obstacles to raising substantially more revenue or substantially reducing the cost of government.

Yet for all its weight, the state and local fiscal crisis did not figure prominently in the 2012 election. This may reflect the popular view that localities, states, and nation are distinctly separate levels of government. Or it may be taken as evidence that for all the ferment going on over the costs of bureaucracy and the welfare state and how to pay for them, neither in city, state, nor nation is there any political consensus as to what to do about it. Our federalist system underscores the variety of the demands that American life places on public life. It also makes clear that, in the largest sense, the issues of Obama's time make their mark on every level of government.[39]

CHAPTER FOUR

. . .

Rough Waters: Finance and the Economy

OBAMA'S 2008 WINNING coalition was energized by his "Hope and Change" campaign: Health care reform! Immigration reform! Education reform! Carbon emissions reduction! Renewable energy! Out of Iraq! Guantanamo closed!

Then the iron law of unforeseen events went to work. The economic downturn that assured Obama's election became the decisive fact of life in his presidency. Topics previously relegated to the back burner—banking and finance; government spending, taxes, and debt; housing and mortgages; above all, unemployment—dominated the political agenda.

The tension between the economic and social policies that Obama wanted to follow and the conditions that reality imposed upon him defined the course of his first presidential term. Halfway through it, what he did and didn't do led to a resounding off-year Democratic defeat. Two years later, his message (and, perhaps in equal measure, his opponent's message) revitalized enough of his core coalition to give him a clear if not decisive victory.

1. THE ECONOMY AND THE POLITY

Obama's opponents believe along with Margaret Thatcher that in economic and social matters "the facts of life are conservative." He thinks otherwise: "The arguments of liberals are more often grounded in reason and fact." His economic policy embodied that view, drawing on Keynesian economics and European social democracy.[1]

But Obama was far from the socialist-minded ideologue portrayed by his conservative critics. When journalist Jon Meacham observed in February 2009, just after he took office, that "we are all socialists now," it was no less a rhetorical flourish than Richard Nixon's declaration (taken from Milton Friedman) 40 years before: "We are all Keynesians."[2]

Obama's principal economic advisers Timothy Geithner and Lawrence Summers subscribed to the moderate Keynesian template that all but defines academic Economics. Those who counseled larger, more assertive federal intervention, such as Paul Volcker and Austen Goolsby, differed in degree but not kind.[3]

But from the Left's perspective, most conspicuously articulated by economist-turned-polemicist Paul Krugman, Obama's response to the finance-jobs crisis was inadequate. He failed to nationalize troubled banks; he had too cozy a relationship with Wall Street; he did not commit enough money to his Stimulus to significantly spur economic expansion; and he shamefully pulled back from socialized medical care. Pundit Ezra Klein concluded, "The reality is that America's anti-business president has led an extremely pro-business recovery."[4]

Critics on the Right found no dearth of intervention in Obama's actions; quite the contrary. Their preferred label (not all that different from the suspicions of the Left) was "crony capitalism": a cozy mutuality with favored unions such as the United Auto Workers, friendly investment bankers, subsidy-hungry renewable energy start-ups, and

Silicon Valley. To certain kinds of big business and certain kinds of big labor could be added certain kinds of big government: social welfare, clean energy, economic regulation. The military-industrial complex that Eisenhower warned against had been replaced, in critics' eyes, by a big union–New Age enterprise complex.[5]

The GOP-conservative opposition was wedded to a very different set of economic assumptions. These descended from Ronald Reagan's supply-side precepts. Paul Ryan's 2010 "roadmap," "A Choice of Two Futures," laid out a supply side–small government alternative to the big spending–big government Obama vision. The Tea Party was the most conspicuous voice of the low tax–low spend mantra, which rooted the prospects of prosperity and growth as solidly in a weak state as the Keynesian Democrats did in a strong one.[6]

In some respects this confrontation between economic perspectives echoed the New Deal–conservative conflict of the 1930s. Once again a larger, international economic malaise colored the American debate. Depressing analogies—with stagnant Japan, with the Euro-crisis-afflicted European Union—coexisted with hopeful references to past American reform triumphs: the New Deal, the Great Society.[7]

The fringe (and not-so-fringe) theories that had some purchase in the Great Depression of 1929–1932—Marxism, fascist-inspired corporatism, gold monetarism—had no place in the debate over the Great Recession of 2008–2009. A few outliers advocated neo-chartalism, the view that government could freely print paper money and thus be able to spend what seemed necessary to fix the economy. An even fewer few adhered to the Austrian School of Economics view that suffering was unavoidable, and any government intervention would delay the natural process of economic recovery.

A government which for three quarters of a century had been wedded to moderate Keynesianism and a partial welfare state was not about to turn to such nostrums. Nor did the administration take seriously the bizarre proposals that surfaced when the need to raise the debt ceiling reemerged in early 2013: that the president do so without benefit of Congress, or that the Treasury magically solve the problem by minting trillion-dollar platinum coins.[8]

The public reaction to the economic policy debate has been ambiguous. Obama's millionaire-billionaire populist motif is an appealing political response to the economic malaise. But so too is the Republican theme that big spending and taxing are more the problem than the solution.[9]

As the election year of 2012 and then Obama's second term unfolded, the economic debate appeared to be fixed in amber. The steep 2008–2009 decline in employment and growth had stopped. But the ensuing "recovery" was as unprecedented as the stagflation that plagued the 1970s. The unsettling mix now was not inflation-cum-unemployment and a stagnant economy, but a frustrating blend of slow growth, stubbornly high unemployment, little inflation, and persistently low (even negative) interest rates on Treasuries and other bonds. Stagcession—or in Larry Summers's words, "secular stagnation"—has succeeded stagflation as the economy's most nagging problem.

New jobs have been created but at far from the pace necessary to keep up with the growth of the potential workforce, let alone end stubbornly persistent unemployment of 6–8 percent and an overall non- and underemployment rate well into double figures. Year after year, the growth rate has edged up and then fallen back.

The neo-Keynesian argument that government stimuli just weren't large enough had diminishing political and even economic appeal. Instead, as in the Carter 1970s, the more imprecise theme of national malaise became an appealing explanation of what had gone wrong. Critics of Obama pointed to the continuing reluctance of companies or investors to venture beyond a hunker-down defensiveness as the major source of the ongoing recession. His defenders dwelt on how much worse things would have been without his policies.[10]

Neither the optimistic Democratic expectation of a rapid recovery nor the pessimistic Republican expectation of a double-dip recession has materialized. The situation is not a uniquely American one. In Europe, China, and elsewhere, both the free market and the Keynesian models seem insufficient. Neither government pump-priming, low interest rates, nor fiscal austerity seems to be the answer to a stalled economy.[11]

A larger perspective may help explain this state of affairs. Democratic and authoritarian states alike are beset by aging populations and overbudgeted, underfunded entitlement commitments. In both the United States and Europe, faith in the capacity of modern, globalized economies to sustain growth is eroding—at a time when the transformative effects of technology have never been higher.

Conservative belief in the curative power of a lightly regulated market flourishes, reflected in the rise of a debate over whether FDR's New Deal policies delayed or fostered jobs and growth. Familiar, too, is the charge that overregulation and excessive taxation impose burdensome costs on business. Both the Right and the Left took on "Wall Street" as they did in the 1930s.[12]

The Democratic-Obama response to the dragging economy has been to resurrect another venerable theme: inequality. But again, the widening gap between the rich and the poor is a larger development, visible in Europe and increasingly so in China. The truth of the matter seems to be what Sylvia Nasar in *Grand Pursuit*, her history of economic theories and theorists, concludes: that economic analysis, like every attempt to comprehend social experience, is prey to the ever-eroding and all-but-unforeseeable factors of contingency and change: "Reality has mostly outstripped imagination."[13]

2. FIXING FINANCE

The banking/financial crisis that erupted in the fall of 2008, at the height of the election campaign, was the first major policy challenge for Obama. During the post-election transition period he showed a confidence-engendering readiness to support Bush's TARP. This reassured the banking and financial communities, if not his liberal base. The prevailing view is that Obama's application of TARP successfully averted further financial meltdown—although with the passage of time, there has been much criticism of the scale of government largesse to the large banks and investment houses, compared to underwater or foreclosed homeowners.[14]

TARP's way was eased in part by continuities of personnel and policy between the outgoing Bush administration (Federal Reserve chair Ben Bernanke, Treasury Secretary Henry Paulson) and the Obama team (Bernanke, Treasury Secretary Geithner, chief economic adviser Summers). The enabling legislation for TARP was passed in the waning days of the Bush administration, by what would soon be regarded as an incredibly bipartisan vote. Perhaps not coincidentally, it turned out to be the most successful policy response to the financial/economic crunch.

The Bush-Obama response to the fiscal crisis in late 2008 and early 2009 resembled that of the Hoover-FDR teams in late 1932 and early 1933. Then as now, there was joint action in the face of a national crisis (though FDR kept his distance from the negotiations). In 1933 the banks reopened successfully and at small cost to the government. Now the banks and financial firms (save Lehman and Bear Stearns) stayed open: again, at little ultimate cost to the government.[15]

Obama's actions after he took office echoed the early New Deal's 1933–1934 quartet of a bank holiday, the Federal Deposit Insurance Corporation, the Securities and Exchange Commission, and the Glass-Steagall banking act, compressed now into the TARP bailouts and the Dodd-Frank financial reform. But unlike the New Deal, which got the benefit of a boost in the 1934 election, the Obama program won little popular endorsement in 2010.[16]

Like Obama's health-care reform, Dodd-Frank is complex and detailed, a bureaucratic blueprint as much as a legislative program. Its 845 pages are 73 times the length of the New Deal's Glass-Steagall banking law. It requires extensive new filing and reporting requirements, with fees and paperwork that add up (as had the Sarbanes-Oxley corporate management act under Bush) to a stiff hike in the cost of doing business.

Yale Law School professor Jonathan Macey cuttingly observed: "Laws classically provide people with rules. Dodd-Frank is not directed at people. It is an outline directed at bureaucrats and it instructs them to make still more regulations and to create more bureaucracies." But in our complex age and in the superheated partisanship of the contemporary Congress, less detailed and specific lawmaking appears not to be in the cards.[17]

As in the case of Obamacare, Dodd-Frank's implementation so far has turned out to be a can of worms. It too set up new regulatory bodies with great if undefined powers: the Financial and Stability Oversight Council and the Consumer Financial Protection Bureau.

Glass-Steagall's straightforward separation of commercial from investment banking was sufficient to the banking ambience of the 1930s. But a far more complex regulatory apparatus is required in the twenty-first century. Four of the five federal agencies charged to enforce the Dodd-Frank rules came up with a 298-page proposal, posing 383 questions and 1,420 subquestions for firms to answer, which a critic said was "unintelligible any way you read it." At the end of 2013, Dodd-Frank's Commodity Futures Trading Commission issued a 498-page directive enacting the "Volcker rule," which restricted proprietary trading by commercial banks in speculative outlets such as hedge and private equity funds.

Dodd-Frank's reliance on hundreds of rules was mother's milk to lobbyists and special interests, and imposed a heavy burden on the bureaucrats who were writing them. In the summer of 2013, three years after Dodd-Frank's passage, the deadline for 279 of the law's rules had passed, but only 104 had been finalized. Meanwhile, state attorneys-general, ever on the *qui vive* for the political and financial benefit to be derived from going after fat financial institutions, were ramping up their own regulatory, investigative, and legal onslaughts.[18]

Problems inevitable in so sweeping a law have come with the evolution of Dodd-Frank. Its Consumer Financial Protection Bureau came under fire as too intrusive and costly in attempting to oversee consumer credit card and mortgage borrowing. Its Financial Stability Oversight Council, chaired by the Secretary of the Treasury, with meetings not open to the press or the public, was accused of threatening the independence of the Securities and Exchange Commission, the Federal Reserve, the Comptroller of the Currency, and the Federal Deposit Insurance Corporation.[19]

Wall Street (in the generic sense of the financial community) was uncharacteristically supportive of Obama in 2008: 51 percent of its campaign contributions that year went to him. That reflected both the changed epicenter of the financial world from industry to information technology and the generational-ideological shift from old WASP to new, often Jewish or Catholic, moneyed givers. But in part because of the hostile tone of Dodd-Frank, the portion of the financial community backing the Democrats and Obama went down to 47 percent in 2010 and 32 percent in 2012.

It emerged that the financial community needn't have worried all that much. Dodd-Frank may have been the biggest financial reform bill since the 1930s, but big wasn't necessarily powerful (a lesson to be learned in other areas of government, from defense to environmental regulation and health care). Wall Street continues to be as financially flush as it is politically unpopular.[20]

3. THE TRIAL OF JOBS

Fixing finance, in the public-political scheme of things, is like a dogfight waged high above the mundane concerns of the average citizen. Unemployment is like trench warfare: of direct and immediate concern to the foot soldiers slogging it out on the battlefield of everyday life.

Job losses grew astronomically in the last Bush and first Obama months. It was not surprising that the new president's first policy initiative was a massive stimulus bill to staunch that decline. The Recovery and Reinvestment Act of February 2009, as universally called the Stimulus as the Patient Protection and Affordable Care Act came to be known as Obamacare, was in the spirit of the New Deal's relief and recovery laws of 1933–1935.

But now was not then. Conservatives in the early 1930s groused about the size of the New Deal's relief and public works expenditures, though few (of the few) congressional Republicans dared oppose them. In 2009–2010 a near-trillion-dollar commitment did not seem outsized. Council of Economic Advisers head Christine Romer proposed a more substantial $1.2 trillion. Economist Paul Krugman complained that the $787 billion (eventually raised to $831 billion) Stimulus was less than a third of what was needed. Chief economics adviser Larry Summers thought anything over a trillion dollars was a political nonstarter, and Obama agreed with him. As in the case of a government-run ("single payer") health-care system, there appeared to be limited support in Congress or public opinion for so much more spending.

It was expected that the relatively restrained Stimulus, a third of it devoted to tax cuts, would attract some Republican support, and Obama did some outreach to achieve this. But a polarized politics, and his decision to let the congressional Democratic leadership craft the bill, worked against that outcome. Only three GOP senators and not a single Republican House member voted for the Stimulus.[21]

More revealing was how the modern response to a sluggish economy and large-scale unemployment differed from the 1930s. The scale of joblessness then was triple that of 2009. With no safety net of unemployment compensation, the great need was to provide outright relief and/or work as soon as possible. In his first two hours as head of the Federal Emergency Relief Administration, Harry Hopkins doled out over $5 million to eight states; within two weeks 4 million unemployed were on the Federal Emergency Relief Administration payroll.[22]

In contrast, about 60 percent of Obama's Stimulus went to infrastructure spending and tax reduction, some 40 percent to entitlements support and aid to the states to meet salary shortfalls for teachers and other public employees. Much of this seemed like a classic payoff to Democratic constituencies. One official admitted, "We should have spent more time thinking about where the money was being spent."[23]

Something more than rewarding friends was afoot. Obama touted Stimulus infrastructure spending as the largest such commitment since Dwight Eisenhower's interstate highway system. But the dams–roads–public buildings "public works" of the past had morphed into the new concept of "investments": not only in steel and concrete and asphalt but in education, health care, renewable energy, and high-speed trains.

Men with shovels took to the streets and the land in 1933–1934. But there were no shovel-ready projects to (so to speak) dig into in

2009. Only $64 billion—8 percent of the Stimulus total—went to traditional public works. The much larger helping hand to over-committed state budgets was more a prop to short-term sustainability than a relief policy.[24]

Michael Grunbaum's *The New New Deal* makes much of the Stimulus's Advanced Research Projects Agency-Energy (ARPA-E) provision. Funded with $400 million (0.5 percent of the total), this body was in line of descent from the Army Research Projects Agency, widely (if overly) credited with having given birth to the Internet. It was intended to make seed money available to clean energy and other New Age projects. ARPA-E may eventually foster new technology of great significance. But it may not, and meanwhile there were jobs to be created or saved.[25]

These considerations reduced the ability of the Stimulus to administer a quick and substantial jolt to the economy. Although some 80 percent of Stimulus spending was authorized by September 2010, only about a third was allocated to specific projects. Most estimates put the saving or creating jobs impact of the Stimulus at 1.5 to 2 million, compared to the 3.5 million predicted by advocates. Nor did it succeed in its goal of bringing unemployment down well below 8 percent.

The content of the Stimulus was understandable, given the administration's belief that it would quickly reduce unemployment and spur economic growth. It was out of that belief that Obama made two decisions that profoundly shaped the course of his presidency.

The first was to turn over not only the passage but the substance of the Stimulus to the House Democratic leadership. Why didn't Obama seek to keep control in the White House? For one thing, his relationship to his party was less hierarchical than FDR's: parties today are not the boss-and-machine-led organisms that they were then. They are far more ideologically cohesive. FDR could not entrust his program to a congressional Democratic leadership dominated by Southerners and northern Irish pols, whose commitment to the New Deal was shaky at best.

Whatever differences Obama may have had with House Speaker Pelosi and Senate Majority Leader Reid, these did not reside in the realm of ideology. They listened to the same voices: organized labor, especially public unions; the environmental lobby; affluent-urban-liberal and new technology donor-constituents; and the liberal media.[26]

The congressional vote on the Stimulus showed how quickly Obama's campaign theme of bi- (or supra-) partisanship fell victim to the realities of contemporary American politics. In part this was because the terms of the Stimulus were already fixed by the Democratic leadership by the time Obama reached out to the House GOP Conference for some support. The same scenario played out in the passage of Dodd-Frank and Obamacare.

Aside from the Stimulus, the administration's most conspicuous jobs-related response to the recession involved the iconic American auto industry, beset by collapsing orders and ever more competitive foreign-owned firms. Using TARP money and a controlled bankruptcy that bypassed the normal process of corporate insolvency, the government bailed out General Motors and Chrysler, the two shakiest firms. Conservative-GOP critics hit Obama hard for favoring the UAW over the industry's bondholders. But most Americans were not committed to the principle that traditional rules as to who gets bailed out first were sacrosanct in a time of trouble. The president's prescience in this matter would be rewarded by Ohio voters in the 2012 election.[27]

The administration's second big decision, to change its focus from jobs to less immediately pressing issues such as health care, banking/financial reform, cap and trade, and renewable energy, did not have comparable political payoff. Obama's own inclinations, and powerful elements of his coalition—affluent liberals, the media—were more interested in these other, more toothsome goals. It is not difficult to see why this was so. Obama's core appeal (and, indeed, his political persona) was not that of a skilled political craftsman á la LBJ but of a Wilsonian purveyor of big ideas and bigger dreams.

Liberals decried the inadequate size of the Stimulus; conservatives, its misdirected objectives. Most public opinion, despite administration assurance that the program had saved millions of jobs otherwise fated to be lost, reacted negatively to its seeming inability to stem a stubbornly high and persisting joblessness. While the mix of taxes, spending, and debt became ever more intertwined and complex, the dominant political reality continued to be the specter of unemployment: the biblical trials of Job transmuted into the modern trial of joblessness.[28]

Nor was much encouragement to be derived from the indices of long-term unemployment, labor force participation, or gross domestic product (GDP). A full-scale depression, as Obama and his supporters rightly observed, had been averted. Their claim that 3.5 million jobs, adding 3 percent to economic growth, had been created or saved by the Stimulus was more doubtful.

According to one estimate, four out of five of the jobs created or saved were in government, although the administration pledged that 90 percent would be private. Nor was the contention that each dollar of Stimulus spending triggered between $1.50 and $2.50 in economic growth beyond question.

In November 2011 the Congressional Budget Office substantially downgraded its estimate of created jobs, and took note of the drag on output imposed by the contribution of the Stimulus to an ever-growing national debt. Summers, echoing Keynes, said that Stimulus spending should be targeted, temporary, and timely. Public works such as routine road repairs were rapid consumers of government funds. But they were not, in a highly mechanized time, prolific job creators.[29]

There is a study of the impact of the Stimulus in Silver Spring, Maryland, the home of many government contractors. The state's governor, beset like so many others by budgetary stringency, quickly reduced Maryland's building expenditure budget by even more than the Stimulus added to it. Maryland's transportation infrastructure spending went down $90 million from 2009 to 2012. So not that much was stimulated by the Stimulus.

There was another, quite predictable problem: favoritism. Three major Bethesda firms got $712 million in Stimulus funds, plus $702 million in other government contracts. This was not necessarily spent on job-creating activities. Palladian Partners, a communications firm that was the biggest client of the National Institutes of Health (NIH), used $800,000 in Stimulus money to collect and disseminate information—on how NIH could spend its Stimulus money. The project produced a website and 29 published articles but only two new employees (who came from other jobs).

These disappointments were national. Half a billion Stimulus dollars were allocated to recruit and train people for new green jobs. The goal was 80,000 new positions. Halfway through the grant period, only 8,000 had materialized. Home weatherizing was another ambitious Stimulus initiative: $5 billion was to benefit some 590,000 homes in this supposedly shovel-ready project. But only 8 percent of the money was spent in the first year of the Stimulus. Maryland's share was 479 homes, 4 percent of the goal.

Why the shortfalls? As a concession to organized labor, Stimulus programs had to abide by prevailing wage rules. So before paying their weatherization workers, the states spent months on surveys to determine the average wages and benefits earned for workers weatherizing homes in each county.[30]

These conditions were not peculiar to Obama's Stimulus, as any student of Defense or any other large-scale government program well knows. What was new was the conflict between the Old Economy of public works, rent-seeking contractors, and union workers, and the demands of new claimants—high tech, greenery, and the like. One-time projects—the 2010 Census, the conversion to digital TV—made work, but not for long. Tens of billions to help states meet Medicaid costs or pay teachers was admirable. But this was stopgap spending, of doubtful job-producing value.

As the 2010 midterm election approached, these shortcomings fed the GOP opposition. In September Obama proposed an additional $50 billion Stimulus, but it was widely dismissed as too little and/or too late.

After his 2010 setback, Obama pledged to focus "like a laser" on the creation of jobs through the "investment" of government spending. He created a Council on Jobs and Competitiveness, headed by General Electric CEO Geoffrey Immelt, in which labor and management were to come up with ways of increasing employment. The council met quarterly for a year, but faded away after its January 2012 gathering. The widening gulf between business and the administration, labor and management differences over outsourcing and other irritants, and most of all the sheer inadequacy of government by committee in an election year put paid to this exercise in Kumbaya.[31]

The precipitate decline of 2008–2009 had stopped. But a quick jobs recovery, as after previous post–World War II recessions, was not happening. The monthly job report took on a political significance not unlike the casualty reports at the height (or depth) of George W. Bush's Iraq war. Only 54,000 net new jobs were reported for May 2011, and unemployment reached 9.1 percent. There was no jobs growth in August. Critics attributed these depressing figures to a big rise in federal spending, negated by business uncertainty over regulation.[32]

In a much-heralded September 2011 address, Obama proposed an American Jobs Act that repackaged familiar standbys of the 2009 Stimulus: more infrastructure spending, subsidizing teachers' salaries, clean energy, and fast rail. He called for a 12-member super committee to add another half trillion to the $1.5 trillion in spending that he had already requested.

Obama insisted: "This isn't political grandstanding. This isn't class warfare." A critic dismissed his remarks as "pathetic, pedestrian": by implication, political grandstanding and class warfare. A sympathizer hailed it as a bold, ambitious attempt to reset a halting presidency. Even a few Republicans found some elements worthwhile, while warning (without much conviction), "Don't let the campaign for this plan become an overt campaign for re-election."[33]

Without fully adopting his left wing's push for much more government spending and a substantial increase in taxes, Obama settled into his economic policy mantra for the run-up to the election: continued Stimulus spending and higher taxes on the wealthy.[34]

But the underlying problem remained: would *either* Keynesian pump-priming *or* free-market policies restore jobs in the world of 2012? If the old free-market model was flawed by the competing demands and complex economic realities of modern America, then so too was the Keynesian model of private sector job-creation through government pump-priming.

The question was how to provide jobs for the rising number of long-term unemployed hobbled by lack of education, age, and appropriate skills. How could companies be induced to invest and expand when they were inhibited by economic and fiscal uncertainty or disinclined because new technology and business methods allowed productivity to rise without a commensurate increase in employment?

In this sense the Great Recession of 2008–2011 echoed the stubbornly job creation–resistant Great Depression of 1930–1933. The recession's sluggish recovery increasingly distinguished it from its predecessors of 1948, 1953, 1957, 1960, 1969, 1974, 1980–81, 1990, and 2001.

Economist Paul Krugman held that if the public could be convinced to increase government spending to prepare for an invasion by space aliens, the slump would end in 18 months. This echoed Keynes's observation that a government program of hole digging and filling would have a stimulative effect. Whatever the theoretical substance of these observations, their political appeal (in the 2010s, as in the 1930s) was minimal.[35]

The sticky politics of jobs creation figured in two controversies during the zero-employment-growth month of August 2011. The National Labor Relations Board (NLRB) sought to stop the Boeing Company from opening a new nonunion plant in Charleston, South Carolina, and the Environmental Protection Agency decided to block the construction of the Keystone XL pipeline.

Boeing's South Carolina plant was designed to build its new Dreamliner plane. Although the factory did not threaten the jobs of the existing unionized workforce in Democratic Washington State, it did mean some 5,000 more nonunionized workers in Republican South Carolina. The NLRB concluded that this was "retaliation" against the union. The Board's ukase was widely seen as overreach, which could encourage companies to avoid union states and/or move their plants abroad. The NLRB pulled back in December 2011, after Boeing and the union came to an agreement, and the union asked the board to drop its complaint.[36]

The XL Pipeline delay won the support of Obama's environmentalist backers and the opposition of his union supporters. With considerable political skill, he first declined to support the pipeline, then supported part of it, and then finessed the issue until after (as it turned out, *much* much after) the 2012 election.[37]

These marginal controversies fed into a larger criticism of excessive regulation that, along with uncertainty over the cost of

Obamacare, weakened business confidence and the job creation that came with it. In a September 2011 poll, only 36 percent of Americans approved of Obama's jobs program. Republicans charged that overspending and an anti-business regulatory environment sapped the confidence necessary to sustain growth. A conservative analyst estimated in July 2011 that the Stimulus cost $278,000 per job. But it was as iffy to estimate its cost as it was to measure its consequences.

There was a more disturbing underside to the data. Underemployment and dropouts from the jobs market put the number of work-deprived people at well over 20 million. The percentage of working-age Americans in the labor force dipped to its lowest level since 1981. The male workforce dropped to 70 percent, the least since relevant data collecting began in 1948.[38]

The situation had not markedly changed by election time 2012. Unemployment stubbornly stayed at around 8 percent; growth in the GDP slowed to about 2 percent. From the Left, Paul Krugman found administration policy "disappointing," not enough "to make any significant recovery or reducing the output gap." Obama, he said, had "presided over unprecedented austerity," not doing anything about state and local government cuts in the purchase of goods and services. Whatever the cause, and whatever the cure, the rate of job creation was generally viewed as unsatisfactory, a perception bolstered by the manifestly better records of countries such as Australia and Germany.[39]

The Obama storyline changed from the number of jobs saved or created to the unexpected depth and severity of the economic situation bequeathed by Bush. Conservatives pounded away at the gap between the administration's projections as to what the Stimulus would accomplish and what in fact it had. The result of the 2012 election implied that a majority of voters agreed with the administration.[40]

4. DEBT AND TAXES

From the 1890s to the 1920s, the Census Bureau published a data series on federal and state wealth, debt, and taxation. This was the first systematic attempt to measure the fiscal condition of the American polity. Now, in our time, government spending, debt, and taxation have joined with unemployment and the financial system to become a first-order economic issue.

How could the country deal with yearly trillion-dollar deficits, and a $17-trillion-plus national debt? How could it meet the current cost and future obligations of Medicare and Social Security, estimated by the Treasury in 2011 to add up to $51.3 trillion? Within a generation, the Treasury feared, the national debt could equal the country's GDP.

Spending and taxation have been staples of American politics since the New Deal. Entitlement add-ons and tax cuts flourished between 1946 and 1981; entitlement cuts and tax increases from 1982 to 1997. Then followed a decade of reduced taxes and increased spending, and (through mortgages and credit cards) a surge in consumer spending and indebtedness.

Debt assumed a more conspicuous place on the national agenda during Obama's first term, though its dramatic upward ascent began in the Bush II years. Taxation, too, commanded more attention. Exemptions and entitlements have grown like barnacles on the tax code to about twice what they were after the last large tax overhaul in 1986.[41]

Tax breaks have come to serve large social programs as well as powerful economic interests. Child benefits, mortgage interest, college tuition loans, and retirement savings are among the major current exemptions. Corporate jets and other fat-cat frills are by contrast small (if irritating). Like an unobserved storm in the night, a looming cloud of unfunded commitments—to retired federal employees and veterans, to Social Security and Medicare and, ultimately, to Obamacare recipients—has been gathering force.[42]

The parties hunkered down on polar views of taxes as either the key palliative for or the key problem behind the debt. The Democrats focused on "revenue raises" on the well-off, and no pullback on entitlements or "investments" (education, clean energy). The Republicans focused on cuts on entitlement and other spending, and no new taxes that might impede "investment" (private) by "job creators" (the rich).

Some more flexible pols floated the idea of reducing or indexing deductions on home mortgages, charity, or employer health-care costs. But this was a tangle of political third rails. Tax enemy Grover Norquist persuaded 235 of 242 House Republicans and 41 of the party's 47 senators to sign a pledge to oppose reductions in tax credits and deductions unless a commensurately lower tax rate was part of the package. On the margin, libertarian Ron Paul and others refloated the venerable flat tax. A few pundits sought to stir interest in a value-added tax.[43]

In early 2010 President Obama called for the creation of a National Commission on Fiscal Responsibility and Reform. Former Wyoming Republican senator Alan Simpson and former Democratic congressman Erskine Bowles headed the group, which was made up of 12 senators and representatives and six outside savants from both parties. At the same time the Bipartisan Policy Center, the creation of GOP grandees Bob Dole and Howard Baker and Democratic ex-senators George Mitchell and Tom Daschle, created a Debt Reduction Task Force headed by former Republican senator from New Mexico Pete Domenici and former Democratic budget director Alice Rivlin (also a member of Bowles-Simpson).

These were attempts by wise men and a wise woman of the Reagan–Bush I–Clinton era to bring back the bipartisan, let's-get-the-job-done spirit that (occasionally) appeared in the politics of the late twentieth century. Safely past the 2010 election, Domenici-Rivlin (in November) and Bowles-Simpson (in December) issued similar reports, calling for a grand bargain that eliminated tax loopholes and exemptions (but did not raise tax rates) and cuts in government spending (but not in Social Security), at a 4–1 ratio of spending cuts to revenue increases. Their shared target was a $4 trillion reduction in the national debt over 10 years.

Then the polarized politics of our time kicked in. Treasury Secretary Geithner and Republican leaders offered vague general endorsements. The commission's report won the support of 11 of its 18 members, short of the supermajority of 14 required to send it to Congress. The stipulation that Bowles-Simpson's recommendations would go before Congress on a take-it-or-leave-it basis was scuttled when six Republicans joined most Democrats to vote against it.

GOP congressman Paul Ryan, on the way to becoming his party's budget guru, led the three Republican commission members opposing the report. The GOP House leadership, sensitive to the no-new-taxes rigidity of its Tea Party component, also shied away from supporting Bowles-Simpson.[44]

Democrats were no more supportive. Four of them on the commission opposed the report. Ex-Speaker Nancy Pelosi found it "simply unacceptable," and President Obama, the commission's godfather, chose not to forward its recommendations to Congress. Instead, in December 2010 he called for reversing the Bush 2002 tax cuts for "millionaires and billionaires" (a rather grandiose label for individuals making more than $200,000 a year and families making over $250,000), with token concessions on entitlements spending.[45]

Eliminating the Bush tax reduction for the rich became a conspicuous part of Obama's take on the deficit-debt problem. Indeed, polls suggested that a large majority favored increased taxes on the wealthy and disfavored cuts in Medicare or Social Security. But *The Economist* concluded that Obama's tax increase for the top 2 percent of households would bring in a modest $34 billion in 2011, enough to cover only nine days of deficit growth. The Congressional Budget Office estimated that if all of the Bush tax cuts were extended, revenue would be 19.6 percent of GDP by 2020; raises on the wealthy would increase it only to 20 percent. During the interim, government spending was slated to rise to 24 percent of GDP.[46]

The Republican position was hardly more realistic. It rested on the unproven proposition that any tax raise for the wealthy stifled investment and entrepreneurship and the undeniable but not necessarily definitive fact that the richest 1 percent of taxpayers provided 40 percent of all federal taxes. Superinvestor Warren Buffett, with good reason to know, pointed out that the lower excess profits tax rate of the very wealthy enabled them to avoid paying more than 20 percent of their pretax income, well under the rate of most of the middle class.[47]

Speaker John Boehner and Majority Leader Eric Cantor floated the prospect of a revenue increase based on the (chancy) elimination of tax loopholes and exemptions, rather than on higher rates. But they soon drew back under fire from the Right. There were in fact instances of (some) Democrats' readiness to consider substantial spending cuts and (some) Republicans' readiness to consider ways of securing additional tax revenues. But more decisive was the core Republican opposition to revenue enhancement without at least commensurate spending reductions and the core Democratic reluctance to accept entitlement cutbacks.

Emboldened by their 2010 gains, the Republicans clashed with Obama over another newly significant fiscal issue: whether to sustain the 2002–2003 Bush tax cuts. A weakened Obama agreed to a two-year extension but secured a reduction of the payroll (Social Security) tax from 6.2 percent to 4.2 percent.

It could be argued that the Social Security tax reduction threatened that program's character as a self-sustaining form of insurance and would eventually turn it into a welfare entitlement like Medicaid and Medicare. But the cut was too popular for the Republicans to resist. Sure enough, this "temporary" reduction was continued in the Budget Control Act of 2011, not to be restored until the January 2013 "fiscal cliff" vote.[48]

The revenue-spending-debt wars engulfed yet another venerable entity of the fiscal realm: the budget. The president's annual budget proposal traditionally was an opening gun for interparty congressional haggling. Now it was enmeshed in the no-end-in-sight gridlock between the parties over the triad of the debt, the deficit, and taxation.

Obama proposed his first (2009–2010) budget soon after he took office. It was 20 percent higher than the preceding Bush budget and projected a deficit of $1.4 trillion; not surprising, given the state of the economy and the Democratic commitment to spending. Solid Democratic congressional majorities assured its passage.[49]

He kept the fiscal pot boiling with a $3.7 trillion 2010–2011 budget, which projected a $1.3 trillion deficit. He proclaimed that his budget would reduce the debt by $1 trillion. The Congressional Budget Office, declaring that it could not score speeches, thought that it would increase it by $2.8 trillion. (The eventual result was an increase of $1.6 trillion.)

The GOP-led House declined to consider Obama's 2011 budget. Senate Republicans put it on the table for a vote, but the Democrats (and the Republicans) unanimously rejected it: Democrats were not inclined to support what they rightly viewed as an empty partisan maneuver. Harry Reid saw to it that Obama's 2012 and 2013 budgets did not come to the Senate floor.

Budget politicization broke more new ground when Paul Ryan, the head of the House Budget Committee, proposed his own blueprint for federal spending in 2011 and again in 2012. Most controversially, he called for block grants to the states to meet Medicaid and Medicare costs. Democratic demonization of Ryan's proposals as a death threat to Medicare and Social Security (and, suggested a TV ad, his grandmother), followed as night the day. Ryan's rising status within the GOP, leading to his choice as Romney's running mate in 2012, followed as day the night.[50]

As Simpson-Bowles faded into the background and budgeting stalled, the politics of debt got new legs with the debt ceiling crisis of 2011. Raising the debt ceiling was hardly something new under the fiscal sun. It went up 18 times under Ronald Reagan and 7 times under George W. Bush (then-senator Obama voting against the 2006 increase as a sign of failed presidential leadership). In the midst of the economic crisis and with a Democratic Congress, Obama got a $3 trillion increase in January 2009, another $700 billion in February, $290 billion in December, and $1.9 trillion in February 2010. The $11.3 trillion debt ceiling of January 2009 had increased to $16.7 trillion.

But this was not enough. If the limit was not raised by March 2011 (later, after some actuarial legerdemain, by early August), the country faced the threat of default, downgrade, and a government shutdown: an attention-getting agenda, indeed.

Democratic analyst William Galston took the White House to task for choosing not to raise the debt ceiling in late 2010, when it still controlled the House. Senate Majority Leader Reid apparently wanted to force the Republicans in Congress to be involved in what was not likely to be a popular act. Analyst

Walter Russell Mead thought that the fight over the debt ceiling underlined the liberal dilemma of the lack of public support for many of the president's policy proposals. A July 2011 Gallup poll found that less than one in four respondents was in favor of raising the ceiling.[51]

The liberal-Progressive dream of wise, effective, compassionate government was being eroded by the looming threat of debt, spending, and an oversized state. As if to underline this concern, a couple of law professors proposed that Obama unilaterally raise the debt ceiling: to understate, politically and legally an iffy step.[52]

Obama and House Speaker Boehner launched negotiations seeking a grand bargain over taxes, spending, and debt reduction reminiscent of the dealings between Reagan and Speaker Tip O'Neill in the 1980s, and Clinton and Speaker Newt Gingrich in the 1990s.[53]

Boehner risked the ire of his Tea Party cohort when he proposed an $800 billion increase in revenue, based on cuts in tax exemptions and deductions. Obama took a similar risk by tentatively agreeing. In truth there was no way of guaranteeing that Congress would pare back popular deductions on contributions to charity, home mortgage interest, or state and local taxes. In addition, the GOP proposal would have its greatest impact on high earners concentrated in Democratic states, which hardly enhanced the likelihood of its passage.[54]

In the midst of this pas de deux, a bipartisan Senate group dubbed the Gang of Six, working in the spirit of Bowles-Simpson, came up with yet another package. It called for over $4 trillion in spending cuts over a decade and a revenue increase of as much as $1 trillion on top of what might come from ending the Bush tax cuts for the wealthy.

Obama could not be seen by his liberal base as having agreed to so much less new revenue than the Gang of Six proposed. So he upped the ante to $1.2 trillion to compensate for cuts in Medicare and Medicaid. Boehner, under his own pressure from the Tea Party wing in the House, seized on Obama's shift to walk away from the negotiations. Obama, for his part, had little taste or talent for the kind of over-the-table bargaining that Reagan and Clinton had. He did big solutions to big problems, not nitty-gritty nitpicking.

There has been much debate over who bore the greater blame for the failure to attain a Grand Compromise. In the wake of the negotiations breakdown, Obama insisted on either more tax revenue or smaller health-care cuts. Boehner claimed to still want a grand bargain, but not at the cost of up to $1 to $2 trillion in new taxes. Both sides were weighed down by party and ideological commitments, making a comprehensive settlement all but impossible.[55]

The Budget Control Act that finally emerged in August 2011 was not a Grand Compromise but a Grand Deferral. It raised the debt ceiling by enough to remove it as an issue in the 2012 election. It created a Congressional Joint Select Committee on Deficit Relations (quickly dubbed the Supercommittee), charged to craft a deficit reduction plan by the end of the year. If the Supercommittee did manage to come up with a proposal, it would go to Congress for a take-it-or-lcavc-it, up-or-down vote: no amendments, no filibuster.

This was Simpson-Bowles on steroids. If the committee failed to offer a bill all fiscal hell would break loose. On January 1, 2013, the Bush and the payroll (Social Security) tax cuts would lapse, and massive spending cuts—a set of "sequesters," in Congress-speak—of $1.2 trillion, split evenly between defense and nondefense spending—would come into effect.

The House vote for the Supercommittee proposal was 269-161; 174 Republicans and 95 Democrats for and 95 Democrats and 66 Republicans against. The still-majority (and less electorally challenged) Democrats in the Senate felt freer to support the bill. Yet 76 of the 87 supposedly obdurate Tea Party–dominated new GOP

House members also voted for it. (A majority of the more politically secure Black Caucus voted against.) While *The Economist* saw the bill as an instance of political dysfunction, Harvard Law School professor Noah Feldman thought otherwise. It was, he said, a vivid example of democracy at work: incoherent but centrist.[56]

Still, much of the Right thought the spending cuts too limited and the tax-cut preservation provision too shaky. One pundit called the budget deal "mostly a triumph of the welfare state over the Pentagon": its projected spending cuts weighed far more on defense than entitlement spending. The Left was just as unhappy, an indication of how hard a row compromise had to hoe in a polarized polity. A "firestorm from the progressive press" greeted the budget deal, over both the spending cuts and the (temporary) preservation of the Bush tax cuts. The deep ideological divide that had come to define the parties—the Democrats hunkering down on entitlements and the Republicans on no new taxes—was hardly narrowed by the Supercommittee stopgap.[57]

In November the Supercommittee confessed failure to come up with a deficit-reduction bill. Slightly more people polled (44 percent) blamed the Republicans than Obama (38 percent), but there was much failure to be shared. Meanwhile the sequester's Day of Reckoning remained, still a relatively small cloud in the stormy skies of the American economy but threatening to become a Category 5 hurricane on January 1, 2013.[58]

Tax policy also was stuck in a Sargasso Sea of gridlock and stonewalling. Democratic senator Max Baucus and Republican congressman Dave Camp, who headed their chambers' tax-writing committees, had been working together for several years to push a Bowles-Simpson-like tax reform act that would lower corporate rates and eliminate distortive exemptions. But their efforts had to face a fearsome wall of precedent, partisanship, and vested interests.[59]

The stage was set for a reprise of the 2010–2011 confrontation over spending, taxation, and the debt limit. *New York Times* columnist David Brooks saw the underlying conflict as between "Cyclicalists" and "Structuralists." The former—Krugmanites in Keynesian clothing—wanted more government spending and borrowing to rev up the economy, deficits and debt be damned. The latter—Hayekians in University of Chicago clothing—blamed the economic malaise on basic long-term changes in technology and globalization, made worse by an unaffordable welfare state and political-regulatory sclerosis.[60]

The rise in spending was spurred by the growth of recession-enhanced benefits: big increases in Social Security disability to about $125 billion a year, up seventeenfold in four decades; food stamp outlays doubling between 2006 and 2011 to about $46 billion; and college tuition loans totaling $1 trillion in 2011. For all their threat to financial stability, these expenditures had in common substantial and growing constituencies of beneficiaries, as opposed to a potential opposition that might be more numerous but certainly was less cohesive.[61]

In an eerily similar replay of the 2011 Grand Deferral, party leaders cobbled together a last minute patchwork New Year's Day 2013 compromise to avoid the much-hyped fiscal cliff. Newly reelected Obama finally extracted Republican consent to raise income tax rates, though they kicked in for individual/family incomes of $400,000/450,000, not the $200,000/250,000 level that he had insisted on until then. He quietly allowed the employee Social Security tax cut of recent years to lapse. But he all but avoided spending reductions: the dollar ratio of cuts to taxes was 1 to 41.

In two months Congress would have to consider raising the debt ceiling again, and without new legislation the sequester spending cuts would take effect. At the end of March the existing budget resolution authorizing federal government spending would end.

But before that the debt ceiling was raised, the sequester kicked in, and a continuing resolution allowed the government to keep working. The administration and its supporters warned that the sequester would bring in its wake insupportable cutbacks and shutdowns. As 2013 unfolded, there was little evidence that anything so dire was happening. Instead, it appeared that "for all the clumsiness of the sequester, it is imposing new rigours."[62]

The politics of debt, spending, and taxes was temporarily overshadowed in 2013 by more compelling issues: the Syrian crisis and the implementation of Obamacare. But the timetable set by past fiscal politics still loomed: funding for the government's activities to be renewed in September 2013 and the $16.7 trillion debt ceiling due to be reached by mid-October.

So in the fall of 2013 the curtain rose once again on the by-now-familiar Kabuki drama of budgetary/spending gridlock, government closedown, and confrontation over raising the debt ceiling. The resolution, after a short shutdown and much damage to the GOP party brand, was yet another short-term stopgap: budget and debt ceiling agreements into early 2014, a congressional committee charged to seek out the elusive Holy Grail of a longer-term compromise.

By mid-second term the core economic issues of jobs, debt, spending, and taxation appeared to be set in amber. Each party was locked into its distinctive, apposite economic policy. The economy was more or less stable, even slowly growing, but at a substantially lower level than in the piping pre-recession days. Unemployment showed at most a slow decline. As much as at any time in American history, the economic prospect of the nation appeared to depend not so much on what Washington did (or didn't) do, but on the resilience, energy, and ingenuity of the American people and their economy.[63]

CHAPTER FIVE

. . .

Home Fires Burning: Social Policy

WITH BANKS SAVED by the Troubled Asset Relief Program and the Stimulus in place, Obama felt free to turn to the more toothsome realm of social policy. He set out to make a new national health-care system the jewel in his presidential crown. Saving the environment by relying more on renewable energy, the Holy Grail of affluent liberals, also had strong appeal. But education and immigration, conspicuous issues in the late Bush years, turned out to be muffled fire bells; or, to change the metaphor, dogs that whined rather than barked.

Did this, when conjoined with Obama's economic program, add up to a new New Deal, a greater Great Society? Or was the bottom line that the era of the active, bureaucratized state, devoted to large, encompassing economic and social goals, was sliding into history's dustbin?

I. OBAMACARE: A NOBLE EXPERIMENT

Obama's legacy will be indelibly linked to the passage and implementation of his Affordable Care Act (ACA). In its scope and aspirations, it deserves the label that Herbert Hoover attached to Prohibition: "a great social and economic experiment, noble in motive and far-reaching in purpose." In a similar vein Ezekiel Emanuel, one of Obamacare's creators, predicted that "the ACA will increasingly be seen as a world historical achievement, even more important for the United States than Social Security and Medicare has been."

Advocates of each cause could point to a long prehistory. Over the course of the late nineteenth century, states and localities imposed an extensive web of constraints on the consumption of alcohol. Over the course of the late twentieth century, insurance companies, employers, and government created a system of individual and group health insurance that covered over 80 percent of the population. But neither satisfied proponents of a more comprehensive approach: national Prohibition, a national health-care program.

Decades of futile attempts preceded the passage of both Prohibition and Obamacare. Prohibition came about through a broad, well-organized public relations campaign, fed by the anxieties of Protestant, small-town Americans and the social engineering of the Progressive movement, and culminating in the idealism unleashed by America's entry into World War I.

Health-care expansion had been an attractive cause since the presidency of Harry Truman. LBJ's Medicare and Medicaid added largely to the existing system. Carter's weakness and Republican disinterest checked further growth, except for the flare-up and die-down of the Clintons' Hillarycare, and George W. Bush's more successful prescription benefits plan. Finally, with the 2008 election of Barack Obama and a Democratic Congress, the way was cleared for a leap forward.

In its early stages Prohibition had broad bipartisan support, except for urban immigrants who saw it as part of a native Protestant backlash that led as well to immigration restriction. The goal of universal health care also was widely popular, though it had a smaller base of strong advocates.

Both noble experiments had difficulties that cast a lengthening shadow over what initially seemed to be hopeful steps forward in social policy. Prohibition, like Obamacare, reflected the all-encompassing vision of its advocates. But in each case some compromises had to be made: the exemption of sacramental wine and that rural staple hard cider in Prohibition; the abandonment of a government-run ("single payer") system in Obamacare.

Problems of implementation and financing quickly afflicted Prohibition. The Volstead Act came into effect in October 1919, its legality ensured by the Eighteenth Amendment to the Constitution. Consumption and the health and social ills of drink at first satisfyingly declined. But in a stunning instance of the workings of the market (in this case, an illegal one), whiskey-running from Canada, Europe, and the West Indies; illicit booze-making at home; and speakeasies, bootleggers, and an endless ronde of law-enforcing and law-breaking rapidly appeared. Prohibition enforcement soon became the most prominent national issue. Finally, in 1933 the unimaginable became inevitable: the Eighteenth Amendment was repealed, and regulation returned to the states and localities.[1]

Does Obamacare have a similar future? Probably not. The fact that it rests on a law of Congress alone and not on a constitutional amendment makes it more susceptible to modification and revision; its outright repeal is likely a nonstarter. Nor does it have the sectional, religious, and cultural baggage that made Prohibition so potent a public issue. Nevertheless the difficulty attending its implementation has resonances with the earlier noble experiment.

The Birth of a Notion

FDR waited until after the supportive November 1934 congressional election to bring forth Social Security. LBJ fathered Medicare in the wake of his 1964 landslide. But Obama put forward the Patient Protection and Affordable Care Act in September 2009, only eight months into his first term. As the election of 2010 showed, this was a momentous decision, with large political costs. As the election of 2012 showed, those costs were not insurmountable.

Universal health care had always been high—perhaps highest—on Obama's must-do list. Some advisers, most notably Peter Orszag and Rahm Emanuel, counseled caution and thought that he should put financial reform first. But he overrode them. When Treasury Secretary Geithner suggested that having avoided a second Great Depression was hardly an insignificant achievement, Obama replied, "That's not enough for me."[2]

The authorship of Obamacare is difficult to pin down. There was no primary drafting committee, as was the case with Social Security. Nancy-Ann DeParle, who directed the White House Office of Health Reform, had a conspicuous role. So did MIT economics professor Jonathan Gruber, who could claim paternity for the idea of the individual mandate, and Rahm Emanuel's bioethicist brother Ezekiel. From the Kennedy School of Government, longtime health-care guru David Cutler and former Senate aide John McDonough were influential voices. House Energy and Commerce Committee chair Henry Waxman was a major player in the bill's crafting, as was Montana senator Max Baucus.[3]

Advocates of single-payer government-run health insurance such as Ted Kennedy were not happy with Obama's readiness to accept the private insurance-mandate approach. Kennedy justifiably noted that the mandate had Republican origins in the 1990s, most directly in GOP governor Mitt Romney's Massachusetts plan.[4]

But moderate Democratic members of Congress were more responsible than the thoroughly excluded Republicans for the rejection of a single-payer plan. Important interests with a large stake in the existing system—the American Medical Association, Big Pharma, hospitals, insurance companies, unions—took center stage, as did questionable arrangements to secure badly needed Senate votes (with Mary Landrieu of Louisiana: the Louisiana Purchase; with Ben Nelson of Nebraska: the Cornhusker Compromise). These enhanced health-care reform's uncomfortable similarity to sausage-making as a product whose mode of production was best left unobserved. (But then, as the movie *Lincoln* suggests, so was the abolition of slavery.)[5]

The Patient Protection and Affordable Care Act became law in March 2010. Its supporters preferred to call it the Affordable Care Act. But a popular culture that referred to the Supreme Court as the Supremes and presidential press conferences as pressers was not likely to stand on such formality. Obamacare (echoing unenacted Hillarycare and enacted Medicare) became the commonly accepted label. In 2012 Obama made his peace with popular usage, declaring that he had no objection to the term.[6]

As with the Stimulus, Obama left the substance and passage of health-care reform to the Democratic congressional leadership. The result, from his perspective, was a triumph: enactment of the most consequential new social policy since Medicare or even Social Security. But to Budget Director Peter Orszag the House bill was a "liberal fantasy of glut and expansion. Everyone in the provider community knew the White House wasn't focused on cost."[7]

Obama regarded the bill's passage as the crowning achievement of his first term. His opponents decried it as a massively complex system whose cost and workability were highly questionable. Both views were justified: which the more so as yet to be determined.

Obamacare did not fill a massive void in public policy, as did Social Security's pension and unemployment coverage and Medicare's health insurance for the elderly. Rather it was superimposed on an existing system, in which over 80 percent of Americans had some form of medical coverage. A majority of those polled by Gallup in July 2009 thought that the current health-care system had large problems. But only 38 percent believed that it needed to be rebuilt. A plurality expected that a government-run program would do a worse job than the private sector.[8]

The primary target of Obama's health-care reform was the numerically substantial (estimates ranged from 30 to 50 million), but limited proportion (less than one in five) of the population who had no insurance coverage. The uninsured were a disparate lot. Some 40 percent were 18- to 34-year-olds, many of whom saw no reason to buy insurance. Up to 30 percent (much overlap here) were illegal immigrants, who were not included in Obamacare. More difficult to estimate were the number of Americans denied insurance because of preexisting conditions; or who were either too poor or uninformed, or too rich or disinterested, to have coverage.[9]

Given the scale of the existing system and the size and variety of interests with a stake in it, a national, government-run, single-payer plan never really had a look-in. But some hoped that such a program would evolve out of Obamacare. The law was designed to bring all existing health coverage into line with its standards. This would come to be a big problem. An expert later observed, "The problem with Obamacare is it's product driven and not market driven."[10]

For all its limitations, the fact remains that Obamacare was a major expansion of America's health-care system, something that none of Obama's predecessors (Truman, Nixon, the Clintons) was able to do. Like Prohibition, this was a considerable achievement. Would it prove, like Prohibition, to be unworkable?

Obamacare's travails since its passage underlines the fact that significant new social policy is no longer the relative slam dunk of the days of Social Security and Medicare. True, those other large entitlements faced problems of cost and implementation that had to be dealt with over time. But even before it began, the structural, financial, political, and constitutional problems of Obamacare were more onerous.

It is difficult to imagine how the situation in which Obamacare found itself might have been avoided. It sought Social Security–like inclusiveness in an unimaginably more complicated society. The size and complexity of the bill reflected that fact. Strong advocate Nancy Pelosi famously—and accurately—held that it was necessary to pass the law to find out what was in it.

Obamacare rested on a system of state exchanges, made up of authorized insurance providers. These would take on millions of new clients as well as those already covered by group or individual policies. Participants were to be drawn in by the carrot of broadly expanded and often subsidized health insurance and the stick of a "mandate" to buy, enforced by escalating penalties for noncompliance by individuals or employers.

If Obamacare disappointed the Left by its failure to come up with a single government system, it alienated the Right by its failure to seek GOP input or support. Some Republican proposals—interstate competition by private insurers and limits on medical liability suits—posed no obvious threat to the program. But they were ignored. In the event, health-care reform passed without a single Republican vote in the House or Senate, and without a conference committee of the two chambers that might have made it more palatable. This cast a cloud over Obamacare from its inception. Very different were Great Britain's National Health Service of 1946, which had the support of all three parties, and Canada's Health Act of 1989, which was passed unanimously by that country's parliament.

Discontent did not noticeably decline with the passage of time. Polls showed opposition stubbornly stuck at a bit over 50 percent, though this included a visible minority who wanted a more socialized system. In late 2011 a third of respondents strongly opposed the plan; only 13 percent strongly supported it. By an 84-14 percent margin, they were against the mandate.[11]

Two years after passage, 61 percent of respondents in a poll placed greatest trust in their own medical decisions; 15 percent trusted their employers; and 5 percent trusted the government. Opposition to Obamacare would rise and fall but remained consistently greater than support.[12]

Structural Challenges

In March 2011, a year after Obamacare's passage, *The Economist* celebrated "a not very happy birthday." Biden's whispered comment to the president at its signing that this was a "big fucking deal" turned out to be true but not in the "mission accomplished" sense implied by the vice president or by Obama's declaration prior to the October 1, 2013, sign-up start: "We're only five days away from finishing the job."[13]

The size and complexity of the law was a problem. By the end of February 2012, regulations totaled almost 2.2 million words, five times the length of the hefty original statute. This was not peculiar to Obamacare; the Dodd-Frank finance reform act underwent a similar evolution. Legislation in a large, complex, rights-and-procedures-ridden society is bound to be complicated. Rules, interpretations, regulations, and regulators are essential (as regulators will be the first to tell you). The implementation of so ambitious a program was no simple matter. The real question: Was it doable?[14]

Obamacare had at its heart a commitment to more centralized policymaking. Influential voices in the media, the academy, and think tanks were wedded to the twentieth-century vision of social engineering by a democratic welfare state. Dr. Donald Berwick, chosen to be the director of Obamacare's Centers for Medicare and Medicaid Services—in effect, the Medicare/Medicaid czar—was an advocate of Britain's National Health Service as against the traditional American fee-for-service system. "The primary function of regulation in health care," he declared, "especially as it affects the quality of medical care, is to constrain decentralized decision making." Perhaps appropriately, Berwick was appointed in the autumn of 2010 without a congressional hearing. Perhaps inevitably, he stepped down a year later after his confirmation was blocked in the Senate.[15]

The capacity of the existing health-care delivery system to absorb Obamacare was far from clear. Third-party payment and fee-for-service, an antiquated hospital system, and inadequate provision for the additional doctors, nurses, and clinics that universal health care would require were problems not substantially addressed by the new law.[16]

The iron law of unanticipated consequences quickly kicked in. In October 2011, Health and Human Services confessed its failure to figure out how to make the Community Living Assistance Services and Support program actuarially sound. It was supposed to provide more economical long-term care, thereby accounting for half of the $140 billion reduction promised in Obamacare.[17]

No more successful was the effort to quickly set up new pools of high-risk uninsured. This was designed to attract at least 375,000 people excluded from health insurance because of preexisting medical conditions. (After 2014, insurance providers would be required to cover them.) But only 8,000 had signed up a year after Obamacare's passage; after two years, only 49,000. The program's $5 billion budget was gone well before 2014.[18]

Waivers began to pop up for some of Obamacare's broadly inclusive dictates. Companies with large numbers of low-paid employees argued that some aspects of their business such as high employee turnover made it difficult to abide by the rule that 80–85 percent of premiums had to go to medical benefits and not administrative costs. By the end of May 2011, waivers of this requirement had been granted to 1,372 businesses, state and local governments, insurers, and unions (who got half the total). These waivers came to a stop in September, but not the problem that gave birth to them.[19]

State exchanges were supposed to be at the heart of Obamacare. They would funnel federal subsidies to recipients and help determine who was eligible for inclusion in Medicaid. A federal exchange would fill the gap if a state chose not to participate.

Given the financial rewards that Obamacare proffered to state exchanges, it seemed likely that there would be extensive participation. But only 14 states and the District of Columbia agreed to run their own exchanges or in partnership with the feds; 36 chose to rely on the federal exchange alone.[20]

Why did Blue states—presumably more sympathetic to a federal-run health-care system—tend to set up their own exchanges? Why were so many Red states content to accept the federal exchange? The answer, not surprisingly, is complicated. Obamacare's subsidies for state exchanges lured some Red states as well as most Blue states. But Red states that wanted to keep their distance from Obamacare or hold down their commitment to Medicaid were inclined to let the feds handle things. Obamacare may have been a big deal, but it was far from a simple deal.

Financial Challenges

There was also the nagging question of Obamacare's financing. This is a systemic issue in large entitlement programs. Medicare and Medicaid have outstripped cost estimates for decades. Social Security's future financial prospect is far from ensured, and the sheer scale of the health-care market is in a class by itself, consuming about a sixth of gross domestic product. In 2012 the health industry spent almost a quarter of a billion dollars on lobbying in Washington, topping the combined spending of finance, other insurance, and real estate interests.[21]

The fee-for-service structure of American health insurance puts care above cost. The result is a program often thought to be more responsive to its users than its British and Canadian national counterparts but more expensive and far from universal.[22]

Obamacare's aim is to add 30 to 40 million participants, half or more of them on Medicaid. To pay for this, its advocates rely in part on the more efficient management of Medicare, hoping to cut that program's costs by as much as half. And they expect to bring in millions of fee-paying younger subscribers, likely to pay in more than the benefits that they get. Less noted, a batch of new or increased taxes are designed to help meet Obamacare's expenses.[23]

Obamacare's cost is overseen by Health and Human Services' Centers for Medicare and Medicaid Services and a 15-member, presidentially appointed Independent Payment Advisory Board—Sarah Palin's famous Death Panel—unaccountable to Congress or the judiciary. Here was another arrow for skeptics' quivers.[24]

The demographic overhang of aging boomers was a danger signal, as was the limited likelihood of savings when millions of people were added to the fully subsidized Medicaid program or given partial subsidies for their Obamacare policies. All of this made the reduced-cost claims of advocates ever more suspect.[25]

On past experience, estimates are guesstimates. New medical technology, a large growth in basic care clinics, and variable coverage might slow down or reverse the hitherto inexorable rise in health-care costs. Supporters insist that more participants and greater efficiency will keep those costs under control. Opponents hold that the history of entitlements dictates otherwise.[26]

In preparation for Obamacare's 2014 unveiling, hospital, clinic, and medical practice mergers increased, as indeed was happening before health reform's passage, and not necessarily a bad thing. Surely the existing system had much waste and fraud. One estimate was that in 2009, unnecessary care cost some $325 billion; fraud and abuse, $175 billion; and administrative inefficiency, $150 billion. These costs are often blamed on the prevailing fee-for-service system. But most health-care providers do not want fee-for-service replaced, and Democrats such as Nancy Pelosi refused to consider any reduction in Medicare benefits.[27]

Defenders of the new plan argued that the uninsured often resorted to expensive emergency rooms, at an estimated cost of more than $40 billion, which Obamacare would substantially reduce. But this was only 3 percent of the cost of health care, and there was no clear evidence that those without health insurance used emergency rooms at a higher rate than the insured. Indeed, an Oregon study showed that Medicaid participants were more inclined to use emergency rooms than were their uninsured counterparts.[28]

Since 2010 the rise in health care spending has appreciably slowed. How much is due to Obamacare's reforms of Medicare pricing, to the recession, or to improved technology is unclear. A large increase in social services is bound to cost more. The real issue is the value of what that expansion is designed to do (incontestably high in this case) and the effectiveness with which it does it (still very much up for grabs).[29]

Obamacare, the Courts, and Politics

Along with structural and financial issues, there rose the problem of Obamacare's constitutionality. Challengers focused on its mandate that everyone had to participate or pay an escalating penalty. Was this a valid application of Congress's power to regulate interstate commerce? Or was it invalid because it *required*, rather than merely *regulated*, participation in a commercial act?

The constitutional debate was fueled as well by the decision to hold Catholic churches, hospitals, and colleges to Obamacare's requirement that contraceptive and abortion aid be provided. A conservative critic summed up his side's objections: "Rarely has one law so exemplified the worst of the Leviathan state—grotesque cost, questionable constitutionality and arbitrary bureaucratic coerciveness."[30]

In June 2012 Chief Justice John Roberts and the four Court liberals found most of the health-care law constitutional, in good part on the ground that its mandate was not a commerce regulation but a tax. For whatever reason—a politically adept solution that protected the Court while hanging the "it's a tax" albatross around the mandate's neck, buckling under in the face of an administration–law school establishment assault, or just being a judge coming to a judicious conclusion—Roberts altered the Obamacare debate.[31]

There were large political implications to Roberts's decision. The Republicans had to face the fact that their own Chief Justice found Obamacare constitutional. Obama had to face the problem that he had been promising not to raise taxes on anyone but the rich. Now the Court said that the mandate fine *was* a tax, and a significant levy for everyone *except* the rich.

Not since the great tariff and currency wars of the nineteenth and early twentieth centuries had a domestic issue of such complexity had so prominent a place in public discourse. It was in good part because of his visibility in the health-care reform debate that Paul Ryan became Mitt Romney's running mate in 2012.[32]

Ryan's entry into the campaign promised to reenergize Obamacare as a political issue. But Romney had the embarrassment of having presided over the passage of a similar law when he was governor of Massachusetts. He argued, without much impact, that one-state Romneycare was one thing; all-states Obamacare was another.

The mandate continued to be a bone of contention. There was some question as to the ability of the Internal Revenue Service to collect the mandate tax (or was it a fine?). Spotting scofflaws would require a substantial expansion of the Internal Revenue Service. But after the spring 2013 revelations of partisan bias, the Internal Revenue Service had a probity problem. In any event, its enforcement power was limited. It couldn't withhold noncompliers' tax refunds, seize their assets, or prosecute them.[33]

The most important political question was whether Obamacare had or could attract public backing on a scale comparable to Social Security and Medicare. Social Security had the support of 73 percent of Americans in early 1937 and 78 percent in 1938. Medicare found favor with 62 percent in early 1965 and 82 percent by the year's end. Obamacare had only 32 percent support at the time of its March 2010 enactment, and failed to get majority support in the run-up to its January 2014 implementation.[34]

Nevertheless it does not appear to have been an issue of great consequence in the 2012 election. Perhaps responding to the polls, Obama was reluctant to tout his crowning legislative achievement. Post-2012 election analyses rarely mentioned Obamacare, nor did Obama in his January 2013 State of the Union address. This is not necessarily a surprise. After all, Medicare for all its popularity did not save LBJ's presidency, and Clinton was not visibly hurt by the defeat of Hillarycare.

The Supreme Court decision to uphold the constitutionality of Obamacare and Obama's reelection ensured that its implementation would go ahead. The GOP-led House continued to pass bills for its repeal—40 times by August 2013. But this was only political posturing: pap for the faithful. More consequential was the fact that, like a fearsome escarpment, the full implementation of Obamacare loomed ever closer.[35]

The Bill's Grim Progress

A campaign to sell participation modeled on the successful sign-ups for Medicare B and D and the Obama get-out-the-vote effort in 2012 began in the summer of 2013. Thousands of "assisters" or "navigators" were recruited to track down and sign up the uninsured: a boon for community organizers and a one-time job stimulus not unlike the Census. In California alone, some 21,000 assisters would get $58 for each enrollee.[36]

But the enabling funds provided by Congress were inadequate for this effort. Enroll America, a 501(c)(3) nonprofit, was created to fill the gap. Health and Human Services secretary Kathleen Sebelius got $10 million from the health-focused Robert Wood Johnson Foundation and half a million from tax preparer H&R Block. She also got much GOP criticism for seeking private money from self-interested parties. Foundations and businesses were reluctant to get involved, as were professional sports leagues approached to pitch participation.[37]

Not surprisingly, a law of great complexity continued to run into a seemingly endless series of glitches. This had been the pattern during the 2010–2013 preparatory period. It proved to be even more so as Obamacare's Opening Day of January 1, 2014, drew nearer.

As befitted a twenty-first-century great leap forward, Obamacare's prime public stage was the Internet: more particularly, the federal Healthcare.gov and 15 state websites, slated to start on October 1, 2013. They were to be Open Sesames to a garden of health insurance delights: ease in signing up, less costly but better policies, millions of new participants benefiting from subsidies or cost-free Medicaid.

But the federal site could not handle the press of traffic, and it showed an impressive capacity to keep users from finding out what they wanted to know and successfully obtaining the plan that they chose. Government-contracted projects are rarely known for the competence of their execution. Canadian firm Consultants to Government and Industry (CGI) got the primary federal website-construction contract from Health and Human Services and the Centers for Medicare and Medicaid Services. Like a celebrity known primarily for being known, CGI's reputation rested on the number of government contracts that it corralled. But its dicey accounting methods, growth primarily through the acquisition of other firms, and the less-than-stellar or cutting-edge quality of its work were danger signals.[38]

It was not only the federal website that ran into trouble. The exchanges of Blue states Oregon, Maryland, Minnesota, Hawaii, and Massachusetts had serious sign-up problems. matching or surpassing those of the federal site.[39]

Yet another embarrassment, one with longer-lasting implications, emerged in late October 2013. Big insurers were sending out termination letters to millions of individual policyholders whose insurance policies were not up to the new law's standards or had been modified or replaced since Obamacare's passage. They would have to plunge into the maze of securing new policies from the exchanges.

As Obama pointed out, this was a small segment of the health insurance universe. And half or more would be eligible for government subsidies or Medicaid. But it embarrassingly contradicted his frequent pledge that if you liked your policy, you could keep it. Even more serious, the same cancellation standard would be applied to group insurance. Small employers were granted a waiver from this until just after the November 2014 election and large ones until 2015. It was clear that the Obamacare mountains were not just an escarpment but a range of peaks extending as far as the eye could see.[40]

The Affordable Care Act had a manifest redistributionist intent. But it cut much deeper than the 99 percent to 1 percent mantra of Occupy Wall Street or Obama's millionaires and billionaires. A large number of people in the distinctly middle-class income range of $50,000 to $90,000 a year were hit hard by Obamacare's cost and the confusion of the roll-out.

Thousands of New York City professionals, artists and writers, and contractors and shopkeepers were caught in the cancellation wave. Most got their insurance through membership in guild-like groups such as the Entertainment Industry Group Insurance Trust, the Society of Children's Book Writers and Illustrators, the New York City Bar Association, and the New York County Medical Society. But it turned out that, under Obamacare, theirs were in fact individual, not group, policies and hence subject to cancellation. "We are the Obama people," one cancellee wailed.[41]

Far from being the pathway to socialized medicine that right-wing opponents feared and left-wing supporters hoped for, Obamacare was a potential boon to private insurers. Millions more would become policyholders; their insurance would be more richly (and expensively) comprehensive; any initial losses by the companies would be covered by a system of risk pools.

But supping with the government had its risks. Obamacare supporters (including Obama) were by no means disinclined to blame the plan's problems on insurers. Changing rules and rolling exemptions were potential obstacles on the companies' high road to profit.[42]

Enrolling was not the same as being covered. That depended on certification by the insurer after it received the enrollee's first premium. This raised the next big problem, the so-called back end of online authentication and premium collection. A government official reported in mid-November 2013 that up to 40 percent of the consolidated website was not yet built: "It's not that it's not working. It's still being developed and tested."[43]

Were these, as the president argued, the inevitable "glitches" that accompany the implementation of a major new public policy? Or were they harbingers of a Prohibition-like "train wreck" (the language of Montana Senator Max Baucus, a onetime booster)?[44]

A frantic repair job on the Healthcare.gov website appeared to overcome the early problems. In full "Mission Accomplished" mode, Obama proclaimed in April 2014 that a target-busting 8 million Americans had enrolled. Who they were—previously insured or uninsured, young or old, well or sick, wholly self-paying or subsidized, first premium paid or not—remained unclear. It seemed ever more likely that a larger-than-expected proportion of Obamacare's participants would be in Medicaid. Hispanic enrollment, too, ran afoul of the complexities of the law and the glitches in its roll-out.[45]

Attention began to focus more on the character of the law itself, and not just its implementation problems. Commentators took note of the gulf between "Pontificators" (policymakers) and "Plumbers" (policy implementers) or of its "fundamental problem," which was that Obamacare's crafters "didn't ask the customer[s] what they wanted."[46]

Then there was the question of Obamacare's political impact. Would it be the defining achievement of the Obama presidency, as Social Security arguably was for FDR's New Deal and Medicare was for LBJ's Great Society? Or was it fated to turn into a failed noble experiment comparable to Prohibition?

The disappointments of Obamacare's early days led to a level of mainstream media criticism not previously experienced by the administration. The major TV networks, newspapers, and websites were not reluctant to report on and adversely judge its defects.[47]

As was the case with Prohibition, substantial remedial proposals short of the mantra of repeal gradually emerged. Most frequent was recurring congressional sentiment, including a number of Democrats, to delay mandate enforcement, to which the administration responded with a series of administrative alterations.

The Republican position moved gradually from a stress on outright repeal to substantial amendment. Wisconsin GOP Senator Ron Johnson, his eyes on the presidential nomination prize, proposed to end the mandate, keep the online exchanges, and expand the range of available insurance options. Congressman Paul Ryan and doctor-Senators Tom Price and Tom Coburn revived old GOP causes: a cap on medical malpractice suits, policies for sale across state lines, health savings accounts, and tax credits for individual enrollees.[48]

As the 2014 election drew nearer, Democrats seemed to be more reluctant to get into the revision game, and Republicans were too fractious to come up with a uniform set of changes. The opposing sides' trenches stabilized, much like the Western front in World War I. Obamacare continued to fail to win widespread public approval, but proponents of repeal were no more successful. A universal health-care system retained its appeal—but the problems of implementation, cost, coverage, and quality that rose so early stubbornly refused to go away. The prospect of congressional tinkering appeared to lie, if at all, in the sober dawn following the 2014 election.

Are Obamacare's difficulties evidence of a more systemic failure of big government? "Maybe the problem is not Obama or Sebelius but rather a government program that requires superhuman technocratic mastery," thought one analyst. Conjoined with the not dissimilar problems of Dodd-Frank financial reform, this was a reasonable question to ask.[49]

But history suggests that the liberal political tradition of a strong state and regulated markets has an appeal comparable to the conservative tradition of a weak state and strong markets. Most voters have malleable memories, and today's losing proposition can become tomorrow's winning one.[50]

2. CLIMATE, ENERGY, AND TRANSPORTATION

The challenge of climate change and the promise of alternative energy sources and high-speed trains strongly appealed to the young, better-educated, and more affluent segments of Obama's coalition; less so to its African-American, Hispanic, working-class components. Most of all, it spoke, with a force second only to health-care reform, to Obama's sense of being a transformative president.

Climate and Energy

Obama initially proposed to use price mechanisms to force consumers out of their coal-oil-gas dependency. Cap and trade promised to lower pollutant emissions by putting a limit on the amount that companies could use. It was supposed to create a market in emission permits that would increase costs for high polluters and financially reward low ones. This had American origins in the late 1960s and early 1970s, was aimed first (and with success) at acid rain, and had the support of Republican administrations.

Candidate Obama said in a January 2008 interview, "If somebody wants to build a coal-fired power plant, they can. It's just that it will bankrupt them because they're going to be charged a huge sum for all that greenhouse gas that's being emitted." But he warned that under a cap-and-trade system, "Electricity rates would necessarily skyrocket." This was of a piece with soon-to-be Energy Secretary Steven Chu's wish to "figure out how to boost the price of gasoline to the levels in Europe."[51]

Not surprisingly, cap and trade and indeed the overall issue of energy and climate change have not had an easy time of it. Cap and trade was an early casualty of political opposition from both parties, fueled (so to speak) by coal and oil interests. The cuddly cause of global warming was not helped when the leaked e-mails of some academic advocates showed a less than full commitment to open scientific inquiry.

The December 2009 Copenhagen conference on climate change made it clear that the energy-hunger of developing countries China and India would not give way to the energy-guilt of Europe and (liberal) America. Nor did Al Gore wear well as a Jeremiah of imminent climate catastrophe.[52]

In the course of the first Obama term, the scientific, political, and geopolitical foundations of the climate change cause gradually eroded. There continued to be abundant confirmation that warming was real. But its sources, pace, scale, and policy implications remained unresolved.[53]

"Global warming" was the doomsayers' label of choice from the mid-1970s to the mid-2000s. Thereafter less in-your-face "climate change" took precedence. Obama's 2009 Earth Day message dwelt on the threat. But in a November 2011 speech on energy, he referred to it only once, and, in his 2012 Earth Day reprise he did not mention "climate." Nevertheless the threat of climate change continued to resonate with the chattering classes (if less so with the public at large), and after his 2012 reelection Obama returned to it.[54]

As with financial reform, jobs, and health care, the politics of anti-pollution policy have proven to be dense and difficult. The ethanol story is a case in point. Mixing ethanol (grain alcohol) extracted from corn with gasoline as a way of reducing the polluting proclivities of the internal combustion engine was at first a noncontroversial fix. A 10 percent ethanol additive became the American norm. If the interest-peddling of the coal and oil states scuttled cap and trade, the influence-peddling of the corn states entrenched ethanol in the American gasoline supply.

But ethanol had its problems. Its pollution-reducing capacity was far from settled. In a sterling display of the law of unintended consequences, the corn-consuming capacity of ethanol production pushed world food prices higher, thus transferring the cost of this palliative to the world's poor: hardly an attractive policy outcome for advocates of environmental change. Even Al Gore turned against the ethanol fix.

Another unexpected result was that the substantial government subsidy to ethanol production made it cheaper than gasoline. The market saw to it that some 400 million gallons of the stuff were sold overseas. Meanwhile, international oil prices remained high. Subsidized ethanol out, costly foreign oil in was not exactly what its supporters had in mind.

In June 2011 a bipartisan majority of 73 senators voted to end the ethanol subsidy of $6 billion a year. But the GOP-led House, its dander up because tax bills were supposed to originate in that chamber, did not go along.[55]

These issues were part of the larger cause of fostering a Green America, in which renewable sources of energy would bring new technology, new companies, new jobs, and a new lifestyle. But here too, as Obama's time unfolded, the inertial heaviness of governing and the unforeseen consequences of technology created a familiar scenario of dashed expectations.[56]

Obama put much stock in the potential of renewable energy to create jobs and economic growth. Its impact hopefully would be like the canal and railroad booms of the nineteenth century and the automobile age of the twentieth. Once again, new technology would lead the way to a new America.

But the *New York Times* reported in August 2011 that "federal and state efforts to stimulate creation of green jobs have largely failed, government records show." There were plenty of sources to blame: intrusive bureaucrats and courts, self-serving companies, over-ideological proponents and opponents of greenery, and, as always, the sheer complexity of organization and administration in modern society.[57]

As so often was the case, reality did not meekly conform to ideology. Electric and (less so) hybrid autos remained resistant to widespread acceptance. The most popular of them, the Toyota Prius, conspicuously lacked the massive government subsidies bestowed on GM's far less successful Chevy Volt. And energy-producing windmills were unsightly, loud, bird-killing, unpredictable, and often expensively far from their users. By the end of Obama's first term, they provided less than 4 percent of the nation's energy.

Solar energy was something else. Like wind, solar was handsomely subsidized by the government, and panels became steadily more abundant and less expensive. They could be used more readily than windmills by homeowners and businesses. But on a commercial scale, they posed economic, environmental, and aesthetic problems similar to those of windmills.[58]

When clean energy rubber (so to speak) hit the entrepreneurial road, old ways of doing public business soon cropped up. Obama devoted over half of his corporation visits to clean technology firms, and $90 billion of the Stimulus was devoted to the cause. But this commitment was plagued by slow and mixed results, and instances of political favoritism that determined who got what. Government initiatives involving large projects tend to attract waste and corruption as jam attracts flies. Problems of cost, waste, and worse rose as night follows day.[59]

The Solyndra scandal hardly compares with such historical benchmarks of malfeasance as Union Pacific's Credit Mobilier of the 1860s or Big Oil's Teapot Dome of the 1920s. But it showed how the old wine of political favoritism could fill the new bottle of renewable energy.

Solyndra was a California solar panel firm with a production technique of questionable economic viability but sterling political credentials. When its prospects darkened in 2010, the administration urged the firm to delay layoffs until after the November election. The company announced its forthcoming bankruptcy in August 2011, despite a $528 million loan guarantee based on Stimulus money.[60]

That, as a *Washington Post* story put it, "politics infused Obama energy programs" has about the same revelatory impact as news that there is gambling at Rick's. Nor was the Solyndra favoritism (or the firm's failure) outsized. Perhaps most important was its reminder that all-too-familiar pitfalls can beset even the very model of a modern social policy.[61]

If past ways of doing things dogged Obama's renewable energy initiative, so did the unpredictable course of technology. The continuing high price of oil and American dependence on the unreliable Middle East and elsewhere increased the appeal of new offshore, Canadian, and domestic sources. With a big boost from technological innovation, their scale and potential took off.

Newly popular terms described the revolution: fracking, horizontal drilling, tar sands, shale gas and oil, tight oil. Oil extraction on private and state land pushed domestic production to its highest level in decades and set the country on course to become the world's largest oil producer. America, it emerged, had natural gas resources, boosted by the fracking process, good for at least a century. (Europe was less fortunate: limited free land, tight government regulation, and a more assertive political greenery stood in the way of fracking.)[62]

Shale gas production, spurred by the new techniques, increased twelvefold between 2000 and 2011. Prices slid: by the spring of 2012 natural gas was competitive with coal, the cheapest extractive fuel. The railroads that hauled coal were hurt; consumers benefited.

Massive sums had been spent to build Gulf Coast plants to handle imports of liquified natural gas. Now the shale revolution made it desirable to convert these plants (at large cost) to reverse the process: to liquify American gas for shipment to cheap-energy-hungry European and Asian markets. The Obama administration, pulled in opposite directions by jobs-hungry workers and hyper-sensitive environmentalists, floundered in a classic policy bind.[63]

All of this had political consequences. The Obama administration initially had the upper hand on the greenery-energy issue, which appealed to much of its constituency and fit well with its active-government stance. The politics of expanding domestic oil and gas use was something else again. Gas had far lower carbon emission than coal or oil. But it posed a major threat to the renewable energy projects that had so prominent a place in the Obama program.[64]

The Environmental Protection Agency accused fracking companies of contaminating drinking water in Texas, Wyoming, and Pennsylvania. But faulty findings, and the politics of well-paying new jobs coming into blighted areas, compelled the agency to back down.

Nor did the indiscretion of yet another inept academician-turned-regulator (for conservatives, a gift that keeps on giving) help. Environmental Protection Agency regional administrator Al Armendariz zestfully poured a pailful of kerosene on the simmering suspicions of the regulated. He compared his approach to regulating Big Oil with the Roman Empire's mode of subjugating a conquered town: crucify the first five people they encountered.[65]

The proposed Keystone XL pipeline, linking Canadian shale oil fields to Texas refineries, was an ongoing point of contention. The pipeline had much appeal: it would provide jobs (though how many was in dispute) and lessen dependence on foreign oil. Environmental objections delayed construction, and Obama chose to wait until after the 2012 election (and, it appeared, after 2014 as well) before resolving the issue. This was attributed to his need to assuage the green wing of his alliance. But he quietly opened the less conspicuous Alaska-Arctic coastline to new oil exploration.[66]

By the time of the 2012 election, the politics of fossil fuels, as of so much else, had changed markedly from four years before. The 2012 Democratic platform was far less apocalyptic on climate change than in 2008, more modest in its proposals to reduce carbon emission, and, while still touting clean energy, more restrained in its criticism of fossil fuels. Newly energized oil, gas, and coal companies spent massive money on TV ad campaigns touting the development of North American fossil fuel production. Environmental-renewable energy groups, very vocal in 2008, maintained a low profile.[67]

Energy and conservation policy continued to be a fruitful source for fans of the law of unexpected consequences. It appeared that the inadequacies of the European Commission's cap-and-trade regime and the declining price of coal as oil-gas fracking took hold conspired to make that dirtiest of fuels the power source of choice in a number of European countries, threatening to outstrip the Americans in the pollution sweepstakes.[68]

Fracking and oil, gas, and shale expansion are likely to keep altering the politics of energy and the environment. Some advocates (e.g., the Environmental Defense Fund, the Natural Resource Defense Council) welcome the boost to natural gas. But the Sierra Club and other devotees of green pantheism condemn continued extraction as a profanation of Mother Earth. The tension between belief and need, between ideology and technology, may be counted on to remain an unresolved feature of Obama's time.[69]

Transportation

The movement of goods and people has been a prime public policy issue since the early days of the Republic. Canal and railroad building in the nineteenth century, and then motor vehicles and the interstate in the twentieth century, have been at the cutting edge of conflict over government (federal vs. state), spending (taxation vs. borrowing), and the clash of economic and social interests (farmers vs. railroads, the urban poor vs. the encroaching Interstate).

So it was in an old and familiar tradition that Obama proposed a federal-state program of new high-speed rail lines. Some $48 billion of Stimulus money went to the Department of Transportation. But in an age of bureaucratic sclerosis, it took a long time to dole out federal subsidies. By September 2010 only about a third of the available total had been spent. For all the appeal of fast trains, other players in the transportation game—bridges, highways, airports, buses, subways, light and suburban rail—had compelling cases to make.[70]

Obama hoped that a new web of fast intercity trains would be the equivalent of Eisenhower's Interstate highways or Kennedy's space program. High-speed trains had a New Tech image, a toothsome alternative to overburdened highways and polluting autos. They offered, too, the frisson of challenging the wasteful individualism of one person–one car.[71]

But they also had a retro aspect: they were *so* twentieth century. Japan had been the king of the bullet train since the 1960s. Elsewhere the lines' financial viability was elusive. In this as in so many areas (universal health care, rigid labor laws, insupportable entitlements and debt) Europe was far ahead of the United States.[72]

Still, China was rushing to get into the high-speed rail game; could we be left behind? Unfortunately, difficulties very much like those afflicting the administration's clean-energy initiative quickly cropped up. The sorry state of Amtrak did not bode well for the future of high-speed rail in so irredeemably a car culture.

Nine billion dollars of the 2009 Stimulus was allocated for high-speed intercity rail service. Over $2 billion went to California, whose citizens in 2008 passed a referendum proposal for a 220-mile-an-hour hookup between Los Angeles and San Francisco. The project was initially supposed to be completed by 2020 and to cost $33 billion. Within a year there was some slippage in the projections: the completion date pushed to 2033 at the earliest, the cost bumped to $100 billion at the cheapest.

The first segment of what was rapidly becoming pie in the sky was a 130-mile stretch between Fresno and Bakersfield, linking two Central Valley cities and traversing farmland, none of which had any pressing need for this benefice. Inevitably it became known as "the train to nowhere."[73]

That proposal and the proviso that construction begin in the fall of 2012 (just before the election) came from the federal government. Its persuasiveness was heightened by the lure of $4.7 billion in federal funds. Governor Jerry Brown, who had a taste for bold ventures, supported the project, summoning up grand analogies with the Suez and Panama Canals.

But polls revealed a steady decline in public support. The Democratic chair of the relevant legislative committee was "staggered" by its cost. Historian of the West Richard White said the project was "a Vietnam of transportation: easy to begin and difficult and expensive to stop." Republicans, one of the state's more conspicuous endangered species, called for a new referendum. But Brown and the Democratic-dominated state legislature held fast, allocating scarce state funds after deeply cutting education spending.[74]

Other states had different politics and different responses. The Republican governors of Florida, Ohio, Wisconsin, and New Jersey rejected federal transportation funds on the ground that their states would incur insupportable new obligations.

The economics and politics of high-speed rail transportation turned out to be not unlike the economics and politics of global warming. Auto traffic, like carbon pollution, was a large, real, and growing problem. In theory, fast trains, like tight emission controls, could go far to remedy things. But vested interests, public skepticism, and shaky economics made these, like many of Obama's domestic initiatives, resemble Gandhi's take on Western civilization: "It's a nice idea."[75]

3. MUFFLED FIRE BELLS: EDUCATION AND IMMIGRATION

Education was deeply, stubbornly embedded in local/state politics and policy. Only a shadow-play debate over the national standards set by the Bush-Kennedy No Child Left Behind (NCLB) Act roiled the calm sea of national political indifference.

In 2009 the Obama administration sought to replace NCLB's competency measurements with Common Core Standards: in effect, establishing a national curriculum. Congress failed to pass the bill, so as elsewhere the administration turned to regulatory tinkering. Education Secretary Arne Duncan stirred up some waves by blaming "white suburban moms" for blocking national tests. A number of states had hearings on the matter, which tended to reinforce the sense that most parents wanted their children's education kept in local hands.

States that adopted the administration's Core Standards plan were exempted from NCLB's requirement that they meet specific math and reading goals by 2014. By April 2014 over half the states had NCLB exemptions, a source of much satisfaction to the teachers' unions.[76]

When education was linked to comparisons of American students' records with other countries, it assumed a more conspicuous place in public discourse. There was much hand wringing and finger wagging over the relatively depressed standing of American schoolchildren. But education in general was too locally embedded and too diverse in the interests at play to gain the sort of attention that jobs, spending, and debt enjoyed. Battles over cost and content played out more conspicuously in states such as Jeb Bush's Florida and Mitch Daniels's Indiana than in the halls of Congress.[77]

On the state level, the issue of education merged into a more general concern over the escalating costs of public employees' pensions and benefits. Opposition to the education establishment took a variety of forms, most conspicuously charter schools, vouchers, and home schooling: all primarily local or state matters.

A new issue, still in an early stage of political development, was the rising cost of higher education. The administration sought to partially subsidize unpaid college loans, now totaling close to a trillion dollars. Education Secretary Arne Duncan adopted a notably bipartisan approach on this as on other school issues, which is testimony, perhaps, to how complex and party-transcending a realm the politics of education was.[78]

No one as yet had a clue as to what to do about the outsized growth of college tuition, and there was growing media interest in the subject. The rise of online courses and programs attracted attention. But it has not so far shown leg as a national political issue. That will-o'-the-wisp the middle class is too largely involved in student loans, without regard to party, for partisan hay to be readily reaped.[79]

Immigration is a more definably national concern. It found a place in the political dialogue of the Bush years, culminating in a failed bipartisan attempt in 2007 to deal with undocumented (a euphemism for illegal) immigrants. But in the early Obama years it was eclipsed by the more compelling issues of the economy and health care.

The primary immigration legislative initiative in the first Obama term was the Dream Act, a cleverly crafted attempt to grant permanent status to toothsome subgroups such as the children of illegals and those who served in the military. It too ran afoul in the face of legislative gridlock. Perhaps more politically consequential was the sharp falloff in new and the emigration of existing illegal immigrants in the wake of the economic downturn.

The most heated politics of immigration went on in states with large numbers of undocumented newcomers. Arizona was the poster child here. Its Republican governor's ongoing confrontation with the administration was the most conspicuous immigration-related political contest of the first Obama term.[80]

Republican conservatives for long had either small or hostile interest in the presence of illegals. But the ever-larger Hispanic preference for Democratic candidates fostered GOP awareness of the noose-tightening potential of that rising demographic. In a larger sense, an issue so deeply embedded in the DNA of what John F. Kennedy called "a nation of immigrants" was bound to have staying power.

During the early stages of Obama's second term, proposals for a Grand Compromise on safeguarding the borders—a concern eased by the virtual cessation of illegal immigration—and legitimizing the 11 million illegals already in the country surfaced again. A bipartisan "gang of eight" senators took the lead, with the president hurriedly following. By no coincidence at all, the most conspicuous Republican advocate of the new legislation was Florida Hispanic senator Marco Rubio, one of the party's more talked-about 2016 prospects.[81]

This was a complex bill of some 1,200 pages, in the modern fashion of legislative draftsmanship. For a time it took pride of place in an otherwise pallid-to-invisible congressional agenda. As before, Republicans defined the issue primarily in terms of the need to secure the Southwest's borders, an attractive stance in that region. Democrats dwelled on the goal of citizenship for illegals, which was widely seen as a fecund source of Democratic votes.[82]

Obama sought to assert leadership in the passage of the bill, though its congressional sponsors showed no great enthusiasm for that. Despite noisy opposition (without much in the way of alternatives) by puristic conservatives, the proposal showed some leg, passing the Senate in June 2013 by a 68 to 32 vote. It then went to the House, where enemies were more numerous and the inclination to follow the Senate's lead was small at best. As the 2014 election drew nearer, the likelihood of legislation diminished. But a refigured Congress and the run-up to the 2016 presidential election might well change the picture.[83]

How does the not inconsiderable economic and social legislation of Obama's time fit into the traditional narrative of the rise of the active national state—the state of the New Deal and the Great Society? These still are, historically speaking, early days. But it does seem evident that neither the high expectations of Obama's boosters nor the deep forebodings of his detractors have been met. Obama has gotten a lot more than his conservative critics wanted but a lot less than his liberal supporters hoped for.

Perhaps the most germane historical issue raised by the Obama domestic policy record is the degree to which it signifies that the active state of the twentieth century faces an uncertain future in the twenty-first. That is a story still playing itself out. But the limited degree to which public policy affects the economy, Obamacare's troubles, and the diminishing American presence abroad do suggest that this issue will figure largely in years to come.

CHAPTER SIX

. . .

Living in the World

THE RELATIONSHIP OF the United States to the world outside has two dimensions. One, the more familiar, is foreign affairs: the diplomatic, economic, cultural, and military interplay between America and other nations. The other is a comparative perspective: how America's public life is similar to, and differs from, that of other countries.

1. FOREIGN AFFAIRS

There are recurring tensions in the history of American foreign affairs. One is between the poles of *realism*, placing national self-interest at the forefront, summed up in the label of *realpolitik* and the aphorism that nations don't have friends; they have interests—and *idealism*, the belief that America's dealings with other nations should be determined by its national ideals and its exceptional character.

These are general terms as much as policy proscriptions. Never has American diplomacy, however drenched in idealistic rhetoric, ignored national self-interest. Nor have its material or strategic goals ever lacked the clothing of idealistic motives.

Another recurring theme is the pressure, on one hand, to sustain the broad character and goals—the continuities—of American foreign policy and, on the other hand, the temptation for a new president, who may well have campaigned for policy change, to foster his own agenda.

There is rarely a sharp disjuncture in the nation's foreign policy, nor is there a single, unchanging American stance in world affairs. Idealism and realism, continuity and change: these are the abiding parameters of American foreign policy.[1]

An Obama Doctrine?

Obama, like most of his predecessors, came into office seeking to set his own brand on American foreign relations. His political rise relied in good part on his opposition to the Iraq war and, more generally, to George W. Bush's neoconservative idealism. Obama offers a variant of the realist foreign policy tradition, one that emphasizes the limits rather than the potential of American power and influence.[2]

The same question may be asked of Obama's foreign as of his domestic policy experience: how well have his transformative goals fared in the pressure-cooker of the real world?

When he came into office, American foreign policy was steeped in continuity. Presidents from Truman to Bush I acted within the same policy framework with their responses to the challenge of Communism and the Cold War. Since then, Clinton, Bush II, and Obama have had to deal with the rise of militant Islam. Relatively limited military conflict has been a persisting reality in both eras: Truman/Eisenhower in Korea, Kennedy/Johnson/Nixon in Vietnam,

George H. W. Bush in the Gulf, Clinton in the Balkans, George W. Bush in Iraq, Obama in Afghanistan.

But not all has been continuity. The old American isolationist strain never fully disappeared. Withdrawal or at least a lower profile abroad, energized by opposition to the Vietnam War, gained new life with the end of the Cold War. It was further strengthened by the Iraq-Afghanistan experience. A Pew poll at the end of 2013 found that isolationist sentiment had reached a 50-year high. There is little reason to think that it has diminished since.[3]

Bush II came into office with little interest in and few opinions on foreign affairs. The Soviet Union was gone, the Balkans were quiet, and Islamic terrorism was marginal. National Security Adviser Condoleezza Rice and Secretary of State Colin Powell had no desire to take out Iraq's Saddam Hussein. Secretary of Defense Donald Rumsfeld was focused more on modernizing the hardware of America's military than using it.

Then, eight months into the administration, came September 11, 2001. The end of the Cold War—indeed, some thought, of history defined as ideological conflict—was suddenly superseded by the onset of the War on Terror. Bush the Indifferent became Bush the Warrior.

America's consequent engagements in Iraq and Afghanistan fired up the antiwar sentiment that had been the defining Left-liberal stance on foreign policy since Vietnam. Just as the Democrats paid a stiff political price for Vietnam in 1968–1972, so too the Republicans paid for Iraq in 2006–2008.[4]

A major theme of Obama's 2008 campaign was to scale back American overseas activism: to end the Iraq war, focus narrowly on getting 9/11 mastermind Osama bin Laden, and mend relations with our adversaries. His opponent John McCain wanted to stay the course in Iraq. *The Economist* thought that "the two versions on offer could hardly present a clearer choice."[5]

As in other policy realms, new president Obama had stronger views than experience in foreign affairs. His anti-Vietnam / anti-Iraq pedigree was consistent and impeccable. He sought to rely on "soft power" and international cooperation instead of a Bushian readiness to use American military power. In this he benefited from a sympathetic consensus among much of the foreign policy elite. The kinds of people who were the most conspicuous interventionists from the late 1930s to the 1960s now had a comparably strong inclination toward disengagement. Not least among the transformations in party identity over the course of the past century has been the reversal of the parties' stances as advocates of isolationist-tinged realism (once the domain of Republicans, now most visible among Democrats) and idealistic internationalism (once most visible among Democrats, now the domain of the GOP).[6]

One way of defining a nation's foreign policy is metaphoric: to perceive the interplay of nations as either a "chessboard" or a "jigsaw puzzle." The chessboard analogy is the more traditional one. It sees the world as a competitive place, with differing and often clashing national models, goals, and strategies. The puzzle analogy sees international relations as a matter of getting the world's nations to work collectively on shared problems such as economic well-being, national security, and human rights.

Obama clearly subscribes to the puzzle model. He came into office with no particular rank order of foreign affairs priorities, beyond ending the Iraq war and improving American relations with the Arab world. Fostering democracy and human rights were lesser goals, as was asserting American military supremacy.

But the realities of Islamic terrorism, the Arab Spring, the Libyan Fall, the Syrian Winter, Iranian and Russian obduracy, and the Chinese challenge quickly and persistently churned the waters of Obama's foreign policy. Here as elsewhere in his presidency, noisome reality and unexpected contingency upset his best-laid plans.[7]

Obama's early diplomatic initiatives reflected his commitment to a new course: hope and change exported overseas. In a 2007 article in *Foreign Affairs* he criticized Bush's wish to impose the American model of freedom and democracy on other countries. He pledged to end the war in Iraq (a process already under way) and to meet with the heads of Iran, Syria, Venezuela, Cuba, and North Korea in the course of his first year in office. As president he made frequent—his critics thought unseemly—reference to the blemishes on America's foreign policy record.[8]

Obama's opposition to the Iraq war and his stark contrast to George W. Bush in policy and personality made him highly attractive to the European Left and (less so) the Muslim world. He met with an enraptured reception when he spoke to a crowd of hundreds of thousands in Berlin during the campaign. The Nobel Peace Prize was bestowed on him when he was barely in office, as much for not being Bush as for being Obama.

Obama came to the presidency with a taste for the noninterventionist foreign policy stance of the American Left. But as was the case with his predecessor, events soon forced him to change course. While ideal-laden belief can struggle mightily against the real world, it takes a truly delusional personality to hold out for long.

International reality inexorably eroded the postulates of nonengagement. For Obama as for Bush, the War on Terror remained by far the most politically fraught issue on his foreign policy agenda. An important part of Obama's 2008 appeal to liberals was his commitment to tone down the American response: to close the Guantanamo terrorist prison camp, eliminate torture ("enhanced interrogation" for the euphemistically inclined), end the war in Iraq, and prosecute accused terrorists in civil rather than military courts.

But Obama also recognized early on that he needed to root his foreign policy, however redefined, in established American tradition. He declared in 2007, "The truth is that my foreign policy is actually a return to the traditional bipartisan realistic policy of George Bush's father, of John F. Kennedy, of, in some ways, Ronald Reagan."[9]

He made Hillary Clinton, his great rival for the nomination, secretary of state. Clinton was closer to the old Democratic-idealist tradition; as a senator she voted for the Iraq war. She made State a haven for Clinton-era idealists. Princeton professor Anne-Marie Slaughter became Director of Policy Planning, Yale Law Dean Harold Koh the department's legal adviser.

But many of Obama's initial foreign policy counselors—Zbigniew Brzezinski, Anthony Lake, Susan Rice—favored an end to Iraq-style intervention and a less pro-Israel policy. Theirs was a Left-liberal realist alternative to the idealist-generated intervention of Bill Clinton in Bosnia/Serbia and the Neocon-inspired Bush war against Saddam Hussein and support for Israel. To some degree the more traditional-minded Secretary of State Clinton and National Security Adviser James Jones were bypassed by younger aides—Ben Rhodes, Mark Lippert, Denis McDonough—who shared with Obama the sense of being post–Cold War, post-Vietnam, and post-Iraq. George H. W. Bushite Brent Scowcroft and the National Security Council vied for influence against the staffers in State. Anne-Marie Slaughter left the administration in February 2010, complaining of gender conflict between the female strategists in the State Department and the male ones in the White House.[10]

But these differences were submerged by the pressure to bring foreign policy into closer accord with the evolving overseas environment and the political priorities of the administration. National Security Adviser Thomas Donilon, Jones's successor, and his deputy McDonough became the "most influential foreign-policy advisers in the White House" as much for their political as their policy smarts.[11]

Both Hillary Clinton and Obama were intensely political animals, an unusual combination. The Acheson-Kissinger model of the professional diplomat gave way to diplomacy as the conduct of domestic politics by other means. Clinton was in constant contact with Obama's White House, holding some 600 meetings by early 2012.[12]

Seeking to stamp his own brand on American foreign policy, Obama initially made conciliatory gestures to Saudi Arabia and China. Clinton proclaimed a "reset" of relations with Putin's Russia. The United States had slid to be the seventh most admired nation by the end of the Bush era in 2008; by the end of 2009 it regained the top slot. Obama's approach had a claim on domestic approval as well, reflecting as it did a growing public desire to pull back from overseas engagements.[13]

One of Obama's first presidential acts was to authorize (but not to implement) closing the Guantanamo Bay detention facility. In a much-heralded Cairo speech on June 4, 2009, full of deference to the region's ways and a disavowal of previous (i.e., Bush-fostered) efforts to intervene there, he called for reconciliation with Islam. He assured his listeners that "no system of government can or should be imposed upon one nation by any other."[14]

But diplomacy as politics by other means had its costs. Brzezinski groused: "He doesn't strategize. He sermonizes." Conservative commentator Charles Krauthammer called Obama's diplomacy "a style, not a doctrine." Others on the Right disagreed, seeing it as a doctrinal replacement of Bush's neoconservative, proactive, pro-democracy approach by a less assertive and judgmental "self-containment" ("constrainment") whose goal was to downplay American power abroad.[15]

Yet evolving reality rather than fixed ideology came to be the most weighty determinant of Obama's foreign policy. From the first, he hedged his anti–Iraq war position by keeping his predecessor's Secretary of Defense, Robert Gates. A week after his conciliatory Cairo speech, the furor that rose over the Iranian repression of protests against what looked like a cooked election suggested that Obama's realism, like Bush's idealism, was subject to the winds of change.

Nowhere was the Obama administration more heavily mugged by reality than in the fraught realm of the War on Terror. Just as a strong anti-military tone was evident in the early Clinton administration (one White House staffer refused to talk to generals), so did anti-anti-terrorism sentiment pervade the early Obama presidency.

Homeland Security Agency head Janet Napolitano substituted "man-caused disaster" for "terrorism" in a Homeland Security Agency document, explaining to *Der Spiegel,* "We had to move away from the politics of fear toward a policy of being prepared for all risks that cause concern." She stirred up more protest, from sources as varied as the American Legion, the American Civil Liberties Union, and the Democratic chair of the House Homeland Security Committee, when her agency released a report warning of the need for vigilance against "right-wing extremism" from "disgruntled" ex-servicemen.[16]

In November 2009 Major Malik Hassan killed 13 fellow-soldiers in Fort Hood, Texas. The administration was reluctant to refer to this as an act of Islamic extremism, and the Department of Defense took the art of euphemism to new heights by labeling it "workplace violence." When on Christmas Day 2009 the "underwear bomber" was foiled in an attempt to bring down a commercial airliner over Detroit, the Holder Justice Department made a strong but politically contentious effort to confine its response to the legal procedures appropriate to a domestic criminal act.

Lessons learned. In the wake of bin Laden's death in 2011, Napolitano stressed the need for a "heightened state of alert." Obama kept Guantanamo Bay open, despite his decree on the first day of his administration that it be closed. He substantially increased drone strikes in Afghanistan, Pakistan, and Yemen: a strategy that inevitably ensured "collateral damage" (the military's euphemism for civilian casualties). He also had a target list, whose selection he participated in, that included American citizens. Obama agreed that the 9/11 conspirators would be tried by a military tribunal in Guantanamo, not by a federal court in lower Manhattan as Attorney General Holder wanted, and he made the killing of bin Laden a milestone in his War on Terror.[17]

A review of America's Afghan policy was the first big test of Obama's evolving place on the realism-idealism spectrum. Increasing America's troops in Afghanistan accorded with his view that getting rid of bin Laden and al-Qaeda took priority over democratizing Iraq. His Special Representative for Afghanistan Richard Holbrooke, in thrall to the Vietnam cautionary tale, wanted fewer troops and more outreach to the Taliban. But Hillary Clinton (whom Holbrooke had supported in 2008) backed a troop increase, and Holbrooke died in December 2010. After an exhaustive review, Obama ordered a Bush-in-Iraq-like surge of 30,000 more soldiers, but pledged to bring them home by the end of 2014.

Technological change created yet another flash point. The administration relied increasingly on pilotless drones to kill terrorist targets. The ethical, ideological, and constitutional issues that this raised were in a tradition that stretched back to FDR's search for ways to aid Britain in 1940–1941. More immediately, enhanced assassination by drones had an unsettling resonance with the enhanced interrogation by waterboarding of the Bush years. Obama's liberal base was not happy with this but muted its objections. Public opinion was tepidly supportive. Obama had joined a long line of presidents who since 1950 had found it necessary to engage in small (and not so small) wars.[18]

The Middle East foreign policy environment took on a new face with the 2009–2010 post-election uprising in Teheran, and the Arab

Spring outbursts a year later. The most conspicuous initiators were students and other middle-class citizens, whose calls for democracy and a secular, tolerant society attracted much Western support.

The administration, still committed to minimal engagement abroad, kept its distance. Obama did not mention the Egyptian uprising in his January 2012 State of the Union address. He adopted a low-keyed role—"leading from behind" was the evocative phrase of *New Yorker* reporter Ryan Lizza—in the effort to remove Libyan dictator Muammar al-Gaddafi, which turned out to be one of his most successful forays abroad.[19]

With the passage of time, the strong militant Islamic presence in the Arab Spring countries made distancing more problematic. Advocates of American global leadership criticized Obama's reluctance to become deeply engaged in the Arab Spring or to support the Syrian rebels fighting against the Assad regime. There was some (not much) reaction to the administration's handling of the killing of the ambassador and other Americans in Benghazi. But the degree to which foreign policy was a nonbarking dog in the 2012 election suggests that Obama's restraint was in accord with mainstream American public opinion.[20]

More troublesome was his rocky relationship with Israel. Many of his core supporters were indifferent-to-hostile toward the traditional America-Israel alliance. Obama told Jewish leaders in the wake of his Cairo address: "Look at the past eight years. During those eight years, there was no space between us and Israel, and what did we get from that? When there is no daylight, Israel just sits on the sidelines, and that erodes our credibility with the Arab states."

In a May 2011 speech he said that the eventual Israel-Palestine border should be based on the 1967 armistice lines, with agreed-upon swaps, a challenge to Israeli leader Benjamin Netanyahu (whom he treated with more cool than warmth in their initial meetings). Canada and American Middle East negotiator George Mitchell thought his statement ill-considered. But some former George W. Bush aides managed to see in it an endorsement of their boss's Israel-Palestine policy.[21]

As with his response to the War on Terror, Obama's stance on the Israel-Palestine issue quickly ran into the headwinds of political reality. He found it expedient to make emollient remarks to the pro-Israel lobbying group AIPAC, and Congress displayed bipartisan sympathy when Netanyahu addressed it.

After his 2012 reelection, Obama made his first in-office visit to Israel, and discomfited his liberal-Left base with a rapprochement of sorts with Netanyahu and a more pro-Israel pivot in his take on how to secure a two-state solution. His pressuring of Netanyahu to mend relations with the Turks suggested that his Israel reset was linked to the dangers posed by the Syrian civil war, the Iranian nuclear *défi*, and the Arab Spring's wintry turn.[22]

Whether Obama was engaged here in subtle diplomatic maneuvering or displaying inexperience and shaky judgment is fodder for speculation. New Secretary of State Kerry has devoted more energy to an Israel-Palestine settlement than his predecessor Hillary Clinton. It is true that so far Kerry and Obama cannot lay claim to anything close to a breakthrough. But who ever had?

Now and Next

The lure of overseas engagement, like the pitfall of scandal, is a recurring theme in presidential second terms. This has had varied political consequences. Woodrow Wilson's embroilment in World War I had disastrous electoral results; FDR's involvement in World War II helped him to be elected to an unprecedented four terms. Against the politically destructive experiences of Truman in Korea, Johnson in Vietnam, Carter with Iran, and Bush II in Iraq may be set the more successful involvements of Eisenhower in Korea, Reagan with the Soviet Union, Bush I in the Gulf War, and Clinton with the Balkans.

And Obama? Under him the country has been disengaging from Iraq and Afghanistan, to general public approval. Much of the groundwork for withdrawal may have been the work of his predecessor, but it was on Obama's watch that the payoff came. America's role in the overthrow of Libya's Muammar al-Gaddafi and in particular the killing of bin Laden were generally viewed as surefooted in their conduct and satisfactory in their outcome.

Despite these successes, Obama did not imitate his doppelgänger Woodrow Wilson in making foreign policy the primary theme of his 2012 reelection campaign. There was no "He Got Us Out of Iraq and Afghanistan" to echo Wilson's 1916 "He Kept Us Out of War." But then Obama didn't have anything like World War I to confront.

There were signs that he wanted to shift his foreign policy focus from the old flash points—Russia and the Middle East—to a still-developing new one, China's economic, military, and geopolitical challenge: from a Russian "reset" to a Chinese "pivot." Obama's pre-2012 election initiatives with regard to China were relatively minor: a statement of concern in a November 17, 2011, speech and the deployment of a small Marine detachment to Australia in 2012. But when China in 2013 sought to assert its primacy over South China Sea air space, he uncharacteristically sent American bombers on a flyover.

There was a symbolic as well as a substantive character to his October 2013 decision to skip major heads-of-state summits in Bali and Brunei on the ground that the domestic budget-debt crisis demanded his presence at home. That the Chinese took advantage of his absence goes without saying—as does the fact that Obama's domestic concerns are likely to continue to outweigh overseas challenges. To call him "The First Pacific President" is to dabble in double meaning.[23]

Despite the ups and downs of a volatile world disorder, a lower American profile abroad remained the primary theme of Obama's foreign policy as his second term unfolded. In historical perspective, this may turn out to be more in sync with the late Bush years than was implied by the rhetoric of fundamental change in his 2008 campaign.

By the close of Obama's first term, the United States was getting out of Iraq, had gotten more into (but was in process of getting out of) Afghanistan, and was conducting the War on Terror in such tried-and-true ways as military tribunals in Guantanamo, drone strikes in Pakistan, and a variety of under-the-radar activities of dubious propriety, all much in the Bush tradition. Obama reluctantly backed NATO in Libya, as Bill Clinton reluctantly backed NATO in Bosnia. Political scientist Thomas Mann observed that Obama's "new dawn of American leadership began to look surprisingly similar to yesterday's dawn."[24]

In acting so, he appeared to be in close accord with the inclinations of the American people. What his critics regarded as lassitude or weakness might also be seen as a politic response to political reality.[25]

Obama's foreign policy record had been less contentious than his domestic one. In a November 2011 poll, 52 percent approved of his performance overseas compared to 40 percent for his economic program. But a spate of policy setbacks, most notably in Syria and with Russia over the Ukraine, eroded his foreign policy standing, much as Obamacare's disappointments sapped his domestic popularity.[26]

Still, Obama's foreign policy has not yet run into popular divisions as deep as those over his domestic initiatives. Withdrawal from Iraq and Afghanistan, successful leading from behind in the effort to rid Libya of Gaddafi, and relative quietude in relations with China have outweighed tensions with Israel, the Benghazi fiasco, the Syrian WMD episode, the ongoing effort to get Iran to drop its quest for nuclear weapons and—so far—Putin's *défi* in the Ukraine.

The Benghazi episode, like Carter's failed attempt to rescue the Embassy hostages in Iran and the Black Hawk helicopter fiasco under Clinton, evoked a negative reaction, but a muted one. It has not secured any great hold on public awareness—in part because it was a relatively limited and discrete failure, in part because the media has not fastened onto it as it did to Carter's hostage crisis or Reagan's Iran-Contra contretemps. Barring some catastrophe like a successful domestic terror attack, there is no reason to expect a substantial disconnect arising between the administration's passivity and public indifference.[27]

Obama can hardly be said to have responded with a firm and consistent hand to the Syrian civil war, and he did some serious waffling on Assad's use of poison gas in the summer of 2013. But pulling back from the use of force was popular, and was followed by seeming Syrian acquiescence in removing the weapons. The longer-term consequences of Russia's rise as a key player in this drama, and what Iran is likely to make of it, are potential more than immediate concerns.[28]

For all the ebb in tension after the poison gas episode, possibly disturbing consequences of the Syrian civil war remain. The support of Russia, Iran, and Hezbollah for Assad's Alawaite-Shiite regime bears some resemblance to the 1930s Spanish Civil War trio of Fascist Italy, Nazi Germany, and Falangeist Franco. The secular and Sunni Syrians, the Sunni Gulf States, and the Islamic militants linked to al Qaeda, who intervened on the side of the rebels, are comparable to the mix of more moderate supporters of the Spanish republican government and the anarchists, Trotskyites, and ultimately controlling Stalinists of the Soviet Union. But this hardly dictates a reprise of the late 1930s. The Islamic terrorist challenge is not (with the limited exception of Iran) state-based, as were Nazism and Stalinism.[29]

In its twists and turns, its mix of verbal bravado and aversion to force, Obama's response to the Iranian nuclear challenge resembles his Syrian record. The late 2013–early 2014 negotiations suggest that his no-Iranian-nukes red line may be as permeable as his no-use-of-Syrian-poison-gas one. But his dealings with Assad on poison gas thus far have worked out better than his critics forecast, and his Iranian strategy remains poised between success and failure.

The challenges raised by Putin's actions in the Ukraine have superseded the Syrian and Iraqi problems. How this new state of affairs will play out is hidden in the fog of the future. But it is likely to figure largely in the remaining time of the Obama administration, and indeed of the presidency that follows it.

As Obama's second term unfolds, the primary questions yet to be answered are these: Will he be confronted by a large-scale crisis that either entrenches him (FDR 1940–, Bush II 2001–) or weakens him (LBJ 1965–, Carter 1979–)? If so, how is he likely to react? Would he reorient his foreign policy approach to embrace military action when it seems necessary (Bush I 1990–1991, Clinton 1999)? Or would he hunker down with his existing policy, as did Carter?

Obama has not yet had to face the peace-or-war decisions that confronted Wilson, FDR, Truman, or LBJ, or even a challenge as stark as Bush's 9/11. His foreign policy agenda continues to be governed by the less traumatic choices that Syria, Iran, China, and Russia (so far) pose. Here as elsewhere, Obama's predilections, solidly rooted in the antiwar, smaller-America outlook of late-twentieth-century liberalism, continue to confront the mugged-by-reality consequences of a nasty world.

Obama's foreign policy to date may best be described as a limited evolution from realist-motivated to idealist-tinged disengagement.

Will he, now that his political future is no longer at stake, move toward a more overtly Wilsonian effort to be an international presence? Even in his less assertive first term, Wilson sent gunboats and cavalry to Mexico, as Obama has sent drones over Pakistan. Would he be inclined to react to a large-scale challenge from Putin as Wilson did to the Germans in World War I? Or would he continue to pursue a more limited, less assertive style of avoiding confrontation? The history of the American presidency, from John Adams's mini-naval war with France in 1799–1800 to Iraq and Afghanistan, suggests that barring something as game-changing as unrestricted German submarine warfare in 1917 or Pearl Harbor in 1941, the latter policy is likely to prevail.[30]

There will be continuing tension between the Left-liberal view of this country as unexceptional and guilt-stained, which certainly was Obama's outlook when he came into office, and the generally more politically attractive view of the United States as having, with all its faults, a responsibility to support democracy and peace. That attitude flourished during the two world wars and the Cold War of the century now past. Short of another 9/11 (which had an impact on the American response to Islamic terrorism that was a muted echo of the impact of Pearl Harbor), the new normal appears to be a toned-down role of the United States as the world's police officer.[31]

That post-Gaddafi Libya, post-Mubarak/post-Morsi Egypt, Assad-led Syria, and Putin's Russia are tangled messes is undeniable. Obama certainly can be held to account for the absence of a discernible American policy toward those hot spots, aside from what an observer called "winging it." But there is every indication that in this he reflects the popular view. It is difficult to say, in a way that would resonate with mainstream American public opinion, that what Obama is doing shouldn't be done or what he's not doing should be done.[32]

For all his enforcement of the Security-Intelligence State, Obama continues to commit his administration to a foreign policy that is reluctant to rely on American military power. Whether his approach is governed by a post-Iraq liberal inclination to disengagement or a canny perception that in a new world order (or disorder) America's response must be different from that of the Cold War and War on Terror era, is a question still to be answered.[33]

One straw in the wind is his second-term foreign policy team. John Kerry, Clinton's successor as secretary of state, gained an early reputation as a vocal opponent of the Vietnam War. Still, he fought in it and voted for intervention in Iraq, and he is hardly a doyen of the antiwar Democratic left. His secretary of defense colleague Chuck Hagel also served in Vietnam, and voted for the Iraqi involvement. Benghazi water carrier Susan Rice, who replaced Hillary supporter Tom Donilon as National Security Adviser, also (though more opaquely) supported the Iraq action. Samantha Power, Rice's successor as UN ambassador, did some fancy waffling on Iraq, but didn't flat-out oppose the American involvement, and is often described as a liberal interventionist. This team is hardly a nest of neo-isolationists.

Indeed, during the Syria flare-up in the summer of 2013, much of the political leadership of both parties rallied to the president and his threat to use the club of force. It was public opinion and ear-to-the-ground members of Congress of both parties who preferred the dove of peace.[34]

Obama, like most of the public, has no taste for Bush-style regime change. At the same time he has retained much of the Cold War / War on Terror Security State: a still-strong (if much reduced) military, active drones, and hyperactive data collecting. If the international status remains more or less quo, his record is likely to continue to be a kind of Kissingerian *realpolitik*: no reset, but uneasy coexistence.[35]

Barring a major game-changer (otherwise called Putin), the foreign policy scene for the rest of Obama's time is likely to remain a cluster of situations of varying concern, none of them on the cusp of a major crisis or major resolution. They include the European Community's economic troubles, continuing to drag their slow length along; the festering post–Arab Spring cold snaps; the very hot and danger-fraught civil war in Syria; the ongoing (though perhaps abating) irritations of Iran and (less so) North Korea; and low-keyed but stubborn tensions with China.

While foreign policy could assume a more commanding place as Obama's second term draws to its close, it does not yet seem likely that a dramatic turn to new directions, such as FDR after 1940, Truman after 1948, or Bush after 9/11, is in the cards. However transformational Obama's domestic policy ambitions may have been (although these, too, have been buffeted in his second term), his foreign policy stance is likely to be cautious, playing rather than changing the game. Surely this is in accord with the prevailing popular sense that America's role since the 1940s as the indispensable world police officer has worn thin.[36]

The current configuration of world affairs may dictate a style of American foreign policy that differs from both nineteenth-century isolationism and twentieth-century interventionism. The fact is that neither politicians or experts have yet come to terms with the post-9/11 world. While relations with Putin's Russia and a surging China echo some Cold War themes, the terms of engagement are quite different. Putin is more like a nationalistic czar than the Bolshevik Stalin. China too is acting more in its ancient tradition of regional commercial and strategic hegemony than with Mao-like ideological assertiveness.

Up to now, what has been called "foreign-policy populism"—support for a powerful military and a readiness to act forcefully if there is a direct threat to national security, and far less support for an American *mission civilisatrice* to bring democracy and prosperity to other lands—is alive and well, more so than at any time since the 1930s. It will take a large game-changer, indeed, to alter this.

2. COMPARATIVE PERSPECTIVES: THE US AND THE EU

Living in the world involves more than foreign policy. There are broad economic, social, and political conditions that cast light on what is shared by and what is distinctive to the American situation, as compared to other nations.

Market economies and representative government are the common coin of the United States, Western Europe, and Japan. Financial crisis and economic recession have afflicted them in recent years. Looking at their responses to a similar set of woes allows a comparative perspective to do what it does best: heighten understanding of one's own country.

The American economy has been buffeted by the bursting of a housing-mortgage bubble, a banking-financial crisis, stubbornly high unemployment, stagnant economic growth, and escalating public debt. Most of these ills are conspicuous as well in Western Europe and Japan. There are signs that, in their very different ways, developing economies—Russia and China, India, and Brazil—are coming to face comparable problems of employment, capital, and growth.

The most meaningful comparison is with the European Union. The causes and character of the Eurobloc countries' troubles vary from too-low tax collection and too-high pension and other benefits in Greece to sclerotic labor laws in Italy and unsound mortgage and construction loans by rogue banks in Spain and Ireland. But the bottom line is a set of troubles that (in less toxic form) has reared its head in the United States as well.

In May 2012 *The Economist* asked of the European Community, "Going for growth, but how?" The basic choice was through low taxes and greater "austerity" in government spending or through a large and recurring stimulus in the form of government "investment."[37]

A comparable economic controversy (however different in its particulars) rages in the United States. It is apparent that in recent decades this country along with Western Europe and Japan has been moving from the economic and political determinants of the post–World War II era, just as from the 1960s on they began to take on a new cultural configuration.

For half a century after 1945, the dominant characteristics of these countries were major-party democracy, expanding welfare states, and deference to American leadership in the Cold War. Since the 1980s, the major facts on the ground have changed. Militant Islam has replaced militant Communism; the War on Terror has replaced the Cold War. Banking, financial, and employment crises have followed decades of generally rising prosperity. The financial burden of the welfare state has begun to erode its popular appeal.

The policy consequences of this changing environment are still very much a work in progress. Problems that for half a century were consigned to a past era have returned with a vengeance. Among them: a lack of will to confront new international challenges (the totalitarianism states before World War II, militant Islam and pesky Putin's Russia now); persistent slowdowns in economic growth that evoke the memory, if not the reality, of the Great Depression; fears of population decline not seen since the 1930s; and rising debt threatening the welfare state. European autarchy and xenophobia are more evident, as is American isolationist sentiment. There is a sense of common decline—of "America and Europe sinking together"—that brings back memories of the 1930s.[38]

Yet as so often in the past, the American and European responses to comparable problems have been very different. Such was the case in the 1930s. There was no European analogue to the New Deal's mix of social welfare and the integration of the nation's new immigrants. Such was the case in the postwar decades, when Europe pursued the course of social democracy and the United States followed its distinctive mix of a limited welfare state and an ever-growing private/corporate sector. And such is the case today: a European backlash against austerity, an American backlash against big government. From a European perspective, there are resonances between America's Tea Party and the xenophobic, anti–European Union parties of Europe's far right. From an American one, the Tea Party is as far from those analogues as the nineteenth-century Populist party was from its Russian namesake.[39]

The past is replete with times in which there were noticeable similarities between American and British public life. Nineteenth-century American Democrats and British Liberals had a number of common qualities, as did American Republicans and English Conservatives. The same was true of British New Liberalism and American Progressivism in the early twentieth century. The pairings of Ronald Reagan and Margaret Thatcher and of Bill Clinton and Tony Blair are in that hands-across-the-water tradition. Obama and Prime Minister David Cameron faced similar difficulties with public and legislative opinion over what to do about the Syrian situation.[40]

Britain's Labor and Conservative parties, like America's Democratic and Republican parties, have tensions between their more ideological/Bourbon wings (learning nothing, forgetting nothing), and younger members aware of the cultural changes that have made adaptation more pressing. Britain's Labor North and Tory South have resonances with America's Blue and Red states. Labor unions in both countries are losing their political edge, as a new politics of cultural identity replaces the old politics of class.[41]

Does the current British Conservative–Liberal Democratic coalition led by David Cameron foretell a comparable convergence of center-Right and center-Left in American politics? So far there is small reason to think so; indeed, the 2012 election suggests that quite the contrary is the case. Up to now, it has been in the American states, more than in the federal government, that the tension between austerity and growth has generated new policy approaches. Nor is it clear how well the British experiment is working out.[42]

Both the relatively healthy economic conditions that set the tone for the politics of Angela Merkel's Germany and the declinist fears that define the politics of François Hollande's France have echoes in the United States. Obama, like Hollande, came into office on a leftist tilt but was nudged toward the center by economic and political reality. The French Right, like the American GOP, appears to be on the upswing. But differences in American society such as the place of immigrants and ethnicity, the structure of the economy, and the institutions of politics and government make more substantive comparison with France or other Continental countries a doubtful enterprise.[43]

Some transnational grass-is-greenerism does exist. Economist-savant Paul Krugman persisted long after it was seemly to look to European-style social democracy as a model for America. European analysts struggling with fiscal and financial autarchy discuss (with comparable irrelevance) the beauties of the American federal state and its untroubled single currency, as created by that unlikely role model Alexander Hamilton.[44]

This is flattering but hardly relevant. The history of the United States has little in common with the past thousand years and more of European history. The European Union Constitution's opening words, "His Majesty the King of the Belgians," just don't have the resonance of "We the People of the United States."

An assault on "austerity" (reductions in government spending) as the antithesis of "growth" (government-sponsored job creation) has recently flourished in Europe, fostered by *The Economist* and its unlikely bedfellow the European Left. A similar argument between free-spending Democrats and purse-pinching Republicans was conspicuous during the 2012 American presidential election. But it did so with little or no reference to the European situation.

Today as in the past, distance, history, and culture conspire to make Americans far less cognizant of what is happening abroad than Europeans are of American developments. For better or worse, America's response to its problems is likely to remain irredeemably insular.[45]

CHAPTER SEVEN

. . .

The 2012 Overture

PRESIDENTIAL ELECTIONS, LIKE the Super Bowl and the World Series, have a large place in a society with a taste for contests ending in playoffs. But the hoopla conceals the more serious purposes of our quadrennial jousts. They are our primary means of allocating public power. They put to the test the rules, institutions, and customs of the political system. They give voice to the anxieties and expectations of the American people.

The election of 2012 was widely expected to cast light on some of the larger issues of modern American politics:

Do we live in an age when party polarization and government gridlock continues (and perhaps worsens)? Or does polarization show signs of easing off?

What is the place of the triad of race, ethnicity, and culture that has figured so prominently for so long in our politics? Is it, too, easing off? Or does it continue to flourish?

Is the election likely to see the establishment of the Democrats as the normal majority party? Or will fluctuation and contingency continue to set the tone of American politics?

Will the election turn out to be a stark confrontation between two opposing views of the role of government in American society: the Democratic model of social democracy and a regulatory state, and the Republican one of limited government and free enterprise?

1. SETTING THE STAGE

In the wake of Obama's solid 2008 victory, visions of a permanent Democratic majority danced in supporters' heads. Left-wing columnist Harold Meyerson declared, "The future in America's politics belongs to Barack Obama's Democrats." Journalist Tom Edsall reported that political pundits foresaw a new normal Democratic majority.[1]

Then came the election of 2010. The Republicans added 63 seats, erasing the Democratic gains of 2006 and 2008. The Democrats barely retained their primacy in the Senate; state legislatures and governorships shifted substantially to the Republicans. The results echoed the election of 1914, when Wilsonian Progressivism was slapped down; or 1938, when the New Deal ran into its first rebuke; or 1994, when Bill Clinton's post-1960s liberalism faced a conservative backlash.[2]

The 2010 election underlined the fragility of coalitions in the modern American political environment. There were early warning signals. A Gallup poll in July 2009 found that the most widely held social and economic views of Americans were "conspicuously incongruous with the results of the 2008 elections." Early 2010 saw the sharpest first-year drop in presidential popularity in polling history.

Majorities opposed expanding the Stimulus, bank bailouts, budget deficits, Obama's health-care reform, cap and trade, and his reset diplomacy.[3]

Did Obama, like Wilson and FDR, respond to his off-year setback by subordinating domestic themes to the allurements of foreign affairs? Did he, like Clinton, triangulate and prevail? Or did he, like Truman, persevere with his previous approach to governance? To raise the question is to answer it. Obama rejected the idea that the 2010 results were anti–big government. Instead, he stuck to the view that a more, not less, muscular state was what an ailing economy needed. And in 2012 he won, though it is debatable whether his policies or his persona and superior campaigning made the difference.[4]

The Political Culture

From 1860 to 1932 only two Democrats, Grover Cleveland and Woodrow Wilson, interrupted the succession of Republican presidents: the inheritance of the Civil War. From 1932 to 1980 only two Republicans, Dwight D. Eisenhower and Richard Nixon, ruffled the procession of Democratic presidencies: the inheritance of the Great Depression.

Since then, Republicans (Reagan, the Bushes) and Democrats (Clinton, Obama) have made the presidency anything but the preserve of one party. "The Emerging Republican Majority" predicted in 1970 turned out to be no more secure than "The Emerging Democratic Majority" foreseen in 2004 is likely to be.[5]

Is this due to the rise of Independent voters, tied to no party and ready to shift their allegiance as the politics of the moment dictate? Or has the character and role of the party system changed so as to all but foreclose the presence of a normal majority?

Analyst Sean Trende holds that the traditional political science talk of normal majorities, major realignments, and critical or sustaining elections are statistical constructs more than descriptions of political reality. He sees indeterminacy, contingency, and variability as the rule in American politics. Like long-gone empires, dominant political persuasions—Federalists, Jeffersonians, Jacksonians, Gilded Age Republicans, New Deal Democrats, Reagan/Bush Republicans—wound up in history's dustbin. That scenario has even greater viability in our current fast-changing, culturally loose-limbed time.[6]

It is customary to speak of today's American politics as uniquely polarized. But there have been other times in the American past when the country and the parties were deeply divided. The most notable of these was the 1850s, dominated by the adamantine issues of slavery and the permanence of the Union.

The consequences of industrialism gave a sharp edge to politics in the 1890s and early 1900s, and so again with the Great Depression and the New Deal of the 1930s. The civil rights movement, the Vietnam War, and cultural upheaval led to profound political strains in the 1960s and early 1970s.

These times of stress played out in different ways, depending on the impact of the issues at stake and the state of the party system. In the 1850s a political culture given over to "an excess of democracy" confronted issues impervious to halfway solutions. The result was the collapse of the two-party system, secession, and civil war.

Since then, outcomes have been less dire. Reform movements—Progressivism around the turn of the twentieth century and the New Deal in the 1930s—eased economic and social discontents.

The triad of civil rights, Vietnam, and culture change in the 1960s and early 1970s posed a weighty challenge, in some respects the greatest since the 1850s. The assassinations of John and Robert

Kennedy and Martin Luther King, the Goldwater election debacle of 1964, the anti-Vietnam movement and the collapse of the Johnson presidency in 1968, the McGovern election debacle of 1972, Watergate and Nixon's departure in 1974: this was indeed the long national nightmare that President Gerald Ford called it.

Yet out of that Sturm und Drang, civil rights emerged as the national norm. The Vietnam War ended without the nation torn apart by it. Both civil society and the political system came to terms of a sort with the cultural revolution.[7]

But that troubled time bequeathed to the nation a recurring sense of political malaise. Polls reveal how low the esteem in which major public institutions—Congress, the Supreme Court, the executive branch, and the media—are held. The semi-impeachment of President Clinton, the bitterly disputed Bush-Gore election of 2000, concern over terrorism and Iraq, and, most of all, the growing belief that the parties and the government cannot effectively respond to the nation's economic problems feed that unease.[8]

This list of ills seems less menacing when viewed in historical perspective. Set against slavery and secession in the 1850s, the immiseration of farmers and workers in the 1890s, the Great Depression of the 1930s, and the conflicts over civil rights, Vietnam, and the counterculture in the 1960s, our current concerns thus far are of a lesser order.

Why, then, are they so difficult to deal with? True, American voters are consistently inconsistent in calling for less government spending while preserving their entitlements. But this does not mean that popular support for a politics (and policies) of compromise and moderation is lacking.

Independents—voters not clearly identified with one of the major parties—are often seen as the 800-pound gorilla in the American electorate room. Polls have shown that the most politically influential bloc of American voters is neither strongly Left nor strongly Right but a muddied middle. George W. Bush was careful to label himself a compassionate conservative in 2000; Barack Obama was similarly careful to don the cloak of post-partisanship in 2008.

Independents make up a third or more of the voting public, but they are a mixed bag. At the tails of the electoral bell curve are Occupy Wall Street (OWS) types disaffected from Obama and the Democrats because they haven't brought true socialism, and Tea Partyites disdaining the Republicans because they haven't done more to dismantle the American state.

More common are citizens who have no particular party leaning and/or are indifferent to politics, and a larger number who prefer one party but are not wedded to it and are drawn to moderate policy positions. They were satirized by British cartoonist David Austin in "Hom. Sap," set in ancient Rome, which pictured a moderates' rally: "What do we want? Gradual change!" "When do we want it? In due course!"[9]

For some time now, Independents have been the fastest-growing category of voters, fed by the weakened structures and deepening polarization of the major parties. They are in effect a third party, wielding a clout comparable to that of Ross Perot in 1992 or the Progressives in 1912. More than 50 members of Congress subscribe to the bipartisan No Labels group chaired by Senator Joe Manchin of West Virginia and 2012 GOP presidential aspirant John Huntsman, which favors solving problems over ideological commitment.[10]

But centrist insurgency is as chancy as its oxymoronic label suggests. Third parties, from the Know-Nothings, Prohibitionists, Liberal Republicans, and Populists of the nineteenth century to the Progressives and the more recent George Wallace and Ross Perot flareups, have a long history of transience. Only two of the 535 senators and representatives, and 80 of 7,383 state legislators, identify themselves as Independents. However disarrayed and unpopular, the two major parties remain the mainstay of our politics.[11]

But if the parties still set the tone and call the tune of elections, why do they remain so polarized, so seemingly disinclined to woo centrists and Independents? The answer lies in part in the rise of an autonomous media, advocacy groups, ideologically driven donors, and the blogosphere and social networks as major participants in the game of politics.[12]

In the past, an intensely partisan press tended to follow the lead of the bosses and parties to whom it gave its loyalty and from whom it got its sustenance. Large interests—business/corporate, agricultural, labor, veterans, ethnic groups—focused on issues of special concern to them. But they were less concerned with the big questions of party ideology. Money and get-out-the-vote activity were funneled through the party machinery. Leadership hierarchies prevailed in state party machines and in Congress. Along with the usual partisan division, a sense of being members of a shared vocation prevailed in the political class.

The parties were composites that put a premium on the art of compromise. The Democrats were an unstable coalition of southern white rural Baptists and Methodists and northern urban Irish Catholics. The Republicans were a brew of businessmen, small and big, Protestants North and West, many industrial workers, and Great Plains farmers.

That political culture has substantially changed. The Democrats' solid South and loyal Irish-Americans are a memory, as are the Republicans' solid North and loyal prosperous Protestants. Presidents and congressional leaders have fewer instruments of control over their party members. The media tail wags the party dog far more than the reverse. Candidates are financially more autonomous, less dependent on party funds, more reliant on ideologically driven money and supporters.

The parties have become more ideologically distinct than at any time since the Civil War era. Conservative Democrats and liberal Republicans are all but vanished breeds. The decline of the North-South divide hastened this process, as did gerrymandering and the primaries' erosion of machine-dictated candidacies.[13]

Partisanship, once part of general American life—elections were social entertainments as much as allocations of power—now is concentrated in ideologically driven segments of the population. This is not unique to the United States: party membership in Europe has declined markedly since the 1980s for similar reasons.[14]

The result is a polarized, populist (but not more popular) politics, one that in the United States has grown to maturity within the traditional party framework. The virtual disappearance of third parties, at a time when cause-driven passions of the sort that traditionally fed them are flourishing, suggests that those impulses now find comfortable homes in the major parties. Third parties bid fair to become an endangered species, to be found primarily in the language of the law and in ménages à trois.[15]

The short, unhappy life of Americans Elect in 2012 underscores the futility of the third-party alternative. Some moderate, enlightened, and well-heeled Democrats (including, in a striking bit of cultural symbolism, former Walt Disney CEI (Chief Executive Illusionist) Michael Eisner) came up with a plan to create an alternative ticket through an Internet referendum. The credulous Tom Friedman of the *New York Times* lent his imprimatur, equating it with such other Now phenomena as Amazon, the blogosphere, and the iPod.

Then reality intruded. If Americans Elect claimed to be a political party, it would have to solicit contributions as a taxable 527 rather than a tax-exempt 501(c)(4). Although $35 million to $40 million was raised, no candidate got more than 10,000 votes online, well below the minimum necessary. By summer, Americans Elect was a rapidly fading memory.[16]

Another sign of the new political culture is the replacement of conventions by primaries in choosing presidential candidates. This has been the case since 1972. Harry Truman regarded primaries as "eyewash," and it would be difficult to argue that the quality of presidential candidates has been higher since they took over. Nor can they claim to have democratized the candidate-selection process: turnout in primaries often is 10 percent or less of eligibles. But there they are: a candidate-choosing device that fits the ideal, if not the reality, of a populist politics.

Meanwhile the national convention has devolved from an occasion when party leaders chose a candidate to a setting for media-driven sales pitches. Republican convention speakers in 2012 steered away from eulogizing (or in some cases even mentioning) candidate Romney. Obama was only lightly and intermittently bashed. The stress instead was on the hard-core party beliefs of small government, low taxes, and patriotism. The Democrats dwelt more on the evils of Romney than on the accomplishments of Obama. They focused on cultural issues with a single-mindedness of the sort usually associated with Republican social conservatives. It is not surprising that neither party got a substantial lift from their shindigs. A deflated ball doesn't bounce very high.[17]

There are other signs of difference from the past besides the demise of third parties, the rise of primaries, and the disappearance of meaningful conventions. Traditional tropes—"labor," "the working class," "the common man"—have been superseded by a portmanteau "middle class." The custom of a (Democratic) president speaking in Detroit on Labor Day has faded away, as indeed has much of Detroit.

There has also been a noticeable decline in the once close campaign interplay between presidential candidates and their congressional and local party fellow-travelers. True, the party-minded George W. Bush ordered his 2004 campaign to do what it could to assist others on the GOP ticket: "I don't want a lonely victory." But Obama and Romney did little endorsing, fundraising for, or money-transferring to House or Senate candidates. The prevailing pattern is for every candidate to paddle his or her own canoe.[18]

The passing of boss-machine politics has had mixed consequences. There is probably less overt corruption in Congress: recent scandals are more likely to involve sex or elections than money. The media are as partisan as they ever were, and with the advent of television became much bigger and more autonomous players in the political game. Whether the cable TV–blogosphere–social networks revolution will lessen that clout has yet to be seen.[19]

One might expect the Democratic party's affluent urban-suburban supporters to coexist uneasily with their black-Hispanic-white working-class partners. That was true of the party's native white southern Protestant and immigrant northern Catholic wings in the past. Similarly, Tea Party, Wall Street, and country club Republicans may be united by shared views on the role of government, but are deeply divided on economic grounds.

These strains do exist, though so far markedly less so than in the past. The fault lines within the parties appear to be less economic, regional, and ethnic, and more cultural and ideological.[20]

2. ADVOCACY, MONEY, AND THE MEDIA

The hallmarks of the new politics are not only new customs and electoral patterns but the enhanced importance of dedicated advocacy groups, big money, and loud media. They have filled much of the void left by the decline of machines and party bosses.

Are these distinctions that don't make a profound difference? After all, special interests, campaign financing, and a large media presence are as old as our political system. Or do differences of intensity and scale add up to something new?

Advocacy

Advocacy groups speaking for big business, agriculture, labor, or veterans have long been part of the American political scene. But as the old party system waned, more ideological, issue-oriented advocacy waxed. Among the conspicuous new players: ideologically defined think tanks; the pro-choice, pro-life, feminist, and gay marriage movements; gun control boosters and opponents; antiwar advocates and environmentalists; organized oldsters.

These groups have the fundraising capacity, the commitment, and the foot soldiers that once were the province of the parties. True, they have precedents: the antislavery, prohibition, and women's suffrage movements, and the Ku Klux Klan. But unlike their predecessors, the new groups show little interest in bipartisan or third-party politics. This is so in part because the major parties are so receptive to them.

Right- and Left-leaning think tanks have become important founts of party policy. The conservative Heritage Foundation made a splash when the Reagan administration adopted many of its policy proposals after the 1980 election. The Center for American Progress had a similar (though lesser) role in the first Obama term.[21]

The American Association of Retired Persons (AARP) claims upward of 40 million members, which makes it second in size to the Roman Catholic Church among American organizations. It lobbies for policies deemed helpful to its constituency, most notably, shielding the major entitlements—Social Security, Medicare, Medicaid—from cuts, and advocated the passage of Obamacare.

Given the enormous government expenditures at stake, AARP may well be the most potent advocacy group. But it began its life in

1958 as a device for selling insurance to the elderly, and this remains a major purpose. A similar mix of advocacy and rent-seeking characterizes prominent members of the green-environmental realm such as the Sierra Club. It was true as well of those old-school outfits the American Legion and the Klan.[22]

Economic interests, as always, are big players in the politics game. The venerable United States Chamber of Commerce has gotten a new lease on life as the leading pro-business voice in Washington. The administration's spending and regulatory policies are opposed by a flock of business-funded advocates, such as the Club for Growth and Karl Rove's American Crossroads. Unions, in particular those representing teachers and service employees, have joined with the United Auto Workers and the AFL-CIO, whose declining hold on the private workforce has if anything encouraged them to invest large money and much commitment in national and state politics.[23]

But the often narrowly defined goals of these groups can constrain their clout. Barack Obama's 2008 and 2012 campaigns showed how a charismatic candidate with an appealing message, a well-tuned campaign, and an opposition in disarray can seize the money-gathering and policy-defining initiative.[24]

Money Talks

In the pre–New Deal past, elections were financed by officeholder assessments, contractor kickbacks, and corporate contributions. Their outcome lay in the hands of party machines, faithful volunteers (paid and unpaid), and voters (unpaid and paid).[25]

There is still much volunteer politicking by committed partisans such as union members, affluent liberals, evangelicals, and the Tea Party folks. But the cost of campaigning in a media-suffused culture demands ever larger, more highly organized, and more productive money-raising instruments. Recent decades have seen an explosion of innovation, the source of a new terminology: political action committees (PACs), soft money, 501(c)s, 527s, and super PACs.

Population growth and the primary system drive political spending upward. But the biggest spurs have been the need to engage in candidate mass-marketing through the media, and the escalating cost of identifying likely supporters and getting them to the polls.[26]

Campaign finance reform has been a conspicuous cause since corporate money became a major fact of political life at the turn of the twentieth century. But laws such as McCain-Feingold and court decisions have not halted the rising flood of getting and spending. In unadjusted dollars, the presidential candidates spent about $92 million in 1980, $192 million in 1992, and $343 million in 2000. Then spending took off: $2 billion in 2004 and $2.75 billion in 2008, followed by a small fallback to $2.6 billion in 2012. This eightfold increase over the past 12 years is college tuition–like in its spiraling magnitude (and ever-less-evident payoff).[27]

The biggest jump (some 62 percent) came between 2000 and 2004, when Democratic 527s and PACs spent more than twice as much as their Republican counterparts. Investor-currency speculator George Soros and insurance magnate Peter Lewis donated over $50 million to the Kerry campaign. But they and their 527, Americans Coming Together, faded after Bush won.[28]

Then came 2008 and Obama's record-shattering $745 million fundraising effort. His campaign tapped millions of small donors on an unprecedented scale and massively bundled the giving of wealthier supporters.

In 2010 the Republicans effectively responded to Obama's 2008 innovations. Crossroads Grassroots Political Strategies, a 501 outfit directed by GOP strategist Karl Rove, raised $70 million. Liberal journals, who ignored Soros, paid much attention (in a there's-gambling-in-Rick's tone) to the Koch brothers, well-heeled libertarian/conservatives who in fact gave a modest $1.3 million to their Americans for Prosperity. Democrats would resurrect the brothers in 2014 as the epitome of political evil, hoping to divert the flow of discourse from the travails of Obamacare and the job market. Meanwhile the Democracy Alliance, a secretive club of wealthy left-leaning liberals, was girding its well-heeled loins for the 2014 and 2016 electoral challenges.[29]

The Supreme Court's *Citizens United* decision of 2010 gave legitimacy to the new culture of fundraising. It held that on free speech grounds corporations and unions had the right to engage in limitless spending for issue advocacy: a green light for big bucks. Super PACs, with no contribution limits and legally required independence from the parties and the candidates, were a made-to-order device for ideology-driven donors. *The Economist* thought that they were changing the face of American politics. (Just what a polarized politics needed.)[30]

The Republicans leapt in first with GOP guru Karl Rove's American Crossroads. Obama initially disdained super PACs—a bit much, given that he refused to accept the constraint of federal campaign funding in 2008. But soon enough reality took over, and Priorities USA appeared in his corner.

Obama showed much skill and devoted much time to big-time money-gathering, though the *New Yorker*'s Jane Mayer questionably concluded that he had a "complicated" attitude toward fundraising and that his donors were more idealistic than their GOP counterparts. He outstripped his predecessors in attending fundraisers, and (successfully) set his sights on a billion dollars in 2012.[31]

While the GOP was mired in its primary follies, the Obama campaign steadily expanded its campaign-funding operation. By as early as mid-summer 2011, it had held over 240 large fundraisers (compared to 47 in 2008), and had 24 bundlers who raised half a million dollars or more. George Soros and other progressive plutocrats set out to collect as much as $100 million to get out the Democratic vote: not so much the politics of ideas as the politics of the machine.[32]

The GOP's traditional money-raising prowess resurfaced. Bush guru Karl Rove's Crossroads Grassroots Political Strategies and the Koch brothers' Tea Party–tinted Americans for Prosperity were bigger super PAC money-getters than their Democratic counterpart Priorities USA, though Rahm Emanuel devoted much time and energy to fill its coffers. The Kochs and Tom Donohue of the United States Chamber of Commerce spoke airily of spending as much as a billion dollars on top of the Romney campaign/Republican National Committee goal of $800 million.[33]

The charge that the two parties are Tweedledee-Tweedledum servants of wealth is as old as American politics. It was indeed the case that they traditionally whipped up enthusiasm and cash by giving voice to the desires and fears of their economic as well as their regional and ethnic constituencies. They are still doing it, with more culturally and ideologically defined bases.

Spurs to spending persist. There is an ever-larger cost to campaigning in a diverse country of a third of a billion people. Consultants and pollsters, a data-gathering infrastructure, mass media outreach, and get-out-the-vote efforts are increasingly expensive. As always, the generous have to be rewarded. Obama paid homage to an old political tradition by appointing a noticeable number of his bundlers (24 of the top 47) to cushy ambassadorships and other administration posts.[34]

The rich do not cluster in one party. Hollywood, Silicon Valley, many Wall Streeters, and top multibillionaires Bill Gates and Warren Buffett favored Obama. Manufacturers, bankers, and small-to-middling businesspeople tended to back Romney. But there was little reason to think that donors unleashed by the Court's *Citizens United* decision strongly affected the level of fat-cat contributions to Romney (or for that matter had a large impact on the candidate's prospects).[35]

Obama's appeal to the well-heeled in 2012 was not what it had been. In 2008 he got some $20 million (compared to the Republicans' $14 million) from major banks and investment firms. Four years later it was another story. But he benefited from the spending that made Washington the affluence capital of the United States. Ethanol, electric, solar, wind energy, and union leaders, enmeshed in close relationships with government, were beholden to the administration.[36]

It appears that for all the rise in political spending, its efficacy has built-in limits. The two parties' 2012 outlays were slightly less than their $1.3 billion in 2008—a leveling off?

If Money Talks, So Do the Media, the Blogosphere, and the Social Networks

One of the distinctive features of the 2012 campaign was the degree to which the media matched and even surpassed big money as a player in the political game. The campaign, money, and the media had a mutually sustaining relationship. Profit-seeking participants in the new populist politics—local TV stations, political consultants, pollsters—were major beneficiaries of campaign spending. Swing-state TV stations welcomed the election as the equivalent of being in a Super Bowl city. Safely one-party states paid a price in foregone advertising and revenue because of their consequent inconsequence.

For some time now it has been beyond serious doubt, except for a few true believers on the Left, that the bulk of the mainstream media has a liberal tilt and looks on Republicans and conservative ideas with a more jaundiced eye than it does on Democrats and liberal ones. This media bent was notably robust in the 2008 election and continued in rude health in 2012.

The closest historical equivalent is the overwhelming newspaper hostility to FDR in the 1936 election. The result then, one of the most lopsided decisions (for FDR) in American political history, suggests that when confronted by the classic (Chico) Marxian dilemma—"What you gonna believe, me or your own eyes?"—the public is inclined to go with the latter.[37]

Media bias is as old as the Republic, and political scurrility is as American as apple pie. That tradition has seamlessly persisted in the new media world of the Internet, the blogosphere, and the social networks.

It is not difficult to cherry-pick instances of slanted reportage. Fox News has a persistent pro-GOP, anti-Obama stance, though it is at times outclassed in the vitriol sweepstakes by MSNBC on the Left. CNN portrays itself as more centrist, though it appears to have a liberal-Democratic tilt. During the campaign its viewership declined as against those of Fox and MSNBC, as one would expect in a political world where strong engagement and strong partisanship go together.

For some years now, talk radio and cable TV news have been conspicuous for their anything-goes style. Once it was the angry Right that led in the defamation sweepstakes: evangelists Jerry Falwell and Pat Robertson and then the Drudge Report and take-no-prisoners Rush Limbaugh (who continues to outrage). The provocative Bush presidency and the age of Obama have enabled voices on the Left to close the gap and then some.

But it is important to keep in mind that the fevered world of cable news attracts a vanishingly small percentage of the electorate. Fox News's 2 million or so viewers add up to eight-tenths of 1 percent of the population.

The liberal *Washington Post* and the conservative *Wall Street Journal* do a creditable job of sustaining a Chinese wall between their news and editorial columns (though the liberal bent of most journalists leaves its mark). The *New York Times* is something else again. Though it sustains a healthy strand of reputable journalism, it is widely seen as the most prominent and consistent voice of a liberal-Left political perspective.

Why? Partly because its now-national readership is of the same political persuasion as its Jewish liberal core in New York, just as the *Journal* taps a countrywide base of the business-and-market-minded. *Times* publisher Arthur Sulzberger Jr. has Left-liberal views comparable to the conservative leanings of William Randolph Hearst and the *Chicago Tribune*'s Robert McCormick in the 1930s, and Fox News's Rupert Murdoch today. "The NYT gets more like MSNBC every day," said one observer.[38]

Is access to political information more narrow and partisan than in the past? Probably not. Surfing, Facebooking, and Twittering may be selective ways of keeping in touch with the ways of the world, But they are not necessarily more confining (arguably, less so) than in the old days of the local *Daily Democrat* or *Republican Sentinel* or, for that matter, the outlooks of Walter Cronkite or Dan Rather in the glory days of TV network news.

Many of the current generation of journalists are the children (only culturally, of course) of Watergate's Bernstein and Woodward. Their model is not objectivity so much as engagement: "making a difference." An outcropping of that mindset was the short, contentious life of JournoList. This was an online cabal of some 400 reporters, academics, think-tankers, and bloggers recruited by *Washington Post* writer Ezra Klein. They shared e-mailed views on how to give the news a liberal-left spin. This was sufficiently at odds with the still-dominant view of good journalism to bring about JournoList's rapid demise.[39]

Was the media as unabashedly in the Obama camp in 2012 as it was in 2008? There was no equivalent to the *Times*'s failed attempt in early 2008 to accessorize McCain with a lobbyist mistress. (That would have been an unlikely line of inquiry indeed, given Romney's Mormonism). A 5,000-plus word *Washington Post* story on Romney's participation in a schoolboy bullying incident did seem excessive. But it had short or no legs.

Romney's Mormonism was as potential a problem as Obama's pre-2008 ties to the radical Reverend Wright. *New York Times* columnist Maureen Dowd and others dipped their toes into a view of Romney's Mormonism and his church that resonated with the anti-Catholic assault on Al Smith in 1928. In general, however, the media-Mormon link was conspicuous for its absence: 2012 was not 1928. *Time* ran a fair-minded cover story on "The Mormon in Mitt." Obama did not raise the issue, as Romney and McCain before him avoided mentioning the Obama–Reverend Wright relationship.[40]

The case can be made that the place of advocacy groups, ideology-driven money, and the media in the current political system, along with the breakdown of the lifts-all-boats American economy, has had baleful effects on both parties.[41]

One consequence is the ever more ubiquitous presence of labels and euphemism in political discourse. There is much talk among the more elevated analysts of tropes and memes: signifiers of post-modern cool but hardly of more substantive political discourse. Little attention was paid to the possible intent of Obama's early talk of a New Foundation and far more to the not quite programmatic "Hope and Change" slogan of his 2008 campaign. This gave way in 2012 to the even less descriptive call to arms of "Forward." The Romney campaign's counterthrust of "Believe" did not add much to the substance of interparty discourse.

Euphemism, not unknown in the nineteenth-century days of "protection" (high tariffs) and "free trade" (low tariffs), is pervasive in our popular culture–infused political world. Liberals like to speak of "undocumented immigrants" and "investment"; conservatives prefer "illegals" and "tax and spend." "Global warming" has given way to less threatening "climate change," and "diversity" sounds better than "affirmative action." Homeland Security secretary Janet Napolitano briefly tried (but failed) to relabel acts of terrorism "man-made disasters."[42]

Polls, Pundits, and Predictions

Reliance on soothsayers and prophets to explain the present and predict the future is as old as human history. Animal entrails and natural phenomena (the stars, comets, storms, earthquakes) were the raw material for this useful mode of social analysis.

Today we have put all that superstitious claptrap behind us. We rely on statistically sophisticated public opinion polling and social network–based trolling to gather data, and on multivariate analysis, probability theory, and the educated insights of an experienced punditry to weigh it. Only one problem: the results are often at variance. Of course, it is true that at least some of the polls will be the most accurate in any given election. But then a stopped clock is on target twice a day.[43]

A media-driven politics and increasingly complex campaigning feed a growing cottage industry of polls, pundits, and predictions. Large-scale political polling has been around since the mid-1930s. It got off to a slow start with the spectacular failure of the *Literary Digest* poll to predict FDR's landslide victory in 1936. That survey relied on telephones, which many in Depression-era America lacked.

But Gallup and Roper pioneered ever more carefully crafted operations, and they became prominent parts of American political life. Over 90 polls were in play during the 2012 election. They even, for a season, became part of the contest: the parties found them deeply flawed and seriously biased when the flow of prediction turned against their candidate, and not when they didn't.

Pundits emerged at about the same time as polls: first, columnists such as Walter Lippmann and Arthur Krock in major newspapers, then newscasters on the mainstream and cable TV news stations, and now bloggers on the Internet.[44]

These developments have grown in pace with the rise of a more populist politics. It feeds on the human desire to know the future, the desire that led the first soothsayer to look up at the stars or down at animal entrails.

Most polling, punditry, and predicting is so bound by partisanship and/or ideology as to be of minimal value. Pro-GOP pundits Dick Morris and Jay Cost predicted a Romney victory and had egg-on-face mopping up to do after the election. The major pollsters—Gallup, Pew, and Rasmussen—were less swayed by political leanings but far from spot-on in their predictions.

The most prescient member of the guild was the *Times*'s Nate Silver, who used a sophisticated set of algorithms to impressively accurate effect, as he had done in the 2010 congressional election. But like the media that sustained them, the impulse of most pollsters and pundits to satisfy fee-paying, candidate-favoring clients (or, in the case of academic pollsters, their status-bestowing colleagues) remained in tension with the impulse to get it right.[45]

3. IDEOLOGY

The parties have always subscribed to distinctive sets of ideas and issues, stitched together to secure a majority. Inevitably they are bedeviled by factional and ideological infighting. To what degree did these facts of political life assert themselves in the 2012 election?

The conventional wisdom is that the right and left tails of the American politics bell curve have grown. But the general judgment of those who study such matters is that while more Americans identify with the Democratic than the Republican party, the number of those who think of themselves as Independents has been rising. Americans are more likely to identify themselves as conservative or center-Right than as liberal or center-Left.[46]

It is a Left-liberal trope that the Right is the more obdurate and virulent force in American politics today. But the mainstream media's treatment of McCain's running mate Sarah Palin is in dramatic contrast with the bargain ride later afforded Kerry's disgraced running mate John Edwards. Nor should the attempt in 2011 led by columnist Paul Krugman and the editorial page of the *New York Times* to link mass murderer Jared Loughner to the rhetoric of the GOP Right be unnoticed before it assumes its rightful place in history's dustbin.

It is not difficult to find comparable excesses in the words of Right-wing avatar Rush Limbaugh or his blogosphere equivalents, or the more heated voices in the Tea Party. There is indeed a symbiosis in the rhetoric as in the mindset of adherents to the political extremes. The Republican Birthers, who question Obama's American citizenship, are like the Democratic Truthers, who see a Bush-Cheney role in the 9/11 attack.[47]

Conservatives, the Right, and the Tea Party

Despite the flood of expectation that Obama's 2008 victory heralded a new era of progressive politics, the first significant sign that his election might have large political consequences was the sudden, unexpected appearance of the Tea Party. In retrospect, that did much to put paid to the belief that an Obama New Foundation comparable to FDR's New Deal or LBJ's Great Society was in the cards. The rise of the Tea Party was as if the anti–New Deal American Liberty League of the 1930s or George Wallace's American Independent Party of the 1960s took on the vestments not of fringe protest but a large-scale political movement.

Flat-out conservatism traditionally had little populist horsepower. There was Ronald Reagan, of course, but like Eisenhower, his appeal lay as much in his persona as in the ideas he championed. The Right had an oppressive political heritage. Visceral hostility to FDR and the New Deal, paranoidal McCarthyite anticommunism, the populist racism of George Wallace, and Nixon's Watergate disgrace were heavy burdens to overcome.

Pat Robinson / Jerry Falwell–style evangelicalism, with Robinson inveighing against "the pagans and the abortionists and the feminists and the gays and the lesbians," may have lured some middle Americans from their FDR-Democratic roots. But this was as politically self-limiting as Colorado GOP congressman Tom Tancredo's black/Hispanic-bashing: "People who could not spell the word vote or say it in English put a committed Socialist ideologue in the White House."[48]

Conservative theorists in their small-circulation magazines and claustrophobic conclaves had been going on for some time about the need to reduce the power, size, money, and role of the government. Libertarians in particular, a minute but highly opinionated band (prominent spokesmen: Congressman Ron Paul and law professor Richard Epstein) beat that drum well before the Obama years.

George Bush may have been in Democratic eyes a demon tax-cutter, but in conservative-libertarian eyes he was a demon budget-and-debt-raiser. Neoconservatism was the foreign policy equivalent of Bush's domestic compassionate conservatism. Together they produced such costly policies as the Iraq war and Bush's prescription drugs add-on to Medicare. By the Obama years, neoconservative doctrine was creaky and outmoded, demonized by the Left and the libertarians, struggling to escape from the incubus of responsibility for the unpopular Iraq war.

The prevailing view in the academy and the mainstream media was that except for a cranky minority, liberalism was, or should be, the default position of most Americans. But for almost half a century, American political reality has been something different. This hardly meant an inclination to be Republican. The party consistently had lower favorability ratings than the Democrats. Nor did it lead to opposing the welfare state. Like Walt Whitman, American voters contained multitudes.

As the era of FDR gave way to the era of Reagan, the more attractive political implications of the conservative small-government creed emerged. Richard Nixon's "We're all Keynesians" of the 1970s was superseded by Bill Clinton's "The era of big government is over" of the 1990s. Neither observation was strictly true. But the paradigm shift in the political environment was clear.

Evangelical Christianity was a major component in the resurrection of the American Right. This is a complex and ambiguous story, with many resemblances to the place of Marxism and postmodernism in the contemporary American Left. The New Left of the 1960s had more than a chronological relation to the New Christian Right that emerged a decade later.

From the 1960s on, Americans became increasingly supportive of black, women's, and gay civil rights, more acquiescent in the expansion of the welfare state, and more accepting of a culture in which sexual and other constraints were loosened. This led to a reaction from traditional-minded elements of the population that had substantial political consequences.

The old Protestant fundamentalism, once a mainstay of Prohibition and substantially opposed to the civil rights revolution, lost its traditional primacy in the politics of the religious Right. Instead, evangelicals (often supportive of black civil rights and mixed in their view of active government) came to the fore. They allied increasingly with observant Catholics and Orthodox Jews, traditional evangelical devil figures, on social issues.

Ronald Reagan came to embody their beliefs and aspirations, as FDR had for immigrants and workers in the 1930s. They brought their votes and their readiness to work in campaigns to the Reagan and post-Reagan GOP, as union members did for the New Deal and post–New Deal Democrats. And the demographics of the Sunbelt fostered a Christian Right heartland as politically consequential for the GOP as the industrial-immigrant cities had been for the Democrats.[49]

Then came Obama, the Stimulus, and a health-care plan and new finance regulation gravid with big spending and big bureaucracy. Obama's reading of his election was that a new era of active government and social change had been mandated.[50]

The consequent rise of the Tea Party sent a different message: not so fast. It said something else as well. It was as ready to turn on the GOP, big business, and banks and investment companies as it was to turn on the traditional conservative bêtes noires of big-spending Democrats, elitist affluent liberals, and a left-leaning media.

Just as liberal-left believers adhered to many of the precepts of nineteenth-century socialism and twentieth-century social democracy, so did the Tea Party identify itself with older American models of thought and action. Its tone was Jeffersonian, Jacksonian, Populist; its totems the Revolution (hence its name), the Declaration, the Founding Fathers and the Constitution, and American exceptionalism. Theirs were not the activist foreign policy neoconservatism or the spending commitments of George W. Bush.[51]

In a sense the Tea Party movement was the early-twentieth-century Progressive movement run backward. Progressivism (and the Populist movement before it) was a political turn to government to deal with the consequences of industrial capitalism. The Tea Party gave voice to an impulse to contain and control a federal government seen as too costly, intrusive, and inefficient.[52]

Pinpointing the origins of a movement is as enticing as it is elusive. The Tea Party's genesis is widely attributed to an outburst on CNBC television by Rick Santelli, who had been reporting for years on the doings of the Chicago Board of Trade. On February 19, 2009, he delivered an impassioned critique of the Obama administration's plans to help bail out delinquent mortgage-holders. He proposed that that protest take the form of a "Chicago Tea Party."

CNBC swiftly uploaded Santelli's call to arms (then and since labeled by the media as a "rant," a "screed," or a "tirade"). The Internet, the blogosphere, YouTube, the Drudge Report, and other purveyors of the new virtual universe made it viral. By Sunday, three days later, it had been viewed nearly 1.7 million times.[53]

Blogosphere events such as this normally have a half-life of microseconds. But Santelli's Tea Party label, and his assault on the Obama administration's spending policies only a month into the Obama term, struck a chord. Keli Carender, a thirty-year-old Seattle math teacher with a pierced nose and weekend Improv appearances—in short, the very model of a 2008 Obama follower—was a pioneering Tea Party activist. Even before Santelli's words went viral, she was sufficiently exercised by the Stimulus to organize what has been called the first Tea Party protest rally.[54]

The media reported that a "potent conservative public relations machine" publicized the nascent movement. Sal Russo, a longtime California GOP publicist, raised millions through a PAC, TP Express, for Tea Party–endorsed candidates in the 2010 election. That the Tea Party was taken over by right-wing Republican fat cats became accepted liberal dogma.[55]

There was indeed this backing, as there were disruptive Tea Party protests at Democratic congressmen's pro-Obamacare town meetings. Its cohorts were called "terrorists" by *New York Times* columnist Joe Nocera and Vice President Biden, and "un-American" by House Speaker Nancy Pelosi.

But neither conspiracy nor extremism is sufficient perspective on a movement so large, so amorphous, and so effective. The Tea Party (but was it a party?) remained diverse and nonhierarchical. The *Washington Post* called it "a disparate band of vaguely connected gatherings": in short, a classic populist movement.[56]

There was a resonance between the Left's and the Tea Party's distaste for bankers, Wall Street, and mainstream Republicans. Liberal journalist Matt Bai noted that in these realms Tea Party rhetoric echoed left-wing Moveon.org. Comparison with the New Left of the 60s was tempting, though the two movements' social makeup, activity, and ideology couldn't have been more different: Wal-Mart instead of Woodstock.[57]

The Tea Party movement tended to shy from divisive social issues. It focused instead on hostility (expressed at times in vigorous conspiratorial rhetoric) to government spending, deficits, taxes, and regulation. No clear leadership emerged, and it had no preferred candidate, though for a while Sarah Palin came close to filling that role.[58]

The age and social makeup of the great majority of Tea Partiers pointed them not in the direction of the street theatre later adopted by the left-wing analogue Occupy Wall Street, but toward traditional political forms of mass demonstrations, lobbying, and voting. Many tens of thousands of supporters flocked to Washington in September 2009 to voice their distaste for TARP, Obama's Stimulus, and in particular his health-care bill.[59]

The Tea Party took credit (perhaps more than was justified) for Scott Brown's acquisition of Ted Kennedy's Massachusetts Senate seat in January 2010. Rising new GOP lights—Marco Rubio in Florida, Rand Paul in Kentucky, Nikki Haley in South

Carolina—were not shy about touting their Tea Party sympathies. As the 2010 congressional election drew near, Tea Party–backed candidates displaced several GOP incumbents.[60]

But there were signs that the Tea Party suffered from the ailments that so often plagued populist movements. Bizarre Tea Party–identified candidates for the Senate in Delaware and Nevada snatched defeat from the jaws of victory in 2010. The inability of the Republican-led House to function effectively dulled the movement's political edge. The Tea Party's general popularity (never very strong) sagged, and the media began to lose interest.[61]

It was easy to overstate the movement's cohesion. In fact it was plagued, as are all populist movements (not least the Populist party of the 1890s), by the tension between political careerism and ideological purity. In the House vote on whether or not to accept the two parties' deficit compromise in the summer of 2011, a larger proportion of the Tea Party Caucus went along than did members of the electorally more secure Black Caucus.

Attention turned to properly vetted GOP candidates for the 2012 election. The Tea Party had the political benefit of more passionate participants. But this came at a cost. As the 2012 election season went into high gear, Tea Party bête noire Mitt Romney led the pack, the movement was polling strongly negative, and it was meet for a columnist to ask, "Is the Tea Party Over?"[62]

Tea Partiers claimed credit for upsetting moderate Republicans in several 2012 primaries, most notably Senator Richard Lugar in Indiana. But Lugar's drawbacks of age, longevity, and remoteness from his constituents may have been as determining as his place on the political spectrum. The Tea Party had its failures, as in the case of its assault on Utah GOP incumbent Orrin Hatch. Membership was down, and so was the movement's visibility in the 2012 election.

Since then its slide has continued, although the 2013 revelations of IRS harassment gave it a fillip. But the "Tea Party" label remained a red flag for liberals, much as "Populist" did for conservatives a century and more ago.[63]

Liberals, the Left, and OWS

After the fervid 1960s slipped into history's mist, the American Left, like the Right in the wake of the New Deal, appeared to be in near-terminal decline. The McGovern campaign of 1972 was a disaster; the stagflation of the seventies did not fit into either the Marxist or the Keynesian explanatory frameworks; the Carter presidency hardly infused new life into the liberal cause. The bland Carter years were followed by the anything but bland Reagan years, and the implosion of Communism in general and the Soviet Union in particular. Then there came the triangulating Clinton presidency, further eroding the Left's appeal.

The 2000 election and its controversial outcome rallied Democratic-liberal foot soldiers, as did the off-putting persona and unattractive policies of George W. Bush. In particular the Iraq war stirred Left-liberal juices dormant since the glory days of the anti-Vietnam movement.

Since the 1960s, Third Worldism has attracted the Left as a substitute for the socialist dream. But 9/11 and, for most Americans, the unsavory qualities of militant Islam, Iran, Palestine, North Korea, the Castros' Cuba, and Hugo Chavez's Venezuela made these causes thin reeds for a revived Left. Even more depressing, Communist China turned from the thoughts of Mao Zedong to the thoughts of Milton Friedman (whose *Free to Choose* became iconic reading there). And the India of Gandhi and Nehru succumbed to the lure of market capitalism.

Still, the Democrats remained politically competitive with and in higher public regard than their Republican opponents. While liberalism as a persuasion kept sliding in opinion polls, spurs to a revival of the Left increased in the new century, culminating in the crash of the American banking-financial system and the election of Barack Obama.

Something like a national health-care system, a big increase in the regulatory state, and quantum leaps in government spending heartened liberals as nothing had since the Great Society's War on Poverty half a century before. Long-quiescent issues—inequality, redistribution, plutocracy, and oligarchy—got a new lease on life.[64]

Would Obama be able to forge a durable new liberal politics? He could lay claim to stronger liberal-Left credentials than his recent Democratic predecessors. His background of elite schooling, community activism, university teaching, a political career in black/Democratic Chicago, and his campaign, a crafty mix of abstract promises (hope and change) and full-throated condemnation of Republican domestic and foreign policy, stirred the Left's expectations to a level not seen since the 1960s.

As the first African-American president, with commanding intelligence, notable oratorical talent, and a magnetic public personality, Obama seemed to be on the cusp of building a durable liberal-Left coalition. His strong appeal to blacks and Hispanics, unmarried women, the college-educated young, and the ever-growing professional-technocratic class gave him the largest potential to recast American politics to the Left since FDR in the 1930s welded together his New Deal coalition of workers and ethnic minorities.

Obama's supporters often called themselves "progressives." The media adopted this, along with the anodyne term "Left-leaning": useful substitutes for "liberal" and "Left," which had a certain disfavor in the public mind.

To what degree has Obama fulfilled these expectations? From the perspective of conservatives, he readily met his left-wing production quota. The Stimulus, Obamacare, an expanded regulatory state, cozying up to Russia and the Arabs: the conservative blacklist went on and on—a toxic brew, in their imaginings, of socialism and Third Worldism.

When the Right was not lambasting Obama as a clandestine socialist, it was accusing him of crony capitalism. Indeed the effort to create a renewable energy industry, like nineteenth-century railroads and the twentieth-century Interstate, would be fertile ground for subsidies to politically favored entrepreneurs. Solyndra and its counterparts demonstrated that the elevated objectives of the new entrepreneurial frontier did not shield it from the ills that come whenever big money, private or public, is at stake.

But there was much to distinguish Obama's New Foundation from FDR's New Deal or LBJ's New Society. After all, the shape of American society and its domestic and foreign challenges were very different from those past times. Now it was the middle class, not farmers or workers, who figured most prominently in political rhetoric. Civil rights had moved from the civil and social equality of African Americans to the more nuanced realm of sexual preference. And it was difficult to find in the Islamic militant *défi* anything like the superficially attractive social and economic rhetoric of socialism and Communism.[65]

Perhaps the closest tie to the New Deal–Great Society tradition was Obama's commitment to extend the regulatory-entitlement state. Regulation and subsidization turned out to be his major interventions in the economy. This was far indeed from the socialist model ascribed by his conservative critics. But it was also far from the transformative presidency that his more progressive supporters hoped for.[66]

For all the sky-is-falling rhetoric of the Right, there was much about the Obama program that fit comfortably into well-established trends in American government. The Stimulus might be seen as a logical extension of New Deal relief and public works, and Bush's TARP. Obamacare could be seen as a logical (if larger-sized) extension of Johnson's Medicare and Medicaid and Bush's prescription health plan. Dodd-Frank had a family tie to Bush's Sarbanes-Oxley corporate regulatory law (though it certainly was a much bigger younger brother). A flourishing crony capitalism and the retention of Guantanamo Bay and a continuing War on Terror testified to the weight of institutional and policy continuity.

It is not surprising that Obama, like FDR, came under fire from the Left. Although union labor and ethnic minorities strongly supported him, he consistently defined his backers as the "middle class," a category that appeared to stretch from the black underclass to investment bankers. Much of his program was directed at what has been called "the post-industrial castes": in finance, technology, and real estate; well-educated younger professionals; and new technocrats.[67]

This bothered many of the Left on both policy and class grounds. *New York Times* columnist Paul Krugman, a reincarnation of John Kenneth Galbraith as the Left's leading economist-savant, was recurrently displeased with what he saw as Obama's timidity over spending, debt-expanding, and bank nationalization.[68]

But just as the disappointment of the Left with FDR's New Deal foundered on the manifest lack of a viable alternative, so was its criticism of Obama a blip, not an outcry. When it came to firepower, Left ideology was reminiscent of the Communism of the 1930s, which appealed to the artistic, literary, and chattering classes but was devoid of a popular base.

Nowhere was the disparity between the social horsepower of the conservative Right and the radical Left more evident than in the contrast of the politically consequential Tea Party with politically inconsequential Occupy Wall Street (OWS).

Discontent with the prevailing state of American affairs led to the movement's sudden appearance in the fall of 2011. OWS elicited a flood of favorable media attention unmatched since the Obama candidacy of 2008. Here, at last, was a counter to the 2009–2010 Tea Party upsurge.

Like the Tea Party, OWS defined itself as the champion of an American political tradition displaced by the faults of modern American society. Although its sources, makeup, and style of protest could not have been more different, it too attacked what it regarded as a corrupt bargain between mainstream politics and privileged interests.

The Tea Party's chief enemy was the large-spending, intrusive state, which it countered with a mix of libertarian individualism and nineteenth-century small-government liberalism. OWS also looked to the past: to old Marxist-populist shibboleths (plutocracy, oligopoly, inequality) and to the 1960s counterculture. There was little attempt to revive New Deal–Great Society social democracy or working-class solidarity. The core theme of OWS was that the deprived 99 percent of the population suffered from the ever-richer and more powerful 1 percent. In this it separated itself from Obama's focus on "the middle class."

Like the Tea Party, OWS had an identifiable forefather: Kalle Lasn. Unlike Rick Santelli, Lasn had a political record. He was born in Estonia in 1942, and when the Russians returned his family fled first to Germany and then to Australia. Lasn eventually made his way to Vancouver, where he started an anti-corporate, anti-consumption magazine called *Adbusters*. It soon had a worldwide following in Marxist, countercultural, and anarchist circles.

Lasn was fiercely pro-Palestine and anti-Israel, and set off a flap when in 2004 he asked in an article: "Why won't anyone say they are Jewish?" He observed that the neoconservatives who came up with the Iraq war included many Jews, and listed 50 members of the neocon persuasion, with helpful asterisks next to the names of those who were Jewish. He insisted, "There's not an anti-Semitic bone in my body." But "if we're going to start wars based on the power of the neoconservatives' influence in foreign policy, I think people should know who they are."

Lasn's most significant contribution to political discourse came when, on July 13, 2011, he sent an e-mail to some 90,000 supporters of *Adbusters*, calling on them to "occupy Wall Street" on September 17. Also prominent in OWS's early stages was anarchist-anthropologist David Graeber, like Lasn a well-known figure in the world of the far Left.[69]

After the initial OWS demonstration in New York, occupiers cropped up in many other cities in America and abroad. Visions of the 1968 student uprisings danced in many graying heads. There was talk of "political disobedience," echoing the civil disobedience model of the civil rights movement.[70]

There were points of resemblance with the Tea Party: outrage over Wall Street, bank bailouts, financial bonuses, and big corporations. But in its small numbers, limited political involvement, and unclear agenda, OWS was very different: as *Wall Street Journal* columnist Peggy Noonan put it, "The difference between acting out and taking part."

The Occupy movement never attracted numbers anywhere near those enlisted by the Tea Party. Tea Partiers indignantly differentiated their movement as more respectful of American institutions, more mainstream, and more seriously engaged in American politics—more real. But this was to miss the point. The media and the social networks made OWS a considerable public force. The organization itself and what it did (and didn't) do was of less consequence.[71]

Media attention, the Internet, and the fact that the OWS message struck a responsive chord among the similarly minded, led to the movement's rapid spread across the nation and abroad. Indeed, the crowds at rallies in Rome, Barcelona, and Madrid were leagues larger than anything in America. Then again they had much more experience with exuberant left-wing street politics, and they had the spur of their governments' austerity programs.[72]

The Pew Research Center found in mid-October 2011 that initially scant and skeptical media coverage had grown virally in size and sympathy. The *New York Times* ran about 1,000 pieces during the movement's October–December 2011 peak, including daily roundups of its often small-bore activities across the country and requests to readers for guidance as to how its coverage should proceed. This was in sharp contrast with the minimal reporting of far more massive Tea Party rallies.[73]

Like flies drawn to honey, Hollywood, media, and pop culture celebrities flocked to the big-city OWS encampments. Left luminaries—Jesse Jackson and Al Sharpton, Noam Chomsky and Oliver Stone—put in requisite appearances. Academics had a field day expounding on the movement's deeper meaning and future prospects. Sociologists, for a time, became almost relevant again.[74]

Labor unions and prominent Democrats such as Al Gore initially offered some support, though more cautiously than Republicans embraced the Tea Party. As the Tea Party's excesses went hand in hand with an influential reminder to the Republicans that they were supposed to be the party of small and limited government, so did OWS offer a wake-up call to an Obama administration whose ideological fervor was in danger of being dulled by the demands of reality and the temptations of power. A survey of OWSers found that while a (surprisingly low) 60 percent of them had voted for Obama in 2008, 75 percent of the protesters disapproved of his subsequent record.[75]

The civil rights movement provided some inspiration. But OWS drew most heavily on the counterculture of the 1960s, the May 1968 days in Paris, and especially the anti–Vietnam War movement. Its posters and slogans echoed the youthful exuberance of Paris and Berkeley 1968. Its primary legacy turned out to be what is nowadays called a meme: the 99 percent and the 1 percent.[76]

The University of California at Berkeley and San Francisco were the most obvious venues for a replay of those gory glory days. But the OWS spinoffs there showed little of their predecessors' passion and energy. San Francisco, after all, was older and richer, and Berkeley's students were more career-conscious.[77]

A more compelling prototype for younger protesters was the Arab Spring and its iconic stage, Tahrir Square. But the democracy and freedom that the Cairo demonstrators sought already was in place in the West. While pro-Palestine / anti-Israel expressions were part of the OWS mix, African Americans were not. Like the Tea Party, this was an overwhelmingly white protest movement, and a disproportionately affluent one.[78]

OWS, like the Tea Party, was easy to parody. One sympathetic article quotes a participant on his comrades' causes: "They're out here because they owe shitloads of money in student-loan debt and can't find a job." (True, true: forgiveness of college loans was a prominent OWS cause.) "Or they can't afford their mortgage." (False, false: these were not homeowners facing foreclosure.)

The OWSers' grasp of the American radical tradition of which they claimed to be a part was limited. Many were surprised to learn that the 1968 demonstrations occurred at the Democratic, not the Republican, convention of that year. The media at times seemed to share in this strand of self-caricature. Nicholas Kristof of the *New York Times* advised the OWSers to demand such esoterica as a financial transactions tax, closing the "carried interest" loophole, and the stricter Basel 3 standards for big banks: not, one would think, concerns high on the demonstrators' agenda.[79]

One observer hazarded the possibility that this "may be the world's first genuine social-media uprising." Economist Jeffrey Sachs saw in OWS the forerunner of a "new Progressive movement." More skeptical conservatives equated OWS with the ill-fated utopianism of the Paris Commune of the 1870s or the Oneida community of the 1840s.[80]

As the OWS encampments got more tattered and in a few cases more violent, and chilly November replaced bracing October, the movement's appeal faded. Street people were attracted to the OWS locations, which provided more creature comforts than they were accustomed to. A shift from romanticized tourist attraction to neighborhood nuisance was not the high road to popularity. Politicians had to take into account growing local protests over sanitation, noise, and economic disruption. The Longshoremen were not likely to go along with an Oakland OWS effort to shut that city's port, and indeed they did not.[81]

Previously sympathetic mayors in Oakland, San Francisco, and New York began to close down the OWS sites. The movement's godfather, Kalle Lasn, thought it might be well to "declare victory" on its three-month December 17 anniversary and go into winter hibernation. After some desultory effort to shift the movement to the presumably more welcoming environment of college campuses, that is what happened.

Ambitious plans for massive demonstrations on May Day 2012 fizzled. There was talk (but little else) of a showing at the party conventions. The last visible OWS locale was Oakland, both geographically and economically distant indeed from Wall Street. By the 2012 election, OWS was little more than a fading memory.[82]

How do the Tea Party and OWS fit into the American tradition of extra-party movements that are ultimately co-opted by the major parties but leave their mark on the parties' policies? Surely that has been the case here. The GOP response to the Tea Party's ideas about big government and the Democrats' response to OWS's ideas about inequality are testimony to that. But there is far less formal integration, in good part because the Tea Party and OWS are not distinguishable parties in the traditional sense. This is yet another sign that in our political culture, the populist political style figures more largely in our public life than does the traditional party political style of the past.

CHAPTER EIGHT

. . .

2012

LET US GET into and out of the November 2012 moment of political truth via the customary narrative for presidential elections: the choice of the candidates, their campaigns, and then the outcome—what that was and why it was.

I. THE CONTEST

Perhaps because of the at times surreal nature of our populist politics, aspirants can eerily echo characters in those seminal works *Alice in Wonderland* and *The Wizard of Oz*. Candidate Mitt Romney often appeared to be channeling *Alice*'s befuddled White Rabbit: "I'm late! I'm late! For a very important date!" as the Disney movie version had it. (An accurate observation, it turned out.) Obama bears more than a little resemblance to the Wizard of Oz: sleight of hand and illusion are part of his stock in trade. Certainly Obama's Washington has come to bear more than a passing resemblance to the Emerald City, gleaming in the reflected glory and ample funding of the expanding state.

Romney in Wonderland

As in *Alice*'s caucus race, an abundance of bizarre contestants endlessly chased one another in the GOP primaries. Candidates-of-the-week rose and fell: Michelle Bachmann, Herman Cain, and Rick Perry from the foot-in-mouth Right; Newt Gingrich reliving the colorful self-destructiveness of his Clinton years; the loopily libertarian Ron Paul; in-your-face conservative Rick Santorum; pallid Tim Pawlenty; Romney clone Jon Huntsman; and, on the furthest edge of the GOP solar system, Donald Trump.[1]

This was not surprising in a troubled, leaderless party. The GOP had an ongoing popularity problem with the young, ethnic minorities, and women. It was a common media-Democratic theme that the GOP was in the hands of toxic, extreme conservatives. Well might the Democrats be "contemplating power without end."[2]

Still, the 2010 off-year election and the declining appeal of the Obama Hope and Change agenda made the 2012 GOP nomination something worth seeking. Some 24 potential candidates were mentioned in the public prints. Several of the more eligible possibles—Mitch Daniels of Indiana, Chris Christie of New Jersey, Jeb Bush and Marco Rubio of Florida—removed themselves, as did Sarah Palin, popular with the faithful but chancy with everyone else.

The seemingly endless series of GOP primary debates reinforced the *Alice* caucus race analogy. Cable TV, hungry for the revenue of heightened viewer ratings, called the tune, ultimately to a staggering 28 encounters, the media tail vigorously wagging the party dog. This may well have kept the more outré candidates in play to the party's detriment. But the debates' reality-show aura attracted viewers and was a toughening ordeal for the survivor.[3]

Last-man-standing candidate Mitt Romney may well have been the best of a questionable lot, but he had problems: a flip-flop image that echoed John Kerry's in 2004; a talent for misspeaking that, while not quite in Biden's world class, was sufficient to stand him in bad stead; his Mormonism; Romneycare; and a pancake personality. *New York Times* columnist David Brooks equated him with Zeppo, the most pallid of the Marx Brothers: "the serious one," earnest, good-looking, and second tier. There was wide expectation that Romney would have a long slog to the nomination. But one observer rightly predicted in February that "the election will come down to Romney and Obama" , though he wrongly predicted that "it will be decided on the economy and on race."[4]

The fight for the nomination was over by April, three months before the convention. Romney showed unexpected fire in the belly, slapping down his chief challengers Gingrich and Santorum (who helped his cause by belaboring each other). He won narrow pluralities in key states: Florida, Illinois, Ohio, Michigan, Pennsylvania, and Wisconsin. He did better than expected with Catholics, evangelical Protestants, and Tea Party adherents. The desire to defeat Obama and the degree to which Romney's expeditious conservatism trumped doctrinal differences played in his favor.[5]

In hoary GOP tradition (Goldwater in 1964 and perhaps Reagan in 1980 were exceptions), a "dispositional" rather than an "ideological" conservative won the nomination. So had it been with Wendell Willkie, Thomas Dewey, and Dwight Eisenhower against Robert Taft in the 1930s, 1940s, and 1950s; with Bob Dole and the Bushes against the likes of Pat Buchanan in the 1990s; and with John McCain against Mike Huckabee in 2008.[6]

There followed the inevitable reorientation of the Romney campaign from feeding the base to wooing the electorate. His negatives were clear enough: the need to heal intraparty primary scars; a hold on unspent primary campaign funds until he was the officially designated candidate; and the might of an Obama campaign fueled by unequalled organization, the power of the presidency, and the preference of the media.

Nevertheless Romney did unexpectedly well in the spring and early summer. There were signs that his popularity rose, or at least that his unpopularity declined. He toned down the social conservatism evoked by the primary season and focused on the economy.

His selection of Paul Ryan as his running mate was as much an outreach to the party's conservative wing as John McCain's choice of Sarah Palin had been in 2008. Now, befitting the times, the attraction was the selectee's stand on economic rather than social issues. One observer called it an "un-McCain campaign": well-funded, Romney seeking to portray himself as a safe and competent president.[7]

It made good sense for Romney to soft-pedal cultural issues. But here as elsewhere, the campaign message was not entirely under his control. He had found it necessary to take hard-line stands on illegal immigrants, abortion, and other tender issues during the primary follies. Rogue political action committees (PACs) and other autonomous players could (and did) dwell on their special causes, however unpopular.[8]

Romney easily met his quota of campaign glitches. His reference to his wife's two Cadillacs and a putdown of the poor during a primary debate hardly enhanced his image. Most spectacularly, in a spring fundraising talk strategically released by a left-wing magazine in September, his dismissal of the near-half of the population who didn't pay income tax suggested that foot-in-mouth disease was not confined to the Vice President.

Just as the Republicans sought to portray Obama as a candidate with a taste for European-style social democracy if not outright socialism, the Democrats more successfully portrayed Romney as a tax-avoiding, jobs-destroying plutocrat. Perhaps in strategic response, corporate America remained conspicuously uncommitted (at least publicly) to Romney.[9]

There was little reason to expect a tectonic shift in popular preference as the election approached. Voters said by a 90-to-8 percent count that they knew what they needed to know about Obama; less so about Romney, but still by a solid 69-to-28 percent spread. The campaign battleground focused on independent or undecided voters in swing states, rather than the electorate at large—and, of course, mobilizing the base, which the Obama organization did spectacularly well.[10]

What appeared to be a tectonic negative shift in Romney's fortunes unfolded in the late summer and fall. Pouring hundreds of millions of dollars into the key swing states, the Obama campaign portrayed him as insensitive, ethically challenged, not quite mainstream. Romney's supposed fundraising advantage was slow to materialize. His campaign operation and strategizing came under question, as is usually the case when things begin to misfire. Much of his Republican base, stretching from the Establishment *Wall Street Journal* to the Tea Party Right, had doubts about his views and his campaign style.[11]

But the major issue remained: Would the election be a referendum on Obama's record, as the Republicans fondly hoped? Or would it be a choice election in which Romney's suitability was the issue, as the Democrats wanted? That was hardly predetermined. Contingency—a candidate miscue; a damaging revelation (the "October surprise" of previous elections); unpredictable events foreign (a terrorist attack) or domestic (a dip in the economy)—were as likely to determine the outcome as turnout, intensity, or campaign money.

When the run-up to the election began in early September, polls showed Obama only marginally ahead. Given the scale of the anti-Romney barrage of previous months, this was a danger signal.

The mid-September revelation of Romney's dismissing the non-taxpaying 47 percent of the population appeared precisely at the time in the campaign when, four years before, the financial crisis broke. This was mother's milk to the Obama campaign and the pro-Obama media. Obama appeared to be pulling ahead decisively in key swing states, and prescient pundits declared the election all but over.[12]

Then there occurred what seemed to be a real October surprise: Romney's decisive win over Obama in their first TV debate. Suddenly—as abruptly as John McCain's implosion when the financial system tanked in 2008, or Jimmy Carter's slide after his first debate with Reagan in 1980—the character of the election appeared to change. Was this Romney rising, Draculalike, from his grave? Was it Obama tuning out because of overconfidence, indifference, or, as the climate-fixated Al Gore suggested, Denver's thin air? November 6 would tell.

Obama: The Wizard of Oz

Obama's massive 2010 setback had barely happened when the presidential election of 2012 began to loom large, as 1996 did for Clinton in the wake of his 1994 reverse. Clinton's response was to respond (successfully, as it turned out) to the restraining message of the 1994 results. What would Obama do?

In 2008 he defined himself as the apostle of a bipartisanship transcending "the bitterness and pettiness and anger that's consumed Washington." At the same time he made it clear that in his lexicon, bipartisanship consisted of the opposition supporting him, which was not unreasonable given his campaign's stress on the iniquity of the Bush administration and the primacy of change. This stance, conjoined with a Republican opposition that in its obduracy came close to the Democrats' portrayal, led not to the Kumbaya politics of Obama's 2008 rhetoric but to muscular confrontation and polarization.[13]

The 2010 defeat inevitably led to criticism of Obama, especially from the party's centrist / Blue Dog survivors and its vocal Left. A couple of Clintonians thought he should not run again, on the ground that his only road to victory was a campaign so negative that it would render him incapable of governing. Prominent spokesmen of the Left Paul Krugman and Robert Kuttner were unhappy over Obama's deviation from the true faith.[14]

In fact, there was no challenge to Obama's renomination. The only visible dissent was over the substance of his presidency. "Tingle down my leg" cable TV admirer Chris Matthews accused Obama of a leaderless "virtual" administration. Analyst Walter Russell Mead equated him with Woodrow Wilson: "a great expounder rather than a great persuader."

Another observer took note of the decline and fall of the "New Foundation" label for Obama's program. Unlike its New Deal and Great Society prototypes, the term dropped into obscurity; Obama did not use it after October 9, 2010. The even less tangible "Win the Future," used nine times in his January 2011 State of the Union address, was further simplified in the 2012 campaign to "Forward."[15]

Obama made a fateful decision in the wake of his 2010 setback: to double down on his first two years. He stuck to this tack tenaciously and won in 2012. The extent of his self-correction was to blame 2010 on his not having acted quickly enough to heal the ailing economy and failing to better communicate his message to the public. There was little sign of an attempt to add to his 2008 base or change the agenda of his presidency.[16]

Obama did subtly recast his message from a Saint-Paul-in-a-hurry quick fix (February 2009: "If I don't have this done in three years, there's gonna be a one-term proposition") to facing an economic abyss far worse than he (or anyone) imagined, real progress made, and future payoff in staying the course. He sought to shift public attention from underwater mortgages, the national debt, government spending, and lack of jobs, to income and wealth inequality and the rich paying more taxes. If the Tea Party's agenda set the tone for the GOP in 2010, a toned-down version of Occupy Wall Street did so for the Democrats in 2012.

True, polls showed that the public valued economic opportunity over economic equality. *New York Times* columnist Charles Blow conceded that 60 percent of Americans regarded themselves as haves rather than have-nots ("the new American delusion"), but hopefully asked, "Is income inequality the new global warming?"[17]

Obama's poll standings were sluggish to negative during the summer and fall of 2011. But this did not dissuade him from hewing to his larger strategy of line-drawing rather than line-crossing. His January 2012 State of the Union address was a full-throated appeal to liberal populism. It set out his campaign mantra: maintenance of entitlements, high taxes on the rich, and relief for the struggling middle class.[18]

Significant new legislation did not emerge from this message: there was no revised New Foundation equivalent of the Second New Deal. Obama intermittently flogged a limited jobs bill that had no real prospect of enactment. His 2012 budget proposal for $1.5 trillion in new taxes for the wealthiest Americans and a hypothetical $3 trillion in deficit reduction over a decade had a "familiar ring" but was hardly a clarion call to legislative arms. That was due in part to the obstructionism of the Republican-led House, and in part to Obama's focus on his reelection campaign.[19]

Nor was there more than marginal change in Obama's style of governing. His circle of confidants shrank, and cautious advisers Summers and Emanuel left. Presidential press conferences became even scarcer. As before, Obama's strength lay in carefully orchestrated campaign appearances, star turns on popular TV programs and social media outlets, and one-on-one interviews with well-disposed journalists.

Hunkering down may have been necessary to preserve his base. The pro-Obama media encouraged his campaign to pursue this course, though Obama's sense of himself and his place in history also dictated it. But it ran the risk of alienating crucial Independents.[20]

He had his share of bloopers: the *Joseph R. Biden* was not the only gaffe-rigged schooner in the Obama fleet. On the eve of the 2010 election loss, he speculated condescendingly on what was going wrong: "Part of the reason that our politics seems so tough right now, and facts and science and argument does not seem to be winning the day all the time, is because we're hard-wired not to always think clearly when we're scared."

During the 2012 campaign Obama gave Romney a run for his money in the embarrassing statements sweepstakes (though ultimately he was outmatched by his more talented opponent). He observed in June, "The private sector is doing fine," when the general sense was that it wasn't. Even more attention-getting was his riff in July on the sources of success in business: "Look, if you've been successful, you didn't get there on your own. . . . If you've got a business—you didn't build that. Somebody else made that happen." His claim that "federal spending since I took office has risen at the slowest pace of any president in almost sixty years" was in the same league as Andrew Jackson's assurance to Alexander Hamilton's son: "Your father never liked banks." Even the media began to take notice.[21]

Obama's ironic, self-confident, hectoring/lecturing style may have contributed to these off-script comments, though all politicians fall prey to the affliction. But they did not have the negative affect of Romney's verbal slips, in part because Romney's were more encompassing, in part because Obama was shielded (as was

Bush before him) by his presidential aura, and in part because of gentler handling by the media.

One rarely noted cost of the Obama campaign (and this was true of Romney's as well) was that its intensely self-referential, autonomous character furthered the separation of presidential from congressional and state politics. A Democratic official observed of the president after the November 2010 election: "He's more of a movement leader than a politician." Obama had little taste for the hands-on camaraderie that members of Congress, party officials, and donors expected, and his demonization of Congress as the primary source of the nation's political malaise did not always distinguish the GOP House from the Democratic Senate.[22]

Sympathetic Ronald Brownstein of the *National Journal* noted the lack of any compelling second-term program for dealing with the sluggish economy. Obama did set out vague goals of a million new manufacturing jobs, 100,000 new math and science teachers, a doubling of exports, and halving oil imports. But it was as though FDR in 1936 or LBJ in 1964 focused almost entirely on their hapless rivals and revealed little of what they would do if they were returned to office.

Obama said of his assault on Romney's record at Bain: "This is not a distraction. This is what this campaign's going to be about." That made sense in terms of defining the election as a referendum on Romney and not on Obama's record. Supporter John Heileman warned: "To a very real degree, 2008's candidate of hope stands poised to become 2012's candidate of fear."[23]

As the campaign swung into higher gear in the spring of 2012, Obama went into an uncharacteristic tailspin. His setbacks included disappointing job numbers, Wisconsin GOP governor Scott Walker's victory in a recall election, falling fundraising figures, and a snooze-inducing 56-minute AST (Academic Standard Time) Obama speech on the state of the economy.

As before, Obama sought solace in channeling with past presidents, a professorial claim to authority through citation. He praised Nixon for the Environmental Protection Agency, Lincoln for the transcontinental railroad, Eisenhower for the Interstate, and Reagan for Social Security reform. It was as though the politics of change had become the politics of nostalgia.[24]

But Obama's 2012 campaign turned out in the long run to be an effective mix of above-the-fray presidential leadership and partisan dismissal of the opposition. The dreamy fervor of 2008 may have faded, but it had been replaced by the hard-nosed self-confidence of a populist president. There was less raw enthusiasm, but a more expertly contrived presentation of self and an even more effective campaign machine. Obama proved to be as skillful in using the political potential of the presidency in 2012 as he had used his star power and uplifting rhetoric in 2008. Like any respectable Wizard, he projected an aura of high and good intentions. Polls consistently rated his persona higher than his policies.[25]

His campaign adopted a take-no-prisoners political style of the sort that Romney had displayed in his primary battles. It went full tilt at the Romney-Ryan personae: Romney supposedly not paying any income taxes for 10 years; his Bain Capital company eliminating a steelworker's job and thus contributing to the subsequent death of the worker's wife from cancer; and Ryan supposititiously pushing his granny off a cliff.

Obama was, a reporter observed, "the competitor in chief," compulsively touting not only the weight, place, and accomplishments of his presidency but also his skill in cooking chili, musical pitch, playing pool, and doodling. This would be rich fare for satirists, if they had chosen to take it on. (Few did.) But it also reflects the confidence, drive, and assertiveness that made Obama so effective a campaigner.[26]

At the same time—and this too spoke to Obama's political wizardry—he did not dwell on those jewels in his legislative crown, the

Stimulus, Obamacare, and Dodd-Frank, for which there was no evident popular enthusiasm. He and his massive Obama for America campaign organization sought to re-create the atmosphere of the 2008 run with rallies including attractive human eye-candy backdrops, the theme of a better future (Forward now; Hope and Change then), and scant talk of a concrete program.

Most important, as it turned out, the organizational excellence of Obama's 2008 run was if anything surpassed. His major campaign headquarters in Chicago was the very model of thoroughly modern campaigning, with over 300 paid staffers. (At a comparable stage in 2004, George Bush had half as many; Clinton in 1996 had 40.) His chief operatives, James Messina and David Plouffe (with 2008 gurus Rahm Emanuel and David Axelrod in the background) were seasoned professionals. Messina declared–"Our efforts on the ground and on technology will make 2008 look prehistoric."

An observer saw in this "a new kind of political engagement—and political persuasion." In fact, politicking of that sort had a rich history. The late-nineteenth-century Pennsylvania GOP machine was reputed to have an 800,000-name card file of party voters, classified as habitual, reliable, doubtful, wavering, or accustomed to "fumble in the booth." The Obama 2008 and 2012 electoral machines owed more than a little to Karl Rove's mobilization of evangelicals in 2004.[27]

But the scale of the Obama 2012 effort and its innovative use of information technology were unprecedented. New computer programs constructed a massive database of donors and voters. Corporate data-mining expert Rayid Ghani was hired to be "chief scientist," flexing his marketing skills. The social media and iPhones were utilized to identify, reach, and bring to the polls every potential supporter far more effectively than e-mails, websites, and cell phones had been used four years before.

Obama met every Sunday evening with a small cadre to review the campaign's progress. The group of 10 included Plouffe, Messina,

Axelrod, close advisers Valerie Jarrett and Peter Rouse, and chief of staff Jack Lew. It did not extend to the Vice President or any cabinet member; this was strictly in-House of Obama.[28]

Still, the race appeared to be stubbornly close. The massive summer assault on Romney yielded disappointingly meager poll results. The September surprise of Romney's 47 percent embarrassment and a more stellar Democratic than Republican convention may have done more for Obama's standing than the hundreds of million dollars' worth of negative advertising.[29]

The post-convention fall campaign—the real campaign—was most striking for its failure to generate substantial change in the candidates' standing. Neither could be said to be firing up the hustings. The economy continued to drag Obama down; Romney continued to drag Romney down.

The Romney campaign focused not on cultural issues but the economy. The Obama campaign, after a try at attaching a War on Women stigmata on Romney, settled down to affix (with considerable success and no small help from Romney himself) the scarlet letters of wealth, privilege, and remoteness from the wants and needs of ordinary Americans.

The generally pro-Obama *Economist* commented, "Mr. Romney is fond of saying that Mr. Obama has no idea how the economy works and how jobs are created. The way the Obama campaign talks about Bain Capital suggests that his criticism is correct." But the GOP iteration that Obama was a European socialist in an American politician's clothing was no less exaggerated. Everything from his declaration that "the free market is the greatest force of economic progress in human history" to his and Michelle's preference for the company and lifestyle of the rich suggested something other than progress on the yellow brick road to socialism.[30]

While the fitfully recovering economy was a diminishing albatross around Obama's neck, foreign policy threatened to compensate. For the greater part of his term, Obama's handling of foreign affairs was popular, if (or because) it was rarely assertive. But leading or evading from behind began to cause trouble during the campaign's last weeks. China and Russia got more persnickety. Most of all, the Arab Spring turned wintry. Egypt's secular democratic future was buffeted by Islamist winds. Syria's civil war—one that most Americans heartily wished to stay out of—got to be more morally troubling, like Bosnia in the 1990s, as the civilian death toll mounted.

The administration at first tried to write off the September 11 killing in Benghazi of the United States ambassador to Libya and three other Americans not as the terrorist attack it was but as a spontaneous reaction to an anti-Mohammed movie. Republican senators and Fox News, the party's media spear-carrier, tried to make the Benghazi affair a latter-day Watergate. This turned out to be a damp squib: partly because the event just didn't attain major-failure status, and partly because the mainstream media were not inclined to pick up on the story.

Romney's unexpected debate success in October only briefly changed the tenor of the campaign. Analyst Sean Trende thought that, over the course of the election cycle, Obama repeatedly met "forces of gravity" that pulled him down, but equally repeatedly he and his campaign reversed things with anti-Romney campaign themes (Bain, Romney's taxes, the 47 percent tape).[31]

In the course of the campaign's final month, the familiar scenario of each candidate donning some of his opponent's clothing played out once more. Romney, at the risk of adding to his already substantial flip-flop image, took on an increasingly moderate, presidential, ready-for-bipartisanship tone. Obama, at the risk of diminishing his above-the-fray presidential aura, became more aggressive and strident.[32]

By the election's eve, polls and predictions clogged the landscape of public discourse. Republican savants—Karl Rove, Michael

Barone, Peggy Noonan—foretold a Romney victory. Their Democratic opposite numbers with equal certitude expected an Obama win. Almost all of the pundits predicted a cliff-hanger.[33]

Obama won handily, but not outstandingly. Why?

2. EXAMINING THE ENTRAILS

One review of the 2008 election (mine, as it happens) concluded that it was not more bitter than its predecessors; there was no October surprise or other unusual nastiness worth noting, and the debates between the candidates had diminished significance. Can something similar be said of 2012?[34]

Familiar Ways

Insofar as there was a surprise in October, it was hurricane Sandy: no contrivance of the campaign or the media. The street theater of protest at the party conventions, whose prototype was the Chicago Democratic gathering of 1968, was conspicuous for its absence, not only because of lots of police and big perimeters around the convention sites but also because, as the short, unhappy life of Occupy Wall Street indicated, 1968-style street politics was so last century.

Did 2012 add anything to the ever-fraught American saga of politics and race? African-American Obama, like Roman Catholic Kennedy, broke new ground. Despite occasional attempts to read race into the election, it is fair to say that in 2012 the primary question was not whether or not a black should be elected president but whether or not Obama's record entitled him to reelection.

The seeming closeness of the campaign raised unsettling possibilities: divergent popular and electoral results á la 2000 or a deadlocked electoral vote with the GOP House deciding who was president (Romney) and the Democratic Senate deciding who was vice president (Biden). But these were marginal concerns. More substantial were the issues of an extended voting period, much favored by Democrats, and voter identification, much favored by Republicans.[35]

Advocates of more voting time argued that this widened participation and lessened the long lines on election day that could deter voters (and impede Obama's super-efficient get-out-the-vote operation). Opponents held that this weakened the idea of voting as a shared civic duty. In fact, there was little indication that a longer voting period led to lower participation—quite the contrary.

Voter ID supporters dwelt on its deterrent effect on cheating. Critics dwelt on its deterrent effect on minority voters. The Supreme Court upheld Indiana's ID law, and there was scarce evidence that the requirement discouraged voting. Nor was there much sign of widespread voting fraud.[36]

About 57.5 percent of eligible voters cast ballots: lower than 2008's 62.3 percent or 2004's 60.4 percent, but higher than 2000's 54.6 percent. The 2012 participation level was precisely that of 1828, just before the party system fully kicked in. For the rest of the nineteenth century, voters generally turned out (or were turned out) at a 70–80 percent rate. The decline of bosses and party machines in the twentieth century went along with a voter slide into the 50–60 percent range, and there it is today.[37]

The liberal read on Obama's victory is summed up by Peter Beinart: "The coalition that carried Obama to victory is every bit as sturdy as America's last two dominant political coalitions: the ones that elected Franklin Roosevelt and Ronald Reagan."

But the vote does not support so portentous a conclusion, as a comparison with previous multi-term presidents suggests:

Year	Winner	Electoral Vote	Popular Vote (%)
1932–1936	FDR	472–59	57.41
	FDR	523–8	60.80
1952–1956	DDE	447–89	55.18
	DDE	457–73	57.37
1968–1972	RMN	301–191	43.42
	RMN	520–17	60.67
1980–1984	RR	489–49	50.75
	RR	525–13	58.77
1992–1996	WJC	370–168	43.01
	WJC	379–159	49.23
2000–2004	GWB	271–266	47.87
	GWB	286–251	50.73
2008–2012	BO	365–173	52.87
	BO	322–206	51.10

NOTE: FDR = Franklin D. Roosevelt. DDE = Dwight D. Eisenhower. RMN = Richard M. Nixon. RR = Ronald Reagan. WJC = William J. Clinton. GWB = George W. Bush. BO = Barack Obama.

Obama's electoral vote and the percentage of his popular vote are the only ones in modern history to have declined from the first election. He may yet turn out to have crafted as stable a liberal Democratic majority as FDR's. But the data suggest that the recent electoral pattern of evanescent superiority is likely to continue.[38]

The view that this was a typically sustaining rather than an untypically transforming election is reinforced by a comparison of congressional results since 1930. Only in 1936 did the reelected president get a strengthened hand in the legislature. In the congressional as in the presidential vote, the gap between the passions of the campaign and the modest change in the result underlines what historian Henry Adams called the "queer mechanical balance" that "holds the two parties even."

At one time the likelihood that the Republicans would take the Senate appeared high indeed, what with 23 Democratic seats in contention compared to only 10 Republican ones. But the GOP's talent for rarely missing an opportunity to miss an opportunity kicked in. The party's Missouri and Indiana candidates threw away likely wins with offensive statements on rape and abortion, sustaining a tradition of electoral ineptitude established by their 2010 counterparts in Delaware and Nevada.

The Democrats wound up with a Senate gain of two seats. They picked up a modest eight seats in the House, further evidence that the Obama coat had short tails. Perhaps the most significant change was a decline in the number of House swing districts and hence a spur to greater congressional polarization. But on the broader stage of elections to the Senate the results were more diverse: 17 states had senators from both parties.[39]

Thirty-one states had divided governments in 1996, compared to only three in 2014. The gubernatorial elections reflected the variance between national and state politics. Since the mid-1990s Republicans have generally outnumbered Democrats in the state houses, by close to a 3-to-2 margin. Obama's 2008 victory brought with it an uncustomary Democratic majority. But the 2010 election restored the GOP ascendancy, and 2012 sustained it.

That was due to the larger number of normally Republican states and to the fact that governors speak to local issues on which GOP candidates are often more likely to strike a popular chord. A Republican candidate for federal office has to deal with the American passion for keeping entitlements. It was easier for a GOP gubernatorial hopeful to take on the state and local costs imposed by public employee unions and federal mandates.[40]

Straws in the Wind

The demographic/cultural revolution going on in modern America was evident in congressional voting. Eighteen women ran for the Senate, 163 for the House: new levels of participation. The post-2012 Senate had 20 women (17 Democrats), the House 77 (57 Democrats). For the first time ever, a majority of one party (congressional Democrats) was less than half white male. Again reflecting the different political culture of the states, four of the six female governors were Republicans.[41]

Other signs of the nation's altered cultural-political face abound. John Barrow of Georgia, the sole white Democratic congressman left in the Deep South, managed to keep his seat. New England remains unencumbered by GOP House members, as has been the case since 2008 when Chris Shays, the last of the breed, succumbed.

The 2012 election saw the first Buddhist come to the Senate, the first Hindu to the House, and the first member to put down "None" when asked to list her religion—all Democrats. But the 90-plus percent black vote for Obama was not accompanied by the election of a Democratic African-American senator. Tim Scott of South Carolina, the region's lone black Republican congressman, was appointed by governor Nikki Haley to fill the Senate seat of retiring Jim DeMint. As of 2014, the sole black Democratic senator was former Newark mayor Cory Booker.

Why such a scarcity of African-American senators and governors, compared to their more proportionate representation in the House? In part because expanding opportunities in business and law lure many potential candidates, and in part because the fact that so many black members of Congress are longtime incumbents in heavily black districts fosters a political style that does not translate well to a larger sphere.

Fifty years ago, Congress was 75 percent Protestant; now it is 56 percent. Today less than half the Democrats are Protestant; Republican Catholics have grown to be a quarter of the GOP total. Jews remained heavily overrepresented in the House with 23 members, all but one Democratic, and 10 seats, none Republican, in the Senate. Congress, like Dorothy, is not in Kansas anymore; although Kansas, with a solidly conservative three-out-of-four white male House delegation, still is.[42]

Beyond who won, we can get a better sense of why by examining the prime determinants of voter choice. This is dense and complex, though heavily explored, terrain. Its most conspicuous markers are *identity* (ethnicity, race, religion, gender, class), *place* (region and state, city, small town or farm, suburbia or exurbia), and *participation* (new ways of using money, the media, and the blogosphere to shape opinion, and new techniques for locating and getting out supporters).

Identity

The strongest constituencies in Obama's victory were blacks (93 percent of those voting), Hispanics (71 percent), and Asians (73 percent). The 56 percent of women supporting him was a bit less than in 2008, heavily concentrated among younger female voters. The 20 percent gender divide between the candidates, composed of Obama's 12 percent female advantage and Romney's 8 percent lead among males, was the largest since Gallup starting measuring it in 1952. But Obama's youth vote went down by six percentage points, from 66 to 60. About 39 percent of white voters supported him, 4 percent less than in 2008.[43]

The black-Hispanic-Asian-female-youth majority for Obama was decisive. Will this turn out to be as groundbreaking as the emergence of FDR's urban–worker–new immigrant–black coalition in 1936?

Besides African Americans and to a lesser extent Jews, no social group is by cultural decree resistant to the siren call of either party. Women in recent decades have favored the Democrats by margins of 10 percent or more. Much was made of Romney's "war against women" in the campaign. Surely there was little about him or his candidacy to appeal to young, unmarried women, who continued to flock to Obama. But women vote with significant variations according to age, marital status, location, and ethnicity, and they are almost as conspicuous in Republican as in Democratic party politics.[44]

Young voters strongly favored Obama, as they did Kerry in 2004 and Reagan in 1984. In each of these cases, they were the preferred candidate's most supportive age group. Along with their erratic voting ways, younger voters have the common denominator of getting older and usually more conservative as life begins to mug them. The 2012 falloff in support for Obama presumably reflected in part the group's unhappiness over the economy and their job prospects.[45]

Hispanics were as drawn to Obama as they were repelled by Romney. But more than 40 percent of them stomached George W. Bush more readily than they did John Kerry in 2004. Asians are still too small a voting body to count for much. But given their social and economic aspirations, their vote for Obama may reflect his appeal to a group with a number of well-educated professionals and technocrats, not culturally disposed to reject active government.[46]

The media and analysts from both parties concluded that native white or minority identity had an outsized place in the election. About 80 percent of the nonwhite vote went for Obama. Romney won almost 60 percent of white voters (who were more than 70 percent of the electorate). But the falloff in the white vote from 2008 to 2012 has been estimated at 5–7 million. Romney arguably was more hurt by this than Obama was helped by the increase in his support from Hispanics.[47]

Then there is class, that ever-elusive category of identity, with an uncertain history in a nation which is supposed to have little room for that sort of line-drawing. The current perception of class in American public life is vibrant, but quite distant from the Marxian-European understanding of the term.

The traditional American designation of "the working class" is deeply buried in political history's dustbin. Much attention is paid to "the rich"—the most affluent 1 or 2 percent—as well it might be in so Mansionizing a society. The residual 98 to 99 percent of the country is commonly identified by a single label, "the middle class," despite the expanding poverty and widening income-and-wealth disparity that characterizes America and, indeed, most other affluent and/or growing economies.[48]

Obama sought to impose a tax increase on "millionaires and billionaires," which at first included anyone making over $200,000 and families with incomes over $250,000. This echoed the spirit, if not the letter, of the 99 percent–1 percent mantra of the Occupy Wall Street movement.

But to what degree does this play into a politics of class? Unquestionably it spoke to popular grievances stemming from the recession and the bloated incomes and tax evasion of the rich. Whether it taps a more profound class resentment is less evident.

Americans remain deeply ambivalent about the lifestyles of the rich. Theirs is a complex mix of envy, admiration, and resentment. The "rich" include folk heroes—sports and rock stars, Megabucks lottery winners, super-entrepreneurs Steve Jobs and Bill Gates—and folk villains—investment bankers and hedge fund managers. It is difficult for class feeling to flourish in a society where little or no hostility prevails in the popular view of Silicon Valley, Hollywood, and professional sports—activities suffused with big money displayed in vulgar ways.[49]

The classic repositories of class feeling in America—an industrialized, unionized workforce and hardscrabble farmers—are social artifacts of a past time. The service and sales workers, clerical employees, and technicians who now dominate our workforce show little class consciousness: less, many would argue, than they should. At the same time there is much reason to think that differences in education, residence, family, marriage, and lifestyle are feeding a growing class divide that transcends and to a degree replaces the old sorting lines of race and ethnicity.

The most noticeable repository of class resentment appears to be the clerisy: academics, media folk, technocrats, and professionals, who are far from poor themselves but react strongly against the grosser displays of wealth. It is the average American who appears to be least concerned about disparities in wealth, another aspect of the social structure that makes our politics so complicated.[50]

Place

There was a time when region meant a lot politically. The heritage of the Civil War defined the Democratic politics of the Solid South and, less markedly, the politics of the Solid North: the Republican band that stretched across the northern tier of states from Portland, Maine to Portland, Oregon.

State and local party machines and national party ideologies reinforced the dominant inclination (to rewrite Gilbert and Sullivan) for every boy and every girl who attains adult political ken / To be either a steady Democrat or else a steady Republican. Dissenters found a voice in third parties, much as dissidents from the major religious sects went off and formed sects of their own.

In our time, state and regional party identity has been thoroughly bent, spindled, folded, and mutilated. The Solid South is still fairly solid, but Republican, not Democratic. So is Appalachia, for all its roots in Jacksonian Democracy. The reverse might be said for New England and indeed for much of the northern tier. The

Midwest and the Southwest are less homogenous. Republican Arizona and Democratic New Mexico are unusual in their political continuity, as is longtime battleground Ohio.[51]

Today's preferred labeling is not so much North and South or even Democratic or Republican as Red and Blue: recognition of the fact that ideology and culture have come to supplant party and region as prime determinants of political identity.

It is appropriate that those labels are a product of our mass-culture-driven time. They were created by the television networks in the 1970s, who wanted to distinguish state political leanings in a way compatible with the arrival of color television. Visual vividness, not political meaning, was the prime motivator. NBC's pioneering 1976 TV map showed Republican states as blue and Democratic ones as red; CBS did the opposite. But in 2000 the media settled down to the GOP-red/Democratic-blue color theme (whereas in England Labor's traditional color is red and the Conservatives' is blue). There it has remained, with the add-on of purple to portray states with mixed party leanings.[52]

What were the most salient political features of location in 2012? The Census of 2010 continued the reallocation of congressional seats and electoral votes from the Northeast and the Midwest to the South, the Southwest, and the Mountain states. The Republicans, in control of more state governments, were better situated to take advantage of congressional gerrymandering after the 2010 Census, as the Democrats previously had with equal assiduity. But it appeared that the Democrats' House problem stemmed more from their greater concentration of support. By one estimate, 29 percent of GOP districts were solidly Republican, compared to 42 percent comparably safe Democratic ones.[53]

The 2012 election does not appear to have significantly altered the prevailing red-blue-purple character of American politics. Much attention was focused on nine "swing states" (an iconic 2012 phrase): Colorado, Florida, Iowa, Nevada, New Hampshire, North Carolina, Ohio, Virginia, and Wisconsin. Only North Carolina went (narrowly) for Romney in 2012, a sign that effective politicking can trump regional or state identity in modern American politics.

Another major place-defined distinction is that of city, suburb or exurb, and small town or farm. From the 1950s on, the suburbs emerged as a major political force. More than the cities and the countryside, they determined the political flow: with Eisenhower in the 1950s, Kennedy-Johnson in the 1960s, Clinton in the 1990s, and Bush and then Obama in the new century.[54]

Here again, 2012 saw little major change in the major divides. Obama won 70 percent of the vote in cities with a population of 500,000 or more and under 60 percent in cities with 50,000 to 500,000 people. Red state suburbs went strongly for Romney; Blue state suburbs went strongly for Obama. Surprising? No. Game-changing? Hardly.

An urban-exurban-rural comparison of the 2008 and 2012 elections reveals that Obama did slightly less well in the urban (and, presumably, suburban) category in 2012 and considerably less well in exurbia and rural America. But 3 million fewer rural voters turned out in 2012 than in 2008. And only 20.5 million of the 128.7 million 2012 voters were from the countryside.[55]

At the same time the cultural and thus the political homogeneity of smaller areas—congressional districts, the zip code–defined areas in which marketers and social scientists locate their subjects—is increasing. In 1976, 26 percent of voters lived in counties where one party won by a margin of 20 percent or more; by 2008 that figure had grown to 48 percent.

The lack of national one-party dominance is related to the declining power of state and regional political cultures. Each party's recent victories (the GOP's in 2002, 2004, and 2010; the Democrats' in 2006, 2008, and 2012) appear to have had more to do with distaste for the opposition and the appeal of cultural issues, both much subject to change, than by inherited behavior rooted in location.[56]

Participation

Identity and ideology do not in themselves guarantee political victory. The political leanings that they breed have to be translated into commitment, engagement, and the act of voting. Enough money to idealize your candidate and defame the opponent, a supportive media presence, and organization to get out your potential vote can be determining. In all of these the Democrats of 2012 excelled, with substantial own-goal help from the opposition.

Those traditional campaign money spigots, corporations and unions, as well as super PACs (the new gorilla on the block) turned out to have their limits. The Obama campaign was very effective at eliciting contributions from millions of individual supporters. But many corporations are loath to have their names too closely associated with a candidate or party. Public employee unions in states that restricted their collective bargaining power suffered sharp declines in dues-paying members and thus of available campaign cash.

The super PACs' money could buy only so much (perhaps too much) TV time. The often uncontrolled take-no-prisoners tone of their campaign ads led to backlash. One estimate was that a presidential campaign might not be able to spend more than half a billion dollars effectively—half of what each one raised. So while the campaigns amassed overflowing coffers, their well-funded cacophonies tended to cancel each other out.[57]

The media's role in pumping up the GOP primary debates, the thousands of reporters that swamped outnumbered delegates at the conventions, the steady drumbeat of punditry and polling, and heavy

TV ad spending in swing states, attest to the fact that big media was as prominent a part of the political scene as big money. Did the media, like money, approach a saturation point (and beyond) in 2012? The heavy pro-Obama bias of the mainstream media in 2008 generally persisted in 2012. Did it matter? Will those mass circuses, the primaries and debates, continue to fill media coffers? Most important, does the ever more absorbing world of social networks and iPhones threaten to erode not only the power of the press but the power of TV? It takes no great effort to raise these questions. But it does seem early on to try to answer them.[58]

Perhaps most decisive in the election of 2012 was the Obama campaign organization's ability to maximize turnout. But a recurring feature of American politics is the tendency of the defeated party to cannibalize the weapons of the victorious one. So it was with the Whigs, who by 1840 figured out how to call and raise the Jacksonian democracy theme with their Harrison-Tyler Log Cabin campaign. They successfully characterized Jackson's heir Martin Van Buren as the epitome of wealth and privilege, much as the Democrats did with Romney. And so it was with the Republicans confronting the Roosevelt–New Deal coalition, turning to moderates Willkie and Dewey and finally finding with Eisenhower and later with Reagan candidates whose charisma approached that of FDR.

Romney hardly solved the GOP's popularity problem. But when set against the alternatives, it is arguable that he was in the Willkie-Dewey mold of holding the line while his party's adaptation to the Obama era went on. This was not enough to counter Obama's personal appeal. Candidates matter, as Reagan, Clinton, and Obama showed in a positive sense, and Michael Dukakis, Bob Dole, Kerry, and Romney showed in a negative one.

It is difficult to argue that Obama's core appeal lay in the attractiveness of his program, the record of his first term, or the state of the economy. Ronald Brownstein foresaw a "towering wave of alienation" threatening both parties; Sean Trende saw a unique confrontation between an unelectable incumbent and an unelectable opponent. But Obama's relative popularity and Romney's lack of it overrode those drawbacks.[59]

Outstanding presidents such as FDR and Ronald Reagan change the public beliefs of their time. Good presidents such as Eisenhower and Kennedy understand and embody them. Run-of-the-mill presidents such as Carter and Bush II are overwhelmed by them. It is not yet clear which of these niches Obama occupies. But it is likely to be somewhere between the second and the third.

CHAPTER NINE

. . .

Looking Around and Ahead

POLITICAL SCIENTISTS SENSIBLY prefer not to predict anything until after it has happened. This cautionary mode goes double for historians. We have trouble enough explaining events even after they occur. It applies still more to a book such as this, which strives to be a history while its subject is alive and kicking.

But the author would be as disappointed as his reader(s) if he failed to give prophecy a try. What follows seeks to draw on my view of the present state and longer-term character of American politics and government. Historical perspective can look around and ahead as well as back.

I. INTO THE SECOND TERM: POLITICS

Observers from both political camps saw 2012 as a fraught and freighted election. (But don't they always?) Typical was journalist Ronald Brownstein's view that it was a confrontation between an

Obama Coalition of Transformation, tapping into new cultural and demographic currents, and a Romney Coalition of Restoration, composed of white voters upset by these changes.[1]

Is Obama's victory likely to revive a Democratic ascendancy that, with the exceptions of the Eisenhower and Nixon-Ford interregna, stretched from FDR to Jimmy Carter? Or does his halved majority, and the fact that no reelected president in modern history (or indeed since Andrew Jackson) did less well the second time around, suggest that relative candidate attractiveness and superior organization were more determining than ideology or issues?

In the wake of Obama's 2012 victory, much was made of a rising American electorate of unmarried women, blacks, Hispanics, and the young, a "coalition of the ascendant." *Time* magazine, naming Obama its 2012 Person of the Year, spoke of him as the "architect of the New America." To paraphrase what Metternich is supposed to have said of Talleyrand's death: What did *Time* mean by that?

Its grammatically challenged editor proposed that Obama was "the beneficiary and the author of a kind of New America, a new demographic, a new cultural America that he is now the symbol of." His primary examples: gay marriage and work permits for illegal immigrants.[2]

In the taxonomy of significant public policy, these are minor species. Indeed, the issues that have stoked liberalism and the Left since the turn of the twenty-first century—inequality, environmentalism, and the War on Terror—were not high on the voters' worry list, and were tucked away in the trunk of the 2012 Obamamobile.

Obama's post-2012 election attempts to capitalize on issues such as gun control, immigration, same-sex marriage, and Obamacare have not had observable political payoff. Indeed, Obamacare bids fair to be a massive liability. The president remains relatively popular and the GOP generally unpopular. But gaining strength every day is a new constraint: lame-duckery, the ineluctable erosion of the power of a president who cannot run again.

Was the 2012 election the GOP's "2012 or never" last chance, as more than one liberal analyst thought? Or was it in the more customary American pattern of a result subject to the winds of contingency and change? In short, was it akin to 1936—FDR's game-altering reelection—or 2004—Bush's evanescent reelection? I would say that the 2012 election was no more decisive a mandate for the winning party than the knell of doom for the losing one. Unforeseen, contingent events are likely to be as important in the future as they have been in the past.[3]

Scenarios to Come

It is not clear that touch-button social and cultural issues will play as important a role in future politics as they did in the past. Clashes over gay marriage, the status of illegal immigrants, or the legalization of marijuana are not likely to match the scale of the great conflicts over civil rights for blacks or abortion. They are causes that mainstream politicos increasingly are inclined to fudge or, in deference to the rising political power of the millennials, to accept.[4]

In the summer of 2013 the Supreme Court sought to avoid a repeat of the long war that followed its *Roe v. Wade* abortion decision. It struck down federal regulation of gay marriage and left it to the states. At the same time it put tighter clamps on federal or state government using race-based criteria in voting rights or college admissions. These decisions were in close accord with the flow of public opinion: the Supreme Court following the polling returns. Since then, public acceptance of gay marriage, and consequent judicial and legislative accommodation, has steadily spread.[5]

Cultural and ethnic diversity will continue to be a significant political dynamic. But the GOP's supposed marginalization in this realm is far from a done deal. The only African-American senators are an appointed GOP conservative from South Carolina and a Democratic centrist former mayor of Newark, New Jersey. The most conspicuous Hispanic politician is GOP Florida senator Marco Rubio. New Texas senator Ted Cruz is a loud voice on the GOP Right. Governors Bobby Jindal of Louisiana, Nikki Haley of South Carolina, Susana Martinez of New Mexico, and Brian Sandoval of Nevada further challenge the view that the Republicans are hopelessly locked into a white, male, European-American persona. Mia Love, a Haitian-American Mormon woman, and Josh Mandel, a Jewish ex-Marine who fought in Iraq, lost in 2012 as Republican candidates for governor of Utah and senator from Ohio. Love is likely to win a Utah congressional seat in 2014. They may not be the face of a new GOP, but surely they aren't typical of the old one.[6]

The economic conservatism and Sun Belt provenance of the new crop of GOP prominenti could mean that the party will continue to be closed out of the presidency, as it was from 1932 to 1952. But party adaptation to social and cultural change remains very much part of the American political scene.

A relevant historical precedent is the political journey of Irish Catholic voters. For a century after they first appeared in numbers they were firm Democrats, at times by the 90 percent or so totals of African Americans today. But over the decades this eroded: in part because of unhappiness with some of the New Deal's tone and substance; then over FDR's alliance with the Soviet Union during the World War II; and most decisively with the Irish-American ascent into the middle class and suburbia, the growing Democratic commitment to racial minorities, and the appeal of GOP candidates Eisenhower and Reagan.

Today "the Catholic vote" in general and "the Irish vote" in particular (about half of Irish Americans are Protestants) are so fractured that it is a stretch to use those terms. They are scattered over the political landscape like Napoleon's army on its retreat from Moscow. It matters more whether a Catholic is white or Hispanic, church-going or unchurched, than whether he or she is Catholic.

Obama won about 52 percent of the Catholic vote, ascribable to his increase in Hispanic support from 68 to 73 percent. Romney made comparable gains among church-going white Catholics. Romney's estimated margin among these voters was 19 points, the largest for a Republican since Nixon in 1972.[7]

Will Hispanics, over time, follow the same course as the Irish? I fall back on the classic historian's response: it depends. If the GOP retains an anti-immigrant, favor-the-rich persona, then probably no. If a Republican candidate has more appeal to Hispanics and offers up more sympathetic policies, then possibly yes. Hispanics—Catholic and Protestant, of Cuban or Mexican of other origin, new immigrant or old settler—are as diverse as the Irish, other European Americans, and Asian Americans. And cultural diversity spells political diversity.[8]

While much has been made of the Hispanic vote, non-Hispanic white voters remain by far the dominant electoral group. The most salient fact about *their* 2012 political behavior is that they cast 5 to 7 million fewer votes than they did in 2008. These voters are heavily lower and lower-middle class, rural, northern: the sort who went for Reagan and Ross Perot. Will they remain mired in indifference or again be mobilized?[9]

Aside from blacks and Jews, who for a complex of reasons remain heavily committed to the Democrats, ethnic political identity is a pale reflection of its former self. Cultural identity that crosses traditional ethnic-religious lines has become much more determining. The evangelical Protestant–churchgoing Catholic voting bloc trumps the Catholic vote or the Protestant vote as a political identifier today.

What once would have been a galactic political event—the Romney-Ryan ticket was the first in American history to have no candidate from a recognized Protestant denomination—went all but unnoticed. Evangelical spokesman Ralph Reed did observe, "It will be ironic if the first ticket in history without a Protestant got the biggest share of the evangelical vote in history." As things turned out, it didn't; Romney's evangelical vote was 3 percent below McCain's. Still, almost 80 percent of voting evangelicals supported Romney, which is testimony to the degree to which cultural predilection can trump theological purity. Yet while the evangelical vote was 27 percent of the total—the highest ever—it could not match Obama's cultural-demographic coalition.[10]

Place is likely to remain a volatile force in American public life. The political action now and in the immediate future is in the cities, the suburbs, and exurbia. There are signs that their old demographic and cultural distinctiveness are changing, in pace with the general erosion of ethnicity and religious identification as political determinants.

Big cities, once the abode of new immigrants, the black underclass, and an embattled white working and lower middle class, are now more varied locales. They have growing numbers of affluent and/or young urban professionals of all shades. Suburbs, once conspicuous for their whiteness, are now home to a majority of black, Hispanic, and Asian Americans. This opens the door to new urban and suburban political patterns.[11]

Does it necessarily mean that the suburbs, like so many large cities, will become Democratic bastions? If ethnicity is political destiny, perhaps. But if the home-family culture of modern suburbia, especially in the more conservative Sun Belt, does to its new arrivals what its post–World War II counterparts did to the Democratic urban refugees of that time, then perhaps not.

The New York and California urban environments—large ethnic and young professional voting blocs, a declining middle class, numerous public sector employees and government-assisted minorities, pro-Democratic wealth in Wall Street, Hollywood, and Silicon Valley—are likely to assure long-term Democratic preponderance. The evolution of the very different Sun Belt urban-suburban environment promises no such thing.[12]

And then there is the inherent erosion of power by the majority. Political predominance such as Obama's carries with it the seeds of decline. That is evident in the field of potential 2016 Democratic candidates. The party's luminaries, from the lame duck president and the superannuated vice president down, embody its past more than its future. This includes former First Lady–former senator–former secretary of state Hillary Clinton and sons-of-governors Jerry Brown of California and Andrew Cuomo of New York. The white male Irish Catholic governors of Maryland, Connecticut, Illinois, New Hampshire, and elsewhere don't exactly embody Hope and Change.

The all-Democratic 38 black congressmen are deeply rooted in black-dominated constituencies, and only a handful represent majority-white districts. This earns them congressional seniority but restricts their access to higher office. Besides the president, Governor Deval Patrick of Massachusetts and Senator Cory Booker of New Jersey are the only African-American Democratic officeholders of some distinction. But Patrick is not an aspirant, and Booker is a newly minted senator. Hispanic Democrats also are thin on the ground. San Antonio's mayor Julián Castro is promising but as yet a minor officeholder, even as the head of HUD.

Newer aspirants, given the Obama presence and the Hillary imminence, are scarce. The latest Kennedy heir to the throne has just entered Congress. There is some talk of Elizabeth Warren as a progressive white (and Cherokee) hope. But an invigorated liberal-Left message does not as yet seem very likely in 2016.[13]

To this may be added another hoary principle of American political life: the ability of one party to adopt the successful campaign devices of the other. Whether the Republicans can do as well as their Democratic opponents in the new world of the social media remains to be seen. That they are trying to do so is already evident.[14]

American political history is often told as the story of the interplay between two traditions: Democratic reform stretching from Jefferson, Jackson, and Wilson to FDR and Truman, Kennedy and Johnson, Clinton and Obama and a Federalist-Whig-Republican line of descent stretching from Washington and the Adamses to Lincoln, Theodore Roosevelt, Coolidge-Hoover, Eisenhower, Reagan, and the Bushes.

What William James said of all social theories may be said of this political one: it leaks at every joint. Jefferson's and Jackson's small-government liberalism was worlds away from the twentieth-century welfare-warfare state of FDR and Truman, Kennedy, and LBJ. Lincoln and Theodore Roosevelt (or, for that matter, Eisenhower, Nixon, Reagan, and the Bushes) can hardly be defined as avatars of shrinking government.

Columnist Ross Douthat took note of the parties' propensity to exaggerate their polar positions: "messianism from the party in power and apocalypticism from the party out of power, regardless of which party is which." The rhetorical divide conceals a larger historical truth: that our parties, our politics, and our government are in fact defined more by the prevailing political culture of the time than by ideological difference.

In my view there have been three such periods. The first saw the deferential Republican regime of colonial times and the Young Republic. It was followed by a Democratic party regime that stretched from Andrew Jackson to the New Deal. In our own time there has risen a populist-bureaucratic regime, in which the media-advocacy-ideological money tail wags the party dog, and an expansive (and expensive) bureaucratic state is the norm.[15]

The issue is not whether a liberal or a conservative tradition will be restored or diminished. Rather, it is whether the contemporary political world of a populist politics and a bureaucratic state will remain in place, and how it can tame the dysfunctional pressures that erode its core mission of governing.

Some saw the 2010 Republican victory as a rebuke to the active state. This turned out to be a stretch. The 2012 election results have been seen as a green light to big government. That too is questionable. Are there other, more revealing portents of our political future?

New political entities are likely to remain marginal at best. The Tea Party has a number of advocates. But it is too diffuse and unorganized to be more than a passing rallying cry. Occupy Wall Street didn't add up to much of an ism; now it's barely a wasm.

Is the rebirth of federalism—the states taking more of their affairs into their own hands—a likely way out of the gridlock that now assails us? Are they, as a century or more ago, Justice Brandeis's laboratories of democracy, in which alternative policy models are tested?

It is true that states and cities are where one is most likely to find Republican officeholders with some awareness of the needs of the less-well-off and Democratic ones with some awareness of the need to rein in current spending and future commitments. One proponent predicts: "A Left-Right federalist compromise would make America a happier, freer, more prosperous and interesting country." But the challenges to the twentieth-century state are likely to transcend the ameliorative powers of federalism.[16]

Republicans and Democrats

So we fall back on the mainstream partisanship that almost always defines our politics. It is widely thought that today there is a degree of party polarization that (save for the Civil War era) is unparalleled in our history. The dominant storyline of current politics is of Democratic assaults on the GOP as intransigent, racist, hostile to the poor, anti–women's rights; and Republican characterizations of the administration as a nest of corrupt, socialist-minded spenders—despite the widespread public desire for more tempered political behavior.[17]

Partisan vituperation in fact is as old as American politics. But the rise of autonomous ideological voices gives a special edge to current political discourse. Polarization is a catchword of our time. Each of the parties has its own form of bloody-mindedness. To understand what these are, and why, is to better comprehend the contemporary political scene.[18]

In the case of the Republicans, the determining elements are the party's minority position in national politics and government and its demographic base: religious, tradition-minded people, concentrated outside the coastal-urban population centers, widely scorned by the mainstream media and the purveyors of popular culture.

These facts of party life have had two consequences. One is the GOP's clunkiness in public relations. Denigrated by most of the media and elite circles, underrepresented in the new world of the social networks, the party fares badly in the publicity wars. Reagan may have been a Great Communicator; Boehner and McConnell surely are not.

Yet in the war of ideas, as distinct from the war of words, the GOP is in a different place. Polls consistently show majority support for a number of Republican postulates: distrust of big government, opposition to Obamacare, support for a strong military. It is not the message so much as the messenger that lacks public approval.

The most visible consequence of this state of affairs is the rise of autonomous political entrepreneurs. The largest, most amorphous instance is the Tea Party: in Democratic demonology the GOP's sinister new Elders of Zion, replacing Wall Street. The fact that almost no one knows the name of a Tea Party leader suggests that this is a hazy conspiracy indeed. Yet there is no doubt that the Tea Party's presence, and its ideas, have had an outsized influence on Republican policy and politics.

That influence often has taken the form of political adventurers identifying with Tea Party ideology, and running with it. Ted Cruz and Rand Paul are the most recent examples; Sarah Palin a less recent one. It is appropriate that a Senate filibuster has been a favored weapon of choice. That word in its nineteenth-century meaning meant "an irregular military adventurer" and only later the Senate vote-delaying tactic. Both meanings aptly apply to the populist pols of the Right.

The Democrats march with a different pace to a different drummer. Obama remains relatively popular; his policies less so. The predictable result is a greater stress on the iniquity of the opposition than on the triumphs of the administration's agenda.

Just as the take-no-prisoners Tea Party agenda of hostility to government spending and programs seems at times to define the GOP, so does the worldview of the liberal-Left media and the chattering classes shape the political style of the Democrats. A revealing example is the prevalence of calls for what might be called the final solution of the Republican question.

CBS political director John Dickerson counseled, "Go for the throat! . . . If he wants to transform American politics, Obama must declare war on the Republican party." *New Republic* writer Noam Scheiber struck a similar note when he proclaimed that "Obama Must Insist on Total Victory over the GOP."

Science writer Chris Mooney's *The Republican Brain* explored the genetic-evolutionary sources of the inability of that party's members to believe in science "or many other inconvenient truths." Former *New York Times Book Review* editor Sam Tanenhaus explained at length why the GOP remains "the party of white people," in thrall to the teachings of John C. Calhoun. Journalist Jonathan Alter's *The Center Holds: Obama and His Enemies*, the first substantial dissection of the 2012 election, called that contest "a titanic ideological struggle" between Obama's centrism and the GOP threat to the social contract that has prevailed in America since the New Deal.[19]

The vituperation of the chattering classes does not necessarily reflect a comparable gulf within the body politic. A January 2014 Pew survey found that 34 percent of Democrats consider themselves liberal, 63 percent moderate or conservative. Republicans are more polar: 67 percent say they are conservative, 32 percent moderate or liberal. A strong difference, but it leaves out the third or more of the electorate without a strong party identification.[20]

Since 1948 there has been only one instance in which an outgoing two-term president has been followed by a party successor: Reagan-Bush I in 1988. Analyst Sean Trende observes that over the past 80 years, "Short-term contingencies occasionally give one party or the other the edge, but a clear tendency exists to revert back to the mean of a 50/50 nation."[21]

Is the current GOP sufficiently locked into a no-win Right view to upset that pattern? As so often is the case, the Republicans after their 2012 loss engaged in a mini-orgy—an "autopsy"—of self-criticism. There were calls for the party to reinvent itself in order to appeal more to Hispanics and women, and to upgrade its campaign tactics. But old dogs don't readily learn new tricks, and the GOP has been around for more than 150 years. The ongoing confrontation over the budget, the debt, and Obamacare has shown that the uncompromising GOP Right is as feisty as the destroy-the-opposition Democratic Left.[22]

Still, the ideological tails are not necessarily bound to wag their party dogs indefinitely. The media makes much of the Tea Party's influence on the Republicans, which is not untrue but a half-truth. The Tea Party caucus currently has about 50 House and five Senate members, hardly commanding. In the 111th Congress (2009–2011), 24 percent of GOP Representatives belonged to the Tea Party caucus; since then, the number has been 21–22 percent, not a sign of deepening identification. The more mainstream Republican Study Committee, which has been around since the 1970s and is the largest House caucus, claims 171 (73 percent) of the 234 congressional Republicans.[23]

The American process of party rebalancing evident throughout our history shows signs of going on within the GOP. There is much to be said for the liberal-media mantra that the Republicans are out of sync with contemporary American culture. But there is also reason to think that, as is usually the case, the party out of power is hungrier and readier to change. The GOP Establishment—congressional leaders, strategist Karl Rove, advocacy groups like the Club for Growth—have been "groping their way to compromise" on the big issues: the budget and the debt ceiling, immigration, Obamacare. The party's commitment to unalloyed social conservatism shows signs of weakening.[24]

Republicans do seem, after 2012, more willing to explore their intraparty differences. Younger voices such as Marco Rubio, Rand Paul, Pat Toomey, Ted Cruz, Chris Christie, and Paul Ryan differ with one another and with older stalwarts such as John McCain and Lindsey Graham, who in turn have their disagreements with the likes of Rick Santorum and Newt Gingrich.[25]

Conservatism, it turns out, is a mansion with as many rooms as liberalism. The Tea Party famously detaches itself from traditional big money–Wall Street Republicanism. The "libertarian populism" of Rand Paul strikes a different note than either the traditional or the Tea Party Right. Paul's Jimmy Stewart–like filibuster against the somewhat less than imminent threat of American drone attacks on citizens at home won him much réclame among Twitter millennials, who not long before seemed wedded to Obama. With much help from the media and his own performance, fellow–political entrepreneur Ted Cruz has a less savory image.[26]

As is usually the case with the party in power, the Democrats are more unified than the GOP. Maintaining or increasing entitlements, now 40 percent of federal spending, is an all but universal party tenet. The Progressive Caucus and the half of the Black Caucus who aren't among its membership were 36 percent of congressional Democrats after the 2008 election, 46 percent after 2010, and 44 percent after 2012, about double the proportion of their Tea Party counterparts.

But that left over half of congressional Democrats without such commitments. The New Democrat Coalition, the successor to the centrist Democratic Leadership Council of the Clinton era, attracted 30 percent of congressional Democrats in 2013's 113th Congress, compared to 14 percent in the 112th and 21 percent in the 111th—less than the liberal-Left wing but not insignificant, and growing.

Tensions, existing and potential, are inevitable among Democrats, as they are among Republicans. Affluent liberals are drawn to quality-of-life issues such as gender and sexual equality or the environment. Billionaire Tom Steyer's readiness to devote large sums to defeat pro-XL Pipeline Democratic senators is a case in point. Their less affluent union, young, female, Hispanic, and black coadjutors, have a greater interest in policies that foster job creation and economic growth.[27]

The confluence of Obama, Iraq, and the financial crisis that made for Democratic victory in 2008, and of Romney's insufficiencies and a super vote-gathering machine in 2012, are not likely to be repeated. It remains to be seen if Hillary can derive from her gender the benefits that Obama derived from his race. A halting recovery will not be as effective a political theme as Bush's financial crisis, and Obamacare and foreign affairs remain dark clouds on the horizon.[28]

2014 and 2016

The broad sweep of American political history suggests that (with the exception of the 1850s and the Civil War) the regional, class, and cultural divisions of American life have been tempered by—what? Perhaps the shared values of our culture, the constraints of our constitutional system, and ever-present contingency—what British prime minister Harold Macmillan is supposed to have said when asked what would effect policy change: "Events, dear boy, events."

For all their sharp divisions over policy, the parties are strikingly alike in the way that they conduct their business. There is little to distinguish between them in their ideological cohesion or their dependence on outside interests: media, advocacy groups, big money. Sometimes one is better at getting out the vote (the GOP in 2004); sometimes the other is (the Democrats in 2008 and 2012).[29]

What does this portend for the 2014 and 2016 elections? One analyst questions the "six-year myth" of the incumbent party losing congressional seats in the election following the president's return to office. Yet this has worked well enough since the 1930s, except for the limited GOP loss in 1986 and the near-equilibrium of 1998.[30]

Is there much reason to expect that 2014 will be another deviation from the norm? The GOP's performance in the budget-debt impasse of the fall of 2013 hardly endeared it to the electorate, though Obama and the Democrats did not fare much better. The troubles afflicting Obamacare threaten to be a heavy burden to bear, and the cultural-demographic advantages enjoyed by the Democrats are much more likely to figure in a presidential than a midterm election.

The continuing decline of swing seats in Congress lessens the likelihood of a galactic move in either direction. One estimate is that in 1998 the Republicans had 148 solid districts and the Democrats 123. Today some 186 are solidly Republican and 159 Democratic, leaving about 90 swing seats: a 45 percent decline.

Obama and his supporters have ascribed the Republican House majority to gerrymandered congressional districts. It is true that evenly balanced districts are declining. Ninety-six percent of House Democrats represent districts that Obama carried; 94 percent of Republicans come from ones that Romney carried. But GOP Red states outnumber Democratic Blue ones, where core Democratic voters are heavily concentrated. Romney won a majority of the nation's congressional districts, and there is little reason to think that a 2014 Democratic upsurge will occur within them.[31]

So perhaps the most likely look ahead to 2014 is no great upheaval in Congress and the states. But there are two flies buzzing around this status quo unguent. One is the disruptive potential of Obamacare. The other is the historically high degree of popular discontent with Congress as an institution and the continuing increase of Americans who think of themselves as political independents. Disapproval of Congress is lodged in the mid- to upper 80 percent range. One poll has more than half of respondents wanting *every* member of Congress (including their own) replaced: equal-opportunity distaste.[32]

As for 2016, here indeed it is too early to tell. If either party succumbs to its ideological tail and nominates a non-mainstream candidate (think Goldwater or McGovern, or latterly, Rand Paul or Elizabeth Warren), then all middling-contingency bets are off.

2. INTO THE SECOND TERM: GOVERNING

Some presidential reelections have more policy significance than others. Lincoln's return in 1864, Wilson's in 1916, and Roosevelt's in 1936 had major consequences; Eisenhower's in 1956, Reagan's in 1984, and Bush's in 2004, less so.

Did Obama's 2012 victory carry with it policy baggage beyond the norm? Or was it, in political science parlance, a sustaining election unlikely to lead to sea change in governance?

In June 2012, *New Yorker* reporter Ryan Lizza looked ahead to what might be expected of a second Obama term. He assumed a close election, a balanced Congress, and a looming sequester cliff, which in fact occurred. The result, he thought, would be much pressure to compromise, to focus on less divisive policies such as immigration reform, climate change, and physical infrastructure (more Interstate repair, less renewable energy). Obama's foreign policy would take a similar tack from "cooperative idealism" to "hard-nosed realism," especially toward Iran and China. He pointed to the Reagan and Clinton second terms as relevant historical models.[33]

What in fact has been happening? What is likely to happen? Do the Republicans recognize that the 2012 election was more of a rebuke to them than a caution to the president? Their initial response to the tax, debt, and health-care issues suggested that the learning process will be slow and painful.

Will Obama recall what he said of Bush's victory in 2004: "Maybe peace would have broken out with a different kind of White House, one less committed to waging a perpetual campaign—a White House that would see a 51–48 victory as a call to humility and compromise rather than an irrefutable mandate"? Again: so far, not likely.[34]

Hope and Change II

As is customary, a reelected (and reempowered) president set out to enact the agenda that he thought was responsible for his victory. That was the case after Bush's return in 2004, Clinton's in 1996, Eisenhower's in 1956, and back to the primeval past of FDR in 1936.

In his Second Inaugural and 2013 State of the Union addresses, Obama reasserted his commitment to greater reliance on regulation and executive fiat, all but rejected compromise with the GOP (a sentiment heartily reciprocated by his opponents), sought to mobilize his 2012 coalition to support his agenda—and defined that agenda much as he had four years ago: defending the all-inclusive middle class against rapacious wealth.

He had ambitious political plans to take the House from the Republicans in 2014. He gave strong signals that Hillary would be next in succession, riding a wave of gender ceiling-breaking as he had that of race. And he had initial successes, most noticeably facing down the House Republicans on the debt ceiling, spending, and taxation.[35]

Obama sought in less provocative ways to exercise greater control over the course of events in his second term. His first cabinet was dominated by a "team of rivals": primaries opponent Hillary Clinton in State, Bush Secretary of Defense Robert Gates staying on, and Clinton-Rubin-Summers associate Timothy Geithner in Treasury. After 2012 they were replaced by the more acquiescent troika of John Kerry, Chuck Hagel, and Jack Lew, a contrast highlighted by Gates's critical memoir *Duty*.[36]

Organizing for America was Obama's most conspicuous fund-raising organization in the 2012 election. It was renamed Organizing for Action in early 2013, charged to use its money and influence to enact Obama's second-term agenda. Organizing for

Action cut loose from its party ties (with some unhappiness in the Democratic National Committee). Its initial goal was to raise $50 million. Among its inducements, donors of $500,000 or more would get quarterly meetings with the president.[37]

This sort of thing is hardly unique to Obama and the Democrats. Major GOP donors are tapped by the Conservative Victory Project, which Karl Rove created out of his 2012 campaign super political action committee, American Crossroads. Its purpose is to foster greater discipline in party nominations, so as to avoid the rogue candidates who cost the GOP winnable Senate seats in 2010 and 2012. It too keeps its distance from the party apparatus.[38]

As the second term unwound, (non-)business as usual reasserted itself. Obama failed to expand gun control and took a backseat on immigration reform. Nor were his second-term hopes bolstered by the revelations of government misbehavior that gathered in the spring of 2013, or the Obamacare rollout embarrassment. With untypical English overstatement, *The Economist* equated Obama's brief day in the post-election sun with Brigadoon, the Scottish village that came to life once a century and then faded into the mist.[39]

Against this was the fact that Obama's personal popularity, while dropping substantially from its 2012-election level, remained relatively high. If unemployment and underemployment continued to hobble the recovery storyline, the slowly improving housing and manufacturing sectors tempered the political cost of a halting economy.[40]

Obama's troubles were hardly unique. Reelections are occasions for much praise, deference, and party unity. But lame-duckery inexorably changes the calculus. Opponents sharpen their knives, while supporters worry that their man has lost his edge. If I'm up for election in 2014, do I cling to or cleave from Obama? This is a no-brainer for Democrats from deep Blue states and districts, though it's an ineradicable part of the Left's (as it is of the Right's) gene pool to scent weakness or deviation in leaders of their persuasion. For others, which includes a number of the party's 2014 senatorial candidates, distance from the president might lend enchantment.[41]

Obama has a second-act problem that is not likely to go away. Polls suggest a substantial disconnect between the issues that concern most Americans—jobs and the economy, the cost and complexity of Obamacare, entitlement reform—and the ones that most concern Obama and his liberal base: gun control, gay marriage and abortion, implementation of Obamacare as is, citizenship for illegal immigrants, climate change, and most of all, inequality.[42]

Obama's hands-off style of governing, the mirror image of LBJ's both-hands-on approach, may protect him from direct involvement in his administration's troubles. But the frustrations inherent in the law-making sausage machine incline him (like other modern presidents) to rely more on the weapons of the executive branch: broad agency discretion for Health and Human Services on Obamacare and the Environmental Protection Agency on the environment, and a clutch of financial regulators on the banking system.

Obama took an expansive view of his power to make interim appointments and showed a readiness, though substantially less than his predecessor Bush, to append signing statements that define (and redefine) the intent of congressional bills. More evident is his penchant for ex officio rejigging of legislation, most notably with Obamacare. These responses to the frustrations of governance, rather than a flurry of new legislative initiatives, are likely to continue to characterize Obama's second term.[43]

As that term unfolds, he has responded to the need for job creation by sticking to his mantra of economic growth through government "investments" in new technology and infrastructure. He festooned his plans with attractive furbelows such as a substantial rise in the minimum wage and universal prekindergarten schooling. He continues to champion immigration reform. And he has called income inequality "the defining issue" of the time.

But other big, unsettled matters are as likely to overshadow the rest of Obama's agenda. One is the recurring gridlock over debt, spending, and taxation. Another is the troubled implementation of Obamacare. A third is the unsettled state of America's foreign affairs.

Bipolarized Misgoverning

Two and a quarter centuries ago, James Madison proposed that the new nation's success depended on governance by large, varied coalitions: in effect, two broadly based political parties. From this perspective there is much reason for concern over the recent evolution of the parties into ever purer repositories of Right or Left ideology.[44]

The solidarity of the major parties may have its comforts. But it also has its costs: most notably, a reduced readiness to respond to new realities in creative ways. That afflicted country-club Republicans in the 1930s and social conservatives in the 1960s and after. The Tea Party mantra of few taxes and little government is also locked into the past.

Now this mindset afflicts policymakers wedded to the model of big government, big labor, big business, and a big welfare state that has flourished over the past three-quarters of a century. It may be that nineteenth- and twentieth-century solutions are equally unresponsive to twenty-first-century problems.[45]

Are we condemned indefinitely to the stalemated polarization of recent years? Or will one (or both) parties seize on the plummiest prize in American politics, an appeal to the public desire for compromise that cuts loose from both the conservative-Right and the liberal-Left mindsets?

In the fall of 2013, like a well-trained ballet troupe, Congress and the president offered up a reprise of their 2011–2012 budget-debt ceiling pas de deux. Might history this time repeat itself as farce?

Indeed it did. Texas senator Ted Cruz launched a Quixotic crusade against the windmill of Obamacare, seeking to defund the entire program in return for refunding the government. This was legislatively impossible. It was broadly unpopular: polls showed that distrust of Obamacare was outmatched by opposition to its dismantling. It was to the manifest political advantage of the GOP to let Obamacare see the light of day. (Ulysses S. Grant: "I know no method to secure the repeal of bad or obnoxious laws so effective as their stringent execution.") Instead, House Republicans dutifully wheeled into line behind the Cruz filibuster (in both the nineteenth-century buccaneer and the twentieth-century senatorial versions of the word).[46]

Obama and the Senate Democrats ran a close second in this orgy of miscalculation. They could have sought a compromise that secured a welcome slowdown of an already troubled Obamacare, while underlining the GOP's preeminence in irresponsible governance. Instead they came up with their own form of obduracy, disdaining the hand-dirtying business of compromise with the opposition.[47]

The polarizing forces within each party were alive and well. The GOP insisted once again on a narrowly supported and politically destructive ideological purity. The Democrats stuck to their unproductive course of demonizing their opponents as a subspecies not worth customary political give-and-take.

Government closedown evoked predictable public backlash, Congressional Republicans hurriedly struck a deal that reopened the government until mid-January 2014, and raised the debt ceiling until February or March. Obama gave little or nothing in return and dodged the debt-ceiling bullet, where he was far more vulnerable in public opinion. Yet another cross-party congressional committee was charged to propose a larger compromise.[48]

Then the administration replaced the Republicans as hell-bent on policy and political self-immolation. It rejected out of hand the proffered gift from the GOP gods of an Obamacare implementation delay. Instead it plowed ahead with a startup that turned into an operational fiasco and a public opinion disaster.

Obamacare remains a work in progress. But both the way in which the administration implemented the program and the politics that have swirled around it reveal the toxicity of and the limits to our polarized politics as clearly as the GOP did with the government closedown.

Why did an administration of all the talents so badly handle the task of setting up the massive Obamacare website, allow the cancellation of millions of existing policies, and incur the political cost of an unsustainable pledge that everyone who wanted to keep their present insurance would be able to do so? GOP hostility to the program may be a partial explanation, but it is hardly a sufficient one. The same may be said of that portmanteau explanation of a government foul-up: bureaucratic incompetence.

The most likely answer is that the intensely political focus of Obama and his aides—How do we get Obamacare passed? How do we fend off Republican criticism?—blinded them to the adverse consequences of their strategy. Much the same might be said of the Nixonians and Watergate, or of the Benghazi, Internal Revenue Service, and Justice abuses. Once again, a polarized political sensibility had adverse policy—and political—consequences.[49]

The GOP-spurred government shutdown and the Obamacare debut fiasco are compelling demonstrations of the cost of bipolarized American governance. That style in full flower could take credit for the following results: Congress, the Republican party, and Obama's favorability plumbed new depths; internal GOP wrangling grew in intensity; and popular distaste for the (non-)workings of American government and politics flourished as much as at any time since that last exercise in take-no-prisoners politics, the Civil War era.[50]

Is there any prospect that more benign and longer-lasting resolutions of the budget-debt and Obamacare problems are in the cards? There are indeed some possible scenarios, plausible perhaps in the wake of the government-closing and Obamacare-opening disasters.

The Paul Ryan–Patty Murray budget deal of late 2013 and the unexpectedly broad bipartisan support it won in both Houses was a shaky harbinger of an American political spring, as inconclusive as groundhog Punxsutawney Phil's forecasts of how much winter was still to come. But it did signify a new readiness on the part of the Republican leadership to open up some space from the Tea Party and conservative advocacy groups.[51]

Growing numbers of Republicans recognize that they would be well advised to let Obamacare continue on its rocky road to implementation and ease off on their unrealistic demand for outright repeal. Some congressional Democrats, anxiously focused on the November 2014 election, began to distance themselves from Obamacare's troubles, further opening the way for modifications that address the program's problems.[52]

The obstacles to a Grand Compromise are as numerous as they are obvious. But there are indications that the more centrist portions of the two congressional parties have been sufficiently shaken by the government shutdown and the Obamacare seize-up to explore a Third Way. However, that may well have to await the outcome of the 2014 election.

3. STATUS AND STATE

What are the issues most likely to figure prominently in American politics to come, barring massive foreign or domestic crises? Two large ones are worth considering: over the creation and distribution of wealth, and over the size and role of government.

Wealth and Inequality

Ours has been an age of major and for the most part positive change in the nation's social makeup. Improvements in the status of African, Hispanic, and Asian Americans and of women and gays add up to a social revolution comparable to the redefinition of civil and religious freedom in the era of the American Revolution and the Young Republic.

But recently we have seen the rebirth of long-muted concerns over inequality in wealth, income, education, and occupational mobility. A mass of data reveals widening disparities of income and wealth, visibly expressed in the mansionizing of the houses and lifestyles of the well-off. Beyond this, there is a widening gap in education, residence, and family between under- and working-class and upper-middle- and high-income Americans. African Americans have undergone major improvement in their civil and social status, but far less so in their economic condition. Social commentators see a growing class divide that transcends the old sorting lines of ethnicity and race. Charles Murray's *Coming Apart* (2012) describes the two cultural-economic nations that appear to be emerging. The most recent poster child of the academic liberal-Left is French economist Thomas Piketty's *Capital in the Twenty-First Century*, a compelling new version of the old Marxian trope of immiseration flowing inevitably from unchecked capitalism.[53]

The sources, extent, and consequences of inequality are more complex than those who worry about it, and those who don't, are ready to concede. Inequality does seem to be linked to economic growth. Over the past 30 years, it has widened even faster in prospering Sweden, Germany, Israel, Finland, New Zealand, and China than in the United States. But a Harvard-Berkeley study in February 2014 found that while inequality in America has grown, social mobility between generations has not declined.[54]

The massive rise of almost a billion of the world's people from poverty was closely related to the shift from planned to market-led economies. And the widespread decline in labor's share of American national income appears to have little or no connection with public policy, and much to do with technology and education.[55]

A December 2011 Gallup poll found that the number of Americans who thought the nation was divided into haves and have-nots had *declined* since 2008, from 49 to 41 percent—although those who saw themselves as have-nots slightly increased. A large majority of respondents still vest their hopes more in economic opportunity and growth than in redistribution. This is further evidence that the 2012 election was a referendum on Obama's popularity and Romney's lack of it, rather than a mandate for particular economic and social policies.[56]

There have been two political responses to the issue of inequality. One is the conservative call to restore economic growth, jobs, and opportunity by reducing the cost of government and freeing private enterprise from onerous regulation and taxation. In its purest form this is the program of the Tea Party, and it is the core of Republican economic policy. Its closest European counterpart is greater government "austerity" (another buzzword of our time). *Bien pensant* thought there, as here, opposes this.[57]

The American liberal-Left antidote for recession and inequality has been the Keynesian remedy of increased government spending and in a modified form the old socialist call for the redistribution of wealth. The 99-percent-against-1-percent theme of Occupy Wall Street is (like the mirror-image impact of the Tea Party on the GOP) the expression in pure form of the Obama-Democratic message of tax hikes for the wealthy and few or no cuts in entitlements. In December 2013 Obama declared that his commitment to reduce inequality "drives everything I do in this office." But his sensitive political antennae led him to hedge his bets. In his January 2014 State of the Union address he referred to "opportunity" ten times, and "inequality" only twice.[58]

The parties' response to the nation's ongoing fiscal-economic crisis is summed up in two highly questionable mantras regarding taxes. Republicans insist that any increase would depress job creation; Democrats claim that higher taxes on the wealthy would solve our fiscal woes. Some mix of the two along the lines of the 2010 Simpson-Bowles proposal for scaled-backed entitlements and a less deduction-encumbered tax code made—and makes—more sense. So far the polarized character of our political culture and the outsized voice of the ideological tails of both parties make its implementation iffy indeed.[59]

This state of affairs has impeded anything beyond toxic deadlock and stopgap Band-Aids. There is a high likelihood that Americans will continue to want their entitlements but not to pay for them, and that most politicians will find it easier to cater to than seek to change this mindset, however dysfunctional it may be. When the issue is more taxes on the wealthy or preserving entitlements, Obama has the advantage. When the issue is reducing federal spending or the threat of a rise in tax rates, the game changes. A final resolution is not likely; a series of half-baked compromises is in the cards.

The drawback from the fabled fiscal cliff, recurring increases in the debt ceiling, public acquiescence in the sequester, the Phoenix-like recurrence of the possibility of a taxing-spending Grand Compromise, and, most of all, the mind-focusing effects of the GOP's government shutdown fiasco, the Democrats' Obamacare troubles, and the 2014 election, may be dashes of cold water in the overheated faces of the parties' ideologues. But one shouldn't expect a policy sea change. There's room for a lot of ruin in a polarized polity dominated by vested interests.[60]

State and Society

Over the course of the twentieth century, the Progressive model of a regulatory-welfare state gradually displaced the nineteenth-century Liberal model of laissez-faire. This was a cross-party enterprise, and stretched through much of the century. However different their approaches, Theodore Roosevelt and Woodrow Wilson had a shared agenda for more regulation of the new industrial-corporate economy. FDR's New Deal, which sought to improve the lives of workers and farmers, was extended rather than reversed by successor presidents, who responded in proactive ways—the Interstate, civil rights, Medicare—to the rise of a middle-class, suburban, increasingly rights-conscious, gradually aging society.

In recent decades the large, active state has come under increasing strain. The triumphs of World War II and the Cold War have given way to the frustrations of coping with militant Islam. The appeal of the benign welfare state is sullied by ever-rising levels of spending and bureaucracy. The achievements of postwar prosperity and the civil rights movement are threatened by the discontents of a halting economy and a society with large school and family problems. Wherever one looks, the Progressive state still is dominant. Everywhere one looks, dissatisfaction with its works is rife.[61]

Our current malaise stems less from a lack of money and policy than from their ineffectiveness. The United States spends as much as or more than other advanced countries on education, health care, welfare, and defense, but with increasingly unsatisfactory results.[62]

Conflict over regulation, taxation, entitlements, and spending—in short, the role of government and its relation to the larger society—has taken center stage in Obama's time. Journalist Charles Lane observed that the country "periodically redefines the role of the federal government in society . . . The post–New Deal consensus about the scope of federal power has broken down amid . . . concern over the welfare state's cost and intrusiveness." When Romney chose Paul Ryan as his running mate, former Obama economic adviser Larry Summers (perhaps prematurely) thought that "it is clear that the central issue in the presidential election will be the scale and scope of government involvement in the economy. How government can best prepare for the pressures that loom, and how greater revenue can be mobilized without damaging the economy, are the great economic questions for the next generation."[63]

This is not a uniquely American dilemma. Between 1870 and 2007, government spending as a percentage of national income rose from 7.3 percent to 36.6 percent in the United States, from 9.4 percent to 44.6 percent in Great Britain, from 10.0 percent to 43.9 percent in Germany, and from 12.6 percent to 52.6 percent in France: by over four times in each country. Throughout the West, mounting welfare (and warfare) costs, debt, recession, and debate over the proper remedy—austerity or stimulus?—have flourished.[64]

Polls tell us that Americans' faith in government, as indeed in most institutions, has been ebbing for more than half a century. Gallup reported in September 2013 that 60 percent of Americans, a record level, thought the federal government had too much power. The big state–social democratic model faces a growing challenge, much as anything-goes capitalism did in the first half of the twentieth century.

A smaller state and more locally grounded institutions have long had theoretical support. See, for example, economists Mancur

Olson's *The Logic of Collective Action* (1965) and E. F. Schumacher's *Small Is Beautiful* (1973); the public choice theory of James Buchanan; and anthropologist–political scientist James C. Scott's *Seeing Like a State* (1998).

High pop-sociology has seized on the theme. Nassim Nicholas Taleb's *Antifragile: Things That Gain from Disorder* (2012) celebrates organic, bottom-up ways of doing things over the "Soviet-Harvard delusions" of "top-down policies and contraptions [i.e., institutions]." Nicco Mele's *The End of Big* (2013) finds "the radical connectivity" of the Internet and the social networks "toxic to conventional power structures" and predicts that "the top-down nation-state model . . . is collapsing."[65]

Social analyst Walter Russell Mead seeks to replace "the Blue Model" (his term for twentieth-century Progressivism) with what he calls "Liberalism 5.0," which relies more on local power and the private sector. He wants the progressive-bureaucratic institutions of the twentieth century to give way to smaller, more private, less intrusive instruments that are more conducive to the creation of wealth and more protective of individual freedom.[66]

In a similar spirit, *The Economist* advocates a new "True Progressivism." This consists of a centrist politics that challenges inequality but does not impede growth; opposes large, vested interests; advocates a shift from subsidies that help the affluent and the elderly to those that foster education and help the poor; and creates a more efficient tax system without distorting deductions.[67]

These views have some resonance in public life. In foreign affairs, there are signs that the interventionist-military experience of much of the twentieth century is drawing to a close. The deeply divisive, arguably failed interventions in Vietnam, Iraq, and Afghanistan have precluded direct involvement in trouble spots like Libya, Syria, Iran, and the Ukraine.

On the domestic side, if Obamacare continues to run into Prohibition-scale difficulties, it may prove to be as large a setback to one-size-fits-all entitlements as Prohibition was to one-size-fits-all social control. And while the rise of the Tea Party and the reaction against outsized state employee perks are not decisive developments, they may well be indicative of a larger trend.

Charter schools, vouchers, and home schooling in effect take on the educational establishment. The Internet and its progeny—social networks, online higher education, more direct seller-buyer links—pose a challenge to elite expertise, the mainstream media, universities, professionals, corporations, and the bureaucracy that were so instrumental in the rise of the twentieth-century state.[68]

Another straw in the wind is Scandinavia, for long the poster child of the social democratic ideal. In recent years the region has adopted a more mixed model: generous social benefits coexisting with Milton Friedman–like experiments in reduced deficits and taxation, and much privatization in education and health care.[69]

But old ways die hard, and the cake of big-government custom, belief, and interest is not easy to slice into. Obama, like FDR and Truman and LBJ before him, has sought to substantially expand the social-democratic welfare state. Now he faces a classic American second-act problem, which afflicts national politics as it does novels and the theater.[70]

The Iraq and Afghanistan wars, with their large gaps between high-minded intent and dismaying results, are likely for some time to severely limit an assertive American foreign policy. Obamacare may produce a comparable discord between high purpose and disappointing performance. It bids fair to be the major battleground for the clash between the big-spending, big-bureaucracy, social-democratic welfare state model of the twentieth century and still nascent smaller-government alternatives.

4. HISTORY LESSONS

It is not difficult to see in certain elections, and certain presidencies, transformative impulses that set the political tone for an extended time to come. It is easy as well to see at other times a political environment that preserves the existing pattern of politics and policy rather than opening the way to new paths. What does history suggest about the character of Obama's time?

Past Presidents, Past Precedents

Woodrow Wilson's reelection in 1916 was predicated on the prospect that the Progressivism of his first term would continue. So too did Obama in 2012 send out signals that he sought not to recalibrate but to double down on his agenda.[71]

The Wilson precedent is not an encouraging one. True, he justified America's entry into World War I in Progressive terms: making the world safe for democracy; taking on the Kaiser and Imperial Germany as he previously took on political bosses and the trusts. But wartime restrictions on civil liberties and controls on agricultural prices fed a political backlash. The Democrats lost 22 House and 6 Senate seats (and control of Congress) in the 1918 congressional election. The inadequacies of the Versailles Treaty, plus the customary postwar reaction against the administration in power, made the 1920 election one of the major landslides in American history. Its victor was not a champion of change, but anodyne Warren G. Harding, who promised not nostrums but normalcy.

The next instance of second-term assertiveness is hardly more promising. After his overwhelming reelection victory in 1936, FDR sought to redefine American politics along explicitly liberal-conservative lines. He hoped to end the Supreme Court's anti–New

Deal majority by getting the power to "pack" it with additional justices. He proposed an Executive Reorganization Act designed to put a number of federal agencies directly under the White House. He set out to eliminate conservative Democratic congressional committee chairs by campaigning against them in the pre-1938 election primaries.

It is hard to imagine a more canny president, more favorably situated politically, more purposefully working to consolidate his and his party's supremacy. The result? Failure.

FDR's Court packing and Executive Reorganization bills were defenestrated by coalitions of varied interests whose toes were being stepped on, and by popular suspicion of executive overreach in the age of the dictators. So too with his "purge" of congressional conservatives: all but one were renominated. The Republicans recovered much lost ground (81 House and 6 Senate seats) in the 1938 election. With candidates Wendell Willkie in 1940 and Thomas Dewey in 1944 and 1948, the GOP came to terms with the New Deal revolution in government.

It was the Second World War that made possible Roosevelt's unprecedented third- and fourth-term reelections. Postwar prosperity undergirded the normal Democratic congressional majorities that lasted until the 1980s. After a predictable postwar congressional setback in 1946—like Wilson's in 1918 or Churchill's in 1945—Truman unexpectedly won in 1948, in sharp contrast to 1920. The GOP's Eisenhower succeeded him, hardly repudiating the New Deal revolution though hardly committed to its extension.

A new liberal challenge came with the Kennedy-Johnson era of the 1960s. Johnson read the 1964 electoral sweep as a mandate to match—or overmatch—the New Deal with his Civil and Voting Rights Acts, Medicare and Medicaid, and War on Poverty.

The broadly popular Second World War was Roosevelt's political salvation; the deeply divisive Vietnam War led to Johnson's downfall. So, to a lesser degree, did his War on Poverty, which brought much civic discord and something of a white backlash in its wake.

Johnson's successor Nixon, narrowly elected in 1968, swept his 1972 bid for a second term against McGovern, as Johnson had with Goldwater in 1964 (and as Harding did in 1920 and Eisenhower in 1952). Nixon accepted the by-now entrenched model of an imperial presidency, an expanding welfare-regulatory state and a proactive foreign policy. But Watergate undid him, much as Vietnam did LBJ.

Thereafter, from Ford and Carter in the 1970s through Reagan, Bush I, Clinton, and Bush II in ensuing decades, a more equivocal attitude toward big government and a more nuanced approach to foreign policy came into vogue. Clinton, like Eisenhower and Reagan before him, had a reasonably successful second term. As in the other cases, this was due more to contingency—domestic and foreign tranquility—than to the president's agenda.

In contrast, Obama's presidency is infused with the grand tradition of the mid-twentieth-century Democratic presidencies. Even when he doesn't explicitly draw parallels, commentators do it for him. His initial response to the Great Recession was widely viewed as a reprise of FDR's 100 Days in 1933. Obamacare is often equated with FDR's Social Security and LBJ's Medicare, his War on Inequality with Johnson's War on Poverty.[72]

What will be history's judgment as to how Obama handled his office, and his domestic and foreign policy legacy? This may be a premature question: neither has fully played out. But I think it is safe to say at this point that Obama's place in history will be defined more by who he was than by what he did.

As I argued earlier, Obama's presidential style and record—his eloquence and intellectualism, his personal detachment, his messianic bent, his electoral record—had many resemblances to Woodrow Wilson. How will his being the first African-American president compare with the impact of that not dissimilar historical event, John F. Kennedy's election as the first Catholic president?

The religious issue, so prominent in the 1960 campaign, faded quickly after Kennedy assumed office. Instead, the star power of his persona and his family became the most noted aspect of his truncated term in office. The political importance of his Catholicism rapidly faded. He was the first icon of the post–World War II mass culture, and it is in this context that he is remembered.

Obama has had a similar experience. Just as Kennedy rapidly transcended his Irish Catholic identity, so has Obama come to be judged more on what he has done (and not done) than on his race. Both men were helped by their distance from prevailing popular perceptions of their group identity. Kennedy was no more a stereotypical Irish Catholic American than Obama was a stereotypical African-American. And Obama has been as attuned to American popular culture in the early twenty-first century as Kennedy was to American popular culture in the 1960s.

The Next New Thing? Or the Same Old Same Old?

Is Obama fated to face the second-term frustrations that dogged Wilson, FDR, LBJ, and Nixon? Or is he riding a change in electoral appeal and domestic and foreign policy that will have long-term consequences comparable to the Lincoln-Republican victory over slavery and disunion, or the long-term success of FDR's response to the Great Depression and World War II?

The view that this is a transformative political time rests on the twin pillars of demography and culture. It points to changes potentially as profound as those that underlay the FDR–New Deal political upheaval.

Then the children of the new immigrants, hardscrabble farmers, and the industrial workforce came of political age. The Great

Depression unleashed long-frustrated pressures for unionism and a welfare state. The economic, cultural, and demographic changes wrought by the Second World War and postwar prosperity cemented this transformation of American politics and government.

Is ours a comparable political time? The argument in favor rests on the belief that generation Xers and millennials—a hundred million of them—have political beliefs and expectations that the Democrats are better able to tap. In this view, Obama seeks to create a "coalition of the ascendants" as effective and long-lasting as the FDR–New Deal coalition of the deprived. His second Inaugural heralded what columnist Ross Douthat called a new "liberal hour." He was ready to give up on lesser-income, culturally conservative whites—Reagan Democrats—who for half a century had been a major component of the Democratic vote.[73]

Obama's attractive Now persona has appealed to his core constituency much as FDR's Benevolent Prince image did to new immigrant and poor Americans in the 1930s. His New Age style of politicking, combined with the sophisticated techniques of the Internet, may be compared with FDR's mix of social democratic policy and urban party machines. But the strongly adverse reaction of millennials to the rollout of Obamacare speaks to the political volatility of the young.[74]

Is it likely that the triad of media, money, and organization that Obama so brilliantly brought together will wag the tail of the American political dog as effectively as machines, bosses, regions, and ethnicity did for a century and more? Certainly the liberal media–Obama administration relationship is deeply entrenched. Complex and widespread family, marriage, social, and ideological connections between them are a characteristic of the Obama years. Will this special relationship continue and shape the political future?[75]

Still to be weighed in the balance is that murky realm of the blogosphere and its hard-breathing successor, the social network world of texting, Facebooking, and tweeting. It turns out that the advent of television was only the first stage of a far more sweeping communications revolution. The impact of this brave new world on the print media is all too evident, and Obama has used it brilliantly. But is social networking closely identified with one party and one political outlook? Will it make politics more tribal or more fluid? These, too, are questions yet to be answered.[76]

The case for Obama not largely changing the political game rests first on voting statistics. There is little evidence of shifts such as those that accompanied the Jefferson, Lincoln, or Roosevelt revolutions. The data more closely resemble the up-and-down pattern of recent decades: a solid win in the perfect storm election of 2008, a large setback in 2010, and a reduced reelection margin in 2012.

Of course, what was is not necessarily what will be. But the historical record weighs heavily against a different outcome in the near future. The party of reelected presidents from 1938 to 2010 lost an average of almost 4 Senate and 38 House seats in the ensuing by-election.

The year 2014 may be different, but there is as yet no reason to expect so. Public opinion (as opposed to politicians' opinion) is divided but not polarized over health care, spending, taxation, and foreign policy. Obama's generally small-bore proposals on immigration, energy, education, jobs, taxes, and spending and his cautious, non-assertive foreign policy are what one would expect of an administration treading second-term water.[77]

History's miniaturizing lens may yet reveal that the Obama and Bush presidencies had more in common than now seems to be the case. Obama spent more and warred less than Bush. But Bush spent and Obama warred more than they were supposed to.

A final caveat: that old game-changer contingency can upset any and all apple carts. Takeoff in the domestic economy or a circle-the-wagons foreign crisis can quickly alter the political calculus.

On the cusp of the president's January 2014 State of the Union address, *New Yorker* editor David Remnick published a 17,000-word article based on a set of interviews with Obama. Familiar themes, of the sort evident from the earliest moments of Obama's time, prevailed: the easy accord of two liberal wordsmiths: the trademark Obama self-knowledge unsullied by self-doubt: "I really want to be a president who makes a difference"; and the shared assumption that Republican obduracy was the chief obstacle to the fulfillment of Obama's goals.

But beneath the customary deference was something else, something new. Obama observed that he had come to realize that a president is "essentially a relay swimmer in a river full of rapids, and that river is history, laden with structural institutional realities." There is more than a hint here of *The Great Gatsby*'s conclusion: "So we beat on, boats against the current, borne back ceaselessly into the past." Or to reiterate the Holmesian insight with which this book began: "Continuity with the past is not a duty, but only a necessity."

At the same time Obama recognized that America's is "a very fast-moving culture", and that as his second term winds down people were looking for something new. His final judgment on his record: "The President of the United States cannot remake our society, and that's probably a good thing." On reflection he added, "Not 'probably.' It's *definitely* a good thing."

What may have been intended as a pre–State of the Union puff piece turned out to be, instead, an elegy. The pro-forma boilerplate about a new birth of presidential leadership was submerged by the undertone of race run, job done. Obama's time, fated by the rules of the game, the cake of institutional custom, and the character of American politics, is inexorably approaching its sell-by date.[78]

Notes

. . .

CHAPTER ONE

1. Ron Suskind, *Confidence Men: Wall Street, Washington, and the Education of a President* (New York: Harper, 2011), 47.

2. David Remnick, *The Bridge* (New York: Knopf, 2010), 274.

3. Morton Keller, *The Unbearable Heaviness of Governing: The Obama Administration in Historical Perspective* (Stanford, CA: Hoover Institution Press, 2011), 2; Ryan Lizza, "The Obama Memos," *New Yorker*, January 30, 2012.

4. Andrew Malcolm, "New Gaffe: Obama Hails America's Historic Building of 'the Intercontinental Railroad,'" http://latimes.blogs.latimes.com, September 23, 2011.

5. James Kloppenberg, *Reading Obama: Dreams, Hope, and the American Political Tradition* (Princeton, NJ: Princeton University Press, 2010); Dinesh D'Souza, *The Roots of Obama's Rage* (New York: Regnery, 2010) and *Obama's America: Unmaking the American Dream* (New York: Regnery, 2012). See also Stanley Kurtz, *Radical-in-Chief* (New York: Threshold Press, 2010); Angelo M. Codevilla, "The Chosen One," *Claremont Review of Books*, Summer 2011, 52–58.

6. John A. Frank, *Obama on the Couch: Inside the Mind of the President* (New York: Free Press, 2011); see also Avner Falk, *The Riddle of Barack Obama: A Psychobiography* (Santa Barbara: Praeger, 2010). For a less favorable view, see Stanley A. Renshon, *Barack Obama and the Politics of Redemption* (New York: Routledge, 2012).

7. Adulatory: Jonathan Alter, *The Promise: President Obama, Year One* (New York: Simon and Schuster, 2010) and (somewhat less so) *The Center Holds: Obama and His Enemies* (New York: Simon and Schuster, 2013). Mixed: Suskind, *Confidence Men*; Bob Woodward, *The Price of Politics* (New York: Simon and Schuster, 2012); Condemnatory: Edward Klein, *The Amateur* (Washington, DC: Regnery, 2012) Charles R. Kesler, *I Am the Change: Barack Obama and the Crisis of Liberalism* (New York: Broadside Press, 2012). See also Keller, *Unbearable Heaviness.*

8. Richard Cohen, "Obama Should Learn from LBJ," realclearpolitics.com, May 8, 2012; Morton Keller, *America's Three Regimes* (New York: Oxford, 2007), Part Four.

9. Maureen Dowd, "Showtime at the Apollo," www.nytimes.com, January 21, 2012; Jeffrey M. Jones, "Obama Ratings Historically Polarized," www.gallup.com/poll, May 12, 2012; Suskind, *Confidence Men*, 302.

10. Robert W. Merry, "The Psychology of Barack Obama," http://nationalinterest.org, October 16, 2013, applies the typology of James D. Barber's *The Presidential Character* (4th ed., New York: Penguin, 2009) to put Obama alongside predecessors such as John Adams, Herbert Hoover, and Wilson as an "Active-Negative" chief executive.

11. "Obama Loves Interviews, Does Not Love Press Conferences or Q&A's, Study Shows," huffingtonpost.com, February 26, 2012; Keith Koffler, "WH Press Corps Goes Seven Weeks Without a Question," www.whitehousedossier.com, August 6, 2012.

12. Suskind, *Confidence Men*, 14, 37.

13. Suskind, *Confidence Men*, 478–481; David Nakamura, "Obama: Biggest Mistake Was Failing to 'Tell a Story' to American Public," www.washingtonpost.com, July 12, 2012.

14. On Obama and Lincoln, Carl M. Cannon, "Obama's Lincoln Demurral Has a Hollow Ring," www.realclearpolitics.com, December 31, 2012; Suskind, *Confidence Men*, 151, 155, 161, 480–481.

15. www.theBlaze.com, December 18, 2011.

16. Suskind, *Confidence Men*, 480–482; Jonah Goldberg, "Obama's Reagan Parallels Are Falling Away," www.usatoday.com, July 5, 2011; Steven F. Hayward, "The Liberal Misappropriation of a Conservative President," *Commentary*, October 2011, 13–19.

17. Jane Harman, "Woodrow Wilson's Second Term May Be Model for Barack Obama's," http://dyn.politico.com, November 7, 2012.

18. Robert Reich, "President Barack Obama Could Learn from FDR," www.sfgate.com, November 7, 2010; Jay Cost, "Would He Rather Fight Than Switch?," www.weeklystandard.com, November 1, 2010.

19. George C. Edwards III, *Overreach: Leadership in the Obama Presidency* (Princeton, NJ: Princeton University Press, 2012).

20. Peter Baker, "The White House Looks for Work," www.nytimes.com, January 19, 2011, 11. See also Michael Grunwald, *The New New Deal* (New York: Simon and Schuster, 2012).

21. Evan Thomas, "Truth or Consequences," www.newsweek.com, November 13, 2010; "Crunch Time," *The Economist*, January 29, 2011, 21; Jay Cost, "Memo to the Media: Obama Is Not Popular!" www.weeklystandard.com; Fouad Ajami, "Barack Obama the Pessimist," *Wall Street Journal*, August 1, 2011.

22. Scott Wilson, "Obama, the Loner President," www.washingtonpost.com, October 7, 2011; Maureen Dowd, "Showtime at the Apollo," www.nytimes.com, January 21, 2011; "Aimless Obama Walks Alone," www.nypost.com, October 9, 2011.

23. Thomas J. Sugrue, *Not Even Past: Barack Obama and the Burden of Race* (Princeton, NJ: Princeton University Press, 2010); Michael P. Jeffries, *Paint the White House Black: Barack Obama and the Meaning of Race in America* (Stanford, CA: Stanford University Press, 2012).

24. "Berry: Obama Said 'Big Difference' Between '10 and '94 is 'Me,'" www.politico.com, January 25, 2010.

25. Mead, "Two Stools"; "The Courage Factor," *The Economist*, March 19, 2011. See also Peter Baker, "Searching for Vision," www.nytimes.com, April 9, 2011; from the right, Linda Chavez, "Obama's Leadership Deficit," www.washingtonexaminer.com, July 29, 2011; from the left, Robert Reich, "The Empty Bully Pulpit," www.huffingtonpost.com, July 29, 2011, and Drew Westen, "What Happened to Obama?," www.nytimes.com, August 7, 2011.

26. Martin S. Indyk et al., *Bending History: Barack Obama's Foreign Policy* (Washington, DC: Brookings Institution, 2012).

27. Matt Bai, "Still Waiting for the Narrator in Chief," www.nytimes.com, October 30, 2012.

28. Franklin Foer, "Putting the President on the Couch," www.tnr.com, November 16, 2012; Kimberley A. Strassel, "Cliff-Top Lessons for the GOP," *Wall Street Journal*, December 28, 2012, A13; Edward-Isaac Dovere, "President Obama's 2nd-term History Lessons," http://dyn.politico.com, November 22, 2012.

29. James Taranto, "What Would Bulworth Do?," http://online.wsj.com, May 16, 2013.

30. Matthew Continetti, "Obama on His Heels," http://freebeacon.com, March 8, 2013; James Taranto, "The Difference Between 43 and 44? Not So Much," *Wall Street Journal*, April 6, 2013, A19.

31. Fred Barnes, "The Decline of Obama," www.weeklystandard.com, April 22, 2013; Maureen Dowd, "President of Scandinavia," www.nytimes.com, May 28, 2013; Mike Allen and Jim Vendenhei, "Behind the Curtain: Obama, Boxed In," http://dyn.politico.com, April 18, 2013; Michael O'Brien, "Obama Leadership Style Raises Question of 'Who Is in Control?,'" http://nbcpolitics.nbcnews.com, October 31, 2013.

32. Peter Baker, "An Onset of Woes Raises Questions on Obama Vision," www.nytimes.com, May 15, 2013; Dan Balz, "Obama's Second Term Clouded by Controversies," www.washingtonpost.com, May 14, 2013; Susan Page, "Obama's Agenda Scorched in Firestorm," www.usatoday.com, June 7, 2013; Maureen Dowd, "Cat on a Hot Stove," www.nytimes.com, October 19, 2013.

33. "How to Save Obama's Second Term," *The Economist*, May 25, 2013, 13.

34. Gerald F. Seib, "Surveillance Shows Obama's Paradoxes," *Wall Street Journal*, June 11, 2013, A8; Ron Fournier, "Do You Trust This Man?," www.nationaljournal.com, June 17, 2013; Lloyd Green, "The Sprawling, Dimming Age of Obama," www.thedailybeast.com, June 30, 2013.

CHAPTER TWO

1. Morton Keller, *The Unbearable Heaviness of Governing* (Stanford, CA: Hoover Institution Press, 2010).

2. Arthur M. Schlesinger Jr., *The Imperial Presidency* (Boston: Houghton Mifflin, 1973); Kimberley A. Strassel, "Obama's Imperial Presidency," *Wall Street Journal*, July 6, 2012, A11.

3. Ben Goad and Julian Hattern, "Regulation Nation: Obama Expands the Regulatory State," http://thehill.com, August 19, 2013.

4. Robert Samuelson, "Big Government on the Brink," www.realclearpolitics.com, April 11, 2011.

5. James Q. Wilson, "'Policy Intellectuals' and Public Policy," in James Q. Wilson, *American Politics, Then and Now* (Washington, DC: AEI Press, 2010), 19–34; Morton Keller, *America's Three Regimes* (New York: Oxford, 2007), chs. 10 and 11.

6. David Malpass, "And the Crisis Winner Is? Government," *Wall Street Journal*, December 16, 2011, A19; "Minds Like Machines," *Economist*, November 19, 2011, 63.

7. Dana Blanton, "Fox News Poll: Trust in Government Hits New Low," www.foxnews.com, July 20, 2011; Nile Gardiner, "Why Barack Obama Could Be America's Last Big Government President," http://blogs.telegraph.co.uk, September 27, 2011.

8. Walter Russell Mead, "Chicken House Rules," http://blogs.the-american-interest.com, December 21, 2011.

9. Stephen Dinan, "Congress Logs Most Futile Legislative Year on Record," www.washingtontimes.com, January 15, 2012; "Capitol Hill Least Productive Congress Ever: 112th Fought 'About Everything,'" www.washingtontimes.com, January 9, 2013; Dinan, "Futility Record: House Republicans Sputter toward One of the Worst Years on Record," www.washingtontimes.com, July 9, 2013.

10. "The Polarization of the Congressional Parties," http://voteview.com, January, 18, 2013.

11. Valerie Richardson, "Press Turns Out a Recent Glut of 'Rare Bipartisan' Breakthroughs," www.washingtontimes.com, December 15, 2011.

12. On McCain, *New York Times*, Oct 25, 2010; "Obama, Boehner Meet for First Time in Seven Months," www.washingtonpost/blogs.com, February 29, 2012.

13. Keller, *Unbearable Heaviness*, 16–20; "Shenanigans and Seriousness," *Economist*, December 18, 2008.

14. Matt Bai, "The Paradox of a Legislative President," www.nytimes.com, August 18, 2010.

15. Peter J. Boyer, "House Rule," www.newyorker.com, December 13, 2010.

16. "The Very Odd Couple," *Economist*, June 30, 2012, 35.

17. "Partisan D.C.: Obama's Broken Promise," Politico.com, January 17, 2012.

18. Charlie Cook, "All Stirred Up," *National Journal*, January 27, 2012.

19. Jesse Weed, "By His Fruits Ye Shall Know Him: Obama's Subversive Appointments," americanthinker.com, April 16, 2012.

20. Glenn Thrush, "Locked in the Cabinet," www.politico.com/magazine, November 2013; Rich Lowry, "Holder's Identity Problem," www.realclearpolitics.com, March 13, 2012.

21. "Room at the Top," *Economist*, November 17, 2012, 27.

22. Suskind, *Confidence Men: Wall Street, Washington, and the Education of a President* (New York: Harper, 2011), 196.

23. Suskind, *Confidence Men*, 143, 151, 195–196, 397.

24. Suskind, *Confidence Men*, 158, 363–365, 375, 380, 442.

25. Jonathan Weisman, "White House's Next Task: Rebuilding Policy Team," *Wall Street Journal*, October 29, 2010, A1.

26. Peter Baker, "The Limits of Rahmism," www.nytimes.com, March 14, 2010; Paul Starobin, "The Rise and Fall of Bill Daley: An Inside Account," *New Republic*, January 18, 2012; Jonathan Alter, "How Bill Daley Died a Death of a Thousand Cuts," www.bloomberg.com, January 12, 2012.

27. John Feehery, "Obama's Real Reelection Problem," www.thehill.com, January 10, 2012.

28. Peggy Noonan, "Amateur Hour at the White House," http://online.wsj.com, September 24, 2011; Roger Cohen, "Obama's Team of Idolizers," www.nytimes.com, August 27, 2012; Jo Becker, "The Other Power in the West Wing," www.nytimes.com, September 1, 2012; Jason Horowitz, "Valerie Jarrett's Latest Role: Shoring up Obama's Support Base," www.washingtonpost.com, October 25, 2011.

29. "The Reorganization Man," *Wall Street Journal*, January 14–15, 2012, A12; Dennis Cauchon, "More Federal Workers' Pay Tops $150,000," www.usatoday.com, November 10, 2010; Ralph Smith, "End of the Federal Pay Freeze Announced," www.fedsmith.com, December 27, 2012.

30. Ross Douthat, "Washington versus America," www.nytimes.com, September 22; 2012; Ross Douthat, "The Wealth of Washington," http://douthat.blogs.nytimes.com, September 26, 2012; Daniel Gade,

"Why the VA Is Buried in Disability Claims," *Wall Street Journal*, June 24, 2013, A17.

31. Carol Morello and Ted Mellnik, "Seven of Nation's 10 Most Affluent Counties Are in Washington Region," www.washingtonpost.com, September 20, 2012; David Leonhardt, "Why D.C. Is Doing So Well," www.nytimes.com, August 4, 2012; Annie Lowrey, "Washington's Economic Boom, Financed by You," www.nytimes.com, January 10, 2013. See also Mark Leibovich, *This Town* (New York: Penguin, 2013), a portrayal of "America's Gilded Capital."

32. Jesse Weed, "By His Fruits," www.americanthinker.com, April 16, 2012.

33. Keller, *Unbearable Heaviness*, 26–27; Sarah Kliff, "Medicare Administrator Donald Berwick Resigns in the Face of Republican Opposition," www.washingtonpost.com, November 23, 2011.

34. Kara Rowland, "Obama Dethrones Czars, Debate Simmers," www.washingtontimes.com, July 22, 2011; Ramsay Cox, "Senate Confirms All Five NLRB Members," www.thehill.com, July 31, 2013. See also Mitchell A. Sollenberger and Mark J. Rozell, *The President's Czars: Undermining Congress and the Constitution* (Lawrence: University Press of Kansas, 2012).

35. Erin Dian Drumbacher, "Senior Executives Give Low Marks to Obama Appointees," www.nationaljournal.com, May 27, 2011.

36. Philip Rucker, "Officials Hail USAID Administrator's Crisis Management Skills," www.washingtonpost.com, January 15, 2010; Jack Shafer, "Beat Sweetener: The Rajiv Shah Edition," www.slate.com, January 15, 2010; Mark Landler, "Curing the Ills of America's Top Foreign Aid Program," www.nytimes.com, October 23, 2010; Dana Milbank, "The Sad Math of U.S. Aid in Haiti: 6 Months, 2 Percent," www.washingtonpost.com, July 13, 2010.

37. Robert Pear, "U.S. Plans Stealth Survey on Access to Doctors," www.nytimes.com, June 28, 2011; Pear, "Administration Halts Survey of Making Doctor Visits," www.nytimes.com, June 28, 2011.

38. Eric Lichtblau and Scott Shane, "In Vast Effort, F.D.A. Spied on E-Mails of Its Own Scientists," www.nytimes.com, July 14, 2012.

39. Sharon LaFreniere, "U.S. Opens Spigot after Farmers Claim Discrimination," www.nytimes.com, April 25, 2013.

40. Jonathan Rauch, *Demosclerosis: The Silent Killer of American Government* (New York: Times Books, 1994); Jonathan Rauch, *Government's End* (New York: Public Affairs Press, 1999).

41. On award, “Return of the Plumbers,” *Economist*, June 18, 2011, 38; Gabriel Sherman, “Revolver,” http://nymag.com, April 10, 2011.

42. Ryan Tracy, “Nuclear Agency Staff Blast Bosses over Yucca Decision,” http://online.wsj.com, June 24, 2011.

43. Keller, *Unbearable Heaviness*, 31; Rich Lowry, “Holder’s Identity Problem,” www.realclearpolitics.com, March 13, 2012.

44. Mike McIntrye and Michael Luo, “White House Opens Door to Big Donors, and Lobbyists Slip In,” www.nytimes.com, April 15, 2012; Paul Bedard, “Obama Rewards Campaign Donors with Ambassador Jobs,” www.usnews.com, June 30, 2010.

45. “How Did Solyndra Get a Sweetheart Interest Rate?,” http://hotair.com, September 7, 2011; Carol D. Leonnig and Joe Stephens, “Solyndra E-mails: Dept. of Energy Was Poised to Approve $469 Million for Firm,” www.washingtonpost.com, October 5, 2011; Matthew Daly, “George Kaiser, Obama Donor, Discussed Solyndra Loan with White House, Emails Show,” www.huffingtonpost.com, November 9, 2011.

46. Editorial Board, “President Obama’s Dragnet,” www.nytimes.com, June 6, 2013; Brett Zongker, “Obama Brings Chilling Effect on Journalism,” www.realclearpolitics.com, October 10, 2013.

47. Peter Baker and David E. Sanger, “Obama Calls Surveillance Programs Legal and Limited,” www.nytimes.com, June 7, 2013.

48. Morton Keller, “Corruption in America: Continuity and Change,” in Abraham S. Eisenstadt et al., eds., *Before Watergate* (Brooklyn, NY: Brooklyn College Press, 1978), 7–19; “The Press and the IRS,” http://online.wsj.com, September 19, 2013.

49. Harry Stein, “Not a Crook—Yet,” www.cityjournal.org, May 14, 2013; Matthew Continetti, “All in the Family: Why the Mainstream Media Failed to Break Obama Scandals,” http://freebeacon.com, June 14, 2013; “ACLU v. IRS v. New York Times,” www.nypost.com, May 14, 2013; Eugene Robinson, “It’s News, Not Espionage,” http:/dyn.realclearpolitics. com, May 21, 2013; Peggy Noonan, “Why This Scandal Is Different,” http://bls.wsj.com, May 31, 2013.

50. Jay Sekulow, “Obama’s Fingerprints All over IRS Tea Party Scandals,” www.foxnews.com, October 20, 2013.

51. Peggy Noonan, “Privacy Isn’t All We’re Losing,” http://online.wsj.com, June 13, 2013.

52. Jonathan Turley, “The Rise of the Fourth Branch of Government,” www.washingtonpost.com, May 14, 2013. See also Dan Balz, “Obama’s

Trust-in-Government Deficit," www.washingtonpost.com, May 18, 2013; Jay Cost, "Our Masters, the Bureaucrats," www.weeklystandard.com, June 14, 2013; Rich Lowry, "The Lois Lerner State," http://dyn.realclearpolitics.com, May 11, 2013.

CHAPTER THREE

1. Morton Keller, *Regulating a New Economy: Public Policy and Economic Change in America, 1900–1933* (Cambridge: Harvard University Press, 1990); Morton Keller, *Regulating a New Society: Public Policy and Social Change in America, 1900–1933* (Cambridge: Harvard University Press, 1994).

2. Philip K. Howard, "One Nation, Under Too Many Laws," www.washingtonpost.com, December 12, 2010.

3. "Over-Regulated America," www.economist.com, February 25, 2012.

4. James Rosen, "Regulation Nation: New Study Finds Obama Is 'No. 1 Regulator,'" www.foxnews.com, March 15, 2012; Uwe E. Reinhardt, "Behind the Burden of Regulation," www.nytimes.com, May 12, 2012.

5. Barack Obama, "Toward a 21st Century Regulatory System," *Wall Street Journal*, January 18, 2011.

6. "The Rule of More," www.economist.com, February 25, 2012; "Breathing Room," *Economist*, September 8, 2012, 31.

7. "Over-Regulated America."

8. Joseph Postell, "A Czar Is Born," *Claremont Review of Books* 10, no. 4 (Fall 2010): 26–31; "Of Sunstein and Sunsets," www.economist.com, February 25, 2012; John M. Broder, "Powerful Shaper of U.S. Rules Quits, with Critics in Wake," www.nytimes.com, August 3, 2012; Cass Sunstein, *Simpler: The Future of Government* (New York: Simon and Schuster, 2013).

9. Keller, *Regulating a New Economy*, chs. 2–4; "Rules for Fools," *Economist*, May 14, 2011, 84.

10. Ezra Klein, "Health-Reform Advocates Have Little to Fear from Judge's Ruling," www.washingtonpost.com, December 13, 2010; Robert Pear, "Changing Stance, Administration Now Defends Insurance Mandate as a Tax," www.nytimes.com, July 18, 2010. For conservative critiques, see Doug Bandow, "Does the Constitution Mean Anything?," http://spectator.org, December 17, 2010; Yuval Levin, "Overruling Obamacare," www.weeklystandard.com, December 27, 2010.

11. Charles Lane, "The Difficult Question of the Health-Care Law's Constitutionality," http://voices.washingtonpost.com, December 14, 2010.

12. Robert Barnes, "How the Roberts Court Could Save Obama's Health-Care Reform," www.washingtonpost.com, March 18, 2012; Adam J. White, "Without Precedent," www.weeklystandard.com, March 19, 2012; "Full-Court Press," *Economist*, March 31, 2012, 37; Philip Klein, "AP Poll: Obamacare Support Hits Record Low of 29 Percent," http://campaign2012 .washingtonexaminer.com, December 16, 2011. See also Tevi Troy, "ObamaCare at the Supreme Court," *Commentary*, February 2012, 20–24.

13. Linda Greenhouse, "Never Before," www.opinionator.blogs.nytimes .com, April 2, 2012; David Dow, "Impeach the Supreme Court Justices if They Overturn Health-Care Law," www.thedailybeast.com, April 5, 2012; Timothy Noah, "Life Sentences," www.tnr.com, April 6, 2012; Ronald Brownstein, "5–4 and 50–50," www.nationaljournal.com, April 6, 2012.

14. George F. Will, "Liberals Put the Squeeze to Justice Roberts," www.washingtonpost.com, May 25, 2012.

15. Charles Lane, "John Roberts's Compromise of 2012," www .washingtonpost.com, June 29, 2012; Sean Trende, "The Chief Justice's Gambit," www.realclearpolitics.com, June 28, 2012.

16. Linda Greenhouse, "The Real John Roberts Emerges," http:// opinionator.blogs.nytimes.com, June 29, 2013; Adam Liptak, "Chief Justice Roberts Plays a Long Game on Supreme Court," www.nytimes.com, June 27, 2013; "A Lesson in Packing," *Economist*, June 8, 2013, 34.

17. Steven Malanga, "Rise of the Republican Governors," *City Journal* 23, no. 2 (Spring 2013): 12–21.

18. Michael Cooper, "States Want to Have Say during Talks over Budget," www.nytimes.com, November 24, 2012; "Political Petri Dishes," *Economist*, September 22, 2012, 65.

19. "All Fall Down," *Economist*, March 17, 2012, 36–37.

20. Keller, *Regulating a New Economy*; Keller, *Regulating a New Society*.

21. Morton Keller, *America's Three Regimes* (New York: Oxford, 2007), ch. 9.

22. Morton Keller, "Debt: The Shame of Cities and States," *Policy Review* 169 (October–November 2011): 3–12; Walter Russell Mead, "Time to Occupy State Pensions," http://blogs.the-american-interest.com, June 25, 2012.

23. Andrew G. Biggs and Jason Richwine, "Overpaid Public Workers: The Evidence Mounts," *Wall Street Journal*, April 11, 2012, A13.

24. Kimberley A. Strassel, "The Reform Governors Who Led the Way," *Wall Street Journal*, August 28, 2012, A15.

25. On Daniels, see "The Right Stuff," www.economist.com, August 19, 2010; on Christie, see Matt Bai, "How Chris Christie Did His Homework," www.nytimes.com, February 24, 2011; Benjamin Wallace-Wells, "What Is Chris Christie Doing Right?," www.nymag.com, August 4, 2012.

26. "Next, Walk on Water," *Economist*, January 28, 2012; Walter Russell Mead, "Cuomo Takes on Unions," www.blogs.the-american-interest .com, May 26, 2012; David Catanese, "The Phlegmatic Andrew Cuomo," www.therun2016.com, June 26, 2013.

27. Michael Cooper, "States Face Tough Choices Even as Downturn Ends," www.nytimes.com, July 10, 2012; Chris Edwards, "The Best and Worst Governors on Growth," *Wall Street Journal*, October 9, 2012, A17; Mary Williams Walsh, "Illinois Debt Takes Toll, Study Finds," www .nytimes.com, October 24, 2012; on Rhode Island, "Improvident," *Economist*, May 5, 2012, 32.

28. Carl M. Cannon and Tom Bevan, "Rising Generation of Wis. Stars Grabs GOP Reins," www.realclearpolitics.com, August 28, 2012.

29. Kimberley Strossel, "Scott Walker's Education Victory," *Wall Street Journal*, June 8, 2012, A11; Ronald Brownstein, "A False Choice," www .nationaljournal.com, June 7, 2012; Charles Lane, "Who's Progressive in Wisconsin," www.washingtonpost.com, February 7, 2012.

30. Kevin Starr, *Golden Dreams: California in an Age of Abundance* (New York: Oxford, 2009); "Fading into Irrelevance," *Economist*, June 30, 2012, 27.

31. Joel Kotkin, "The New Class Warfare," www.cityjournal.org, April 30, 2012; "Not Quite Greek, but Still Weak," www.economist.com, June 16, 2012; "The Great California Exodus," *Wall Street Journal*, April 21–22, 2012, A13.

32. Ira Stoll, "Jerry Brown's Vetoes and the Limits of Progressivism," http://reason.com, October 1, 2012; Brooks Barnes, "Californians Face Rival Ballot Initiatives That Would Raise Taxes and Aid Schools," www.nytimes .com, September 10, 2012; "Brownian Motion," *Economist*, November 17, 2012, 25; Conn Carroll, "The California Spending Rush," http://washington-examiner.com, February 25, 2013; Walter Russell Mead, "State 'Recovery' Is Figment of Blue Imagination," http://blogs.the-american-interest.com, June 1, 2013; "Ruinous Promises," *Economist*, June 15, 2013, 13.

33. Arthur B. Laffer, "The States Are Leading a Pro-Growth Rebellion," *Wall Street Journal*, February 11, 2012; Keller, "Debt," 6; Brian Barry,

"Blue States' Fiscal Woes Test Obama," wwwbloomberg.com, January 9, 2013.

34. Ethan Epstein, "One Tough Nutter," *City Journal* 23, no. 2 (Spring 2013): 54–60.

35. Lyndsey Layton, "Democratic Mayors Challenge Teachers Unions in Urban Political Shift," www.washingtonpost.com, March 31, 2012; Anthony Flint, "The Next Big Financial Crisis That Could Cripple Cities," http://www.theatlantic.cities.com, September 28, 2012; Mary Williams Walsh and Danny Hakim, "Public Pensions Faulted for Bets on Rosy Returns," www.nytimes.com, May 28, 2012; Rich Yeselson, "Bill de Blasio's America," www.politico.com, August 29, 2014.

36. Danny Hakim, "Amid Gains, Municipalities in Dire Straits," www.nytimes.com, March 14, 2012; Malia Wollan, "Mediation Fails, Pushing Stockton Toward Bankruptcy," www.nytimes.com, June 27, 2012; Michael Cooper and Mary Williams Walsh, "San Diego and San Jose Lead Way in Pension Cuts," www.nytimes.com, June 6, 2012; "Mayors to the Rescue," *Economist*, October 26, 2013, 36; Matthew Dolan, "Record Bankruptcy for Detroit," www.onlinewsj.com, July 19, 2013; Bill Vlasic, "In Testimony, Michigan Governor Says Bankruptcy Was Right Call for Detroit," www.nytimes.com, October 29, 2013.

37. "Rambo vs. Springfield," *Wall Street Journal*, May 30, 2012, A12; Aaron M. Renn, "The Second-Rate City?," www.city-journal.org, Spring 2012; Stephanie Banchero and Caoline Porter, "With Strike Over, Chicago Faces Another Test," *Wall Street Journal*, September 20, 2012, A7; Tim Cavanaugh, "Unions vs. Democratic Mayors," http://reason.com, November 19, 2012; "Class Dismissed," wwww.economist.com, March 30, 2013.

38. "State of Renewal," *Economist*, June 2, 2012, 18; "Upswing," *Economist*, June 2, 2012, 35.

39. Mary Williams Walsh and Michael Cooper, "Gloomy Forecast for States, Even if Economy Rebounds," www.nytimes.com, July 17, 2012; Michael Corkery, "Pension Crisis Looms Despite Cuts," *Wall Street Journal*, September 22–23, 2012, A1.

CHAPTER FOUR

1. Randall Hoven, "Liberal Myths vs. Reality," www.nypost.com, December 18, 2010.

2. Jon Meacham, "We Are All Socialists Now," www.thedailybeast.com, February 6, 2009; on Friedman, *Time*, February 4, 1966.

3. Ron Suskind, *Confidence Men: Wall Street, Washington, and the Education of a President* (New York: Harper, 2011).

4. Ezra Klein, "The Anti-Business President's Pro-Business Recovery," www.washingtonpost.com, August 8, 2010; John Cassidy, "Replay," www.newyorker.com, March 26, 2012.

5. Jay Cost, "The Store Is Closed," www.weeklystandard.com, August 24, 2012.

6. Ryan's plan can be found at www.roadmap.republicans.budget.house.gov; Robert Samuelson, "The Crisis of the Old Order," www.realclearpolitics.com, July 25, 2011.

7. David Leonhardt, "The Gridlock Where Debts Meet Politics," www.nytimes.com, November 5, 2011; Victor Davis Hanson, "A Tottering Technocracy," www.nationalreview.com, August 9, 2011.

8. "A Bipartisan Triumph," *Wall Street Journal*, October 14, 2011; "Marginal Revolutionaries," *Economist*, December 31, 2011, 51; "Toss a Coin," www.economist.com, January 12, 2013.

9. "Unbottled Gini," *Economist*, January 22, 2011, 71; "The Rich and the Rest," *Economist*, January 22, 2011, 13; "The Beautiful and the Damned," *Economist*, January 22, 2011, 90.

10. Caroline Baum, "Keynesians Revive a Depression Idea," www.bloomberg.com, December 4, 2013; Robert Samuelson, "Behind the Economic Pessimism," www.realclearpolitics.com, July 30, 2012; "American Idiocracy," *Economist*, August 13, 2011.

11. John C. Michaelson, "The High Costs of Very Low Interest Rates," http://online.wsj.com, August 11, 2010; "Not Open for Business," *Economist*, October 12, 2013, 78.

12. Amity Shlaes, "What Paul Krugman Misses about 1937 Redux: Echoes," www.bloomberg.com, June 6, 2011; Matthew Continetti, "The Zombie Recovery," http://weeklystandard.com, August 16, 2010; on regulation, see "Someone Will Pay," www.economist.com, September 16, 2010, "Clause and Effect," www.economist.com, October 29, 2011, 88.

13. Sylvia Nasar, *Grand Pursuit: The Story of Economic Genius* (New York: Simon and Schuster, 2011), 462.

14. Gretchen Morgenson, "The Rescue That Missed Wall Street," www.nytimes.com, August 27, 2011; Gretchen Morgenson, "Into the Bailout Buzz Saw," www.nytimes.com, July 21, 2012; Neil Barosky, *Bailout: An*

Inside Account of How Washington Abandoned Main Street While Rescuing Wall Street (New York: Free Press, 2012); Sheila Bair, *Bull by the Horns: Fighting to Save Main Street from Wall Street and Wall Street from Itself* (New York: Free Press, 2012).

15. Morton Keller, *The Unbearable Heaviness of Governing: The Obama Administration in Historical Perspective* (Stanford, CA: Hoover Institution Press, 2010), 37–41.

16. Keller, *Unbearable Heaviness*, 63–64.

17. Macey quoted in "Too Big Not to Fail," www.economist.com, February 18, 2013. See also Robert Kaiser, *Act of Congress: How America's Essential Institution Works, and How It Doesn't* (New York: Knopf, 2013).

18. "Law and Disorder," *Economist*, October 13, 2012, 83–85; Gretchen Morgenson, "How Mr. Volcker Would Fix It," www.nytimes.com, October 22, 2011; "Dodd-Frank, Nearly Three Years Later," http://apps.washingtonpost.com, July 6, 2013; Nicole Gelinas, "Too Convoluted to Succeed," *City Journal* 23, no. 4 (Autumn 2013): 21–29.

19. "Fed Writes Sweeping Rules from Behind Closed Doors," *Wall Street Journal*, February 21, 2012, A1.

20. Lawrence Lessig, "The Roots of the Next Financial Crisis: How Wall Street Undermines Reform," www.thedailybeast.com, June 23, 2013; Gretchen Morgenson, "Trying to Slam the Bailout Door," www.nytimes.com, April 28, 2013.

21. Suskind, *Confidence Men*, 153; Ryan Lizza, "The Obama Memos," www.newyorker.com, January 30, 2012.

22. Keller, *Unbearable Heaviness*, 43–44.

23. Suskind *Confidence Men*, 162.

24. Keller, *Unbearable Heaviness*, 41–55.

25. Michael Grunwald, *The New New Deal: The Hidden Story of Change in the Obama Era* (New York: Simon and Schuster, 2012); William Voegeli, "The Same Old Deal," *Claremont Review of Books* 13 (Winter 2012–2013): 12–18.

26. Suskind, *Confidence Men*, 19.

27. Kimberley Amadeo, "The Auto Industry Bailout," www.useconomy.about.com, November 27, 2013.

28. Michael Grabell, "How the $800B Stimulus Failed," *New York Post*, January 29, 2012.

29. Timothy Conley and Bill Dupor, "The American Recovery and Reinvestment Act: Public Sector Jobs Saved, Private Sector Jobs Forestalled,"

www.web.econ.Ohio-state.edu, May 17, 2011; "CBO: Stimulus Hurts Economy in Long Run," www.washingtontimes.com, November 22, 2011.

30. Jim Epstein, "Why Obama's Stimulus Failed: A Case Study of Silver Spring, Maryland," www.reason.com, December 8, 2011; Ron Hart, "Where Did the Stimulus Money Go?" www.ocregister.com, March 26, 2013. See also Peter Suderman, "Down the Drain," http://reason.com, April 15, 2013.

31. Josh Gerstein, "President Obama's Jobs Panel Missing in Action," http://dyn.politico.com, July 18, 2012.

32. Phil Gramm, "Reagan and Obama: A Tale of Two Recoveries," *Wall Street Journal*, August 30, 2012, A15.

33. Michael Barone, "Obama's Pathetic, Pedestrian Speech," www.realclearpolitics.com, September 12, 2011; Clive Crook, "Obama's New Stimulus," www.theatlantic.com, September 9, 2011.

34. "Hunting the Rich," *Economist*, September 24, 2011, 13; "Diving into the Rich Pool," *Economist*, September 24, 2011, 83.

35. "No More Mr. Nice Guy," *Economist*, September 24, 2011, 35; Tim Cavanaugh, "They Gave a Recovery and Nobody Came," http://reason.com, September 15, 2011; Josh Sanburn, "Paul Krugman: An Alien Invasion Could Fix the Economy," www.time.com, August 16, 2011.

36. Joe Nocera, "How Democrats Hurt Jobs," www.nytimes.com, August 22, 2011; "Boeing Bullied," *Economist*, December 17, 2011, 115.

37. "Keystone XL Pipeline: Obama Administration Announcing It Will Not Go Forward with Controversial Plan," www.huffingtonpost.com, January 18, 2012; Jackie Calmes, "In Oklahoma, Obama Declares Pipeline Support," www.nytimes.com, March 22, 2012.

38. Catherine Rampell, "U.S. Added Only 115,000 Jobs in April; Rate Is 8.1%," www.nytimes.com, May 5, 2012.

39. Nelson D. Schwartz, "Many Rival Nations Surge Past the U.S. in Adding New Jobs," www.nytimes.com, June 7, 2013; Walter Russell Mead, "The Jobs Crisis: Bigger Than You Think," http://blogs.the-american-interest.com, May 10, 2013; Gretchen Morgenson, "New Jobs! If Only It Were True," www.nytimes.com, August 24, 2013.

40. Cavanaugh, "They Gave a Recovery"; Richard W. Stevenson, "Early Economic Projections Could Haunt Obama in 2012," http://thecaucus.blogs.nytimes.com, November 4, 2011.

41. Dylan Matthews, "Everything Obama Has Done—and Wants to Do—on Taxes in One Post," www.washingtonpost.com, July 10, 2012.

42. Gretchen Morgenson, "U.S. Has Binged. Soon It'll Be Time to Pay the Tab," www.nytimes.com, May 28, 2011; Lori Montgomery, "Ever-Increasing Tax Breaks for U.S. Families Eclipse Benefits for Special Interests," www.washingtonpost.com, September 17, 2011; Bruce Bartlett, "The True Federal Debt," http://economix.blogs.nytimes.com, January 3, 2012.

43. Bruce Bartlett, *The Benefit and the Burden: Tax Reform: Why We Need It and What It Will Take* (New York: Simon and Schuster, 2012); Joshua Green, "The 3-Word Phrase That Signals Obama's Intentions on Taxes," www.theatlantic.com, April 23, 2011; "The Grover Norquist Tax Myth," www.washingtonpost.com, November 24, 2011; "Paul, Cain and Romney: Loving the Flat Tax in the GOP," www.washingtontimes.com, October 31, 2011; William G. Gale and Benjamin H. Harris, "A VAT for the United States: Part of the Solution," www.brookings.edu, March 3, 2011.

44. Suskind, *Confidence Men*, 476.

45. "Confronting the Monster," *Economist*, November 20, 2010, 29.

46. "Someone Will Pay," www.economist.com, September 16, 2011; "Where the Tax Money Is," *Wall Street Journal*, April 18, 2011, A14.

47. Alan Reynolds, "Obama's Soak-the-Rich Tax Hikes Won't Work," *Wall Street Journal*, April 14, 2011, A17; "Diving into the Rich Pool," *Economist*, September 24, 2011, 83.

48. Ari Fleischer, "Calling Obama's Payroll Tax Bluff," *Wall Street Journal*, December 16, 2011; Ira Stoll, "The Payroll-Tax Holiday from Hell," *Commentary*, February 2012, 25–28.

49. Naftali Bendavid and Greg Hitt, "Congress Approves Obama's 3.6 Trillion Budget," www.wsj.com, April 3, 2009.

50. "President's Budget Sinks, 97–0," http://thehill.com, May 25, 2011; Paul Ryan, "The GOP Budget and America's Future," *Wall Street Journal*, March 20, 2012, A15; Ross Douthat, "Budgeting for Opportunity," www.nytimes.com, April 10, 2011.

51. William Galston, "The White House's Three Biggest Blunders in the Debt Ceiling Fight," www.tnr.com, August 2, 2011; Walter Russell Mead, "The Progressive Crisis," www.blogs.the-american-interest.com, August 2, 2011; Ross Douthat, "Some Advice for Democrats," http://douthat.blogs.nytimes.com, August 4, 2011.

52. Eric A. Posner and Adrian Vermeule, "Obama Should Raise the Debt Ceiling on His Own," www.nytimes.com, July 22, 2011.

53. On Reagan and O'Neill, Keller, *America's Three Regimes*, 236–237; on Clinton and Gingrich, Steven Gillon, *The Pact: Bill Clinton, Newt Gingrich, and the Rivalry that Defined a Generation* (New York: Oxford, 2008).

54. Michael Barone, "Put Tax Breaks for Mortgages, Local Taxes on Table," www.realclearpolitics.com, November 21, 2011; Alan Zibel and John D. McKinnon, "Uneven Bite of Limiting Deductions," *Wall Street Journal*, November 19, 2012, A4.

55. Matt Bai, "Obama vs. Boehner: Who Killed the Debt Deal?," www.nytimes.com, March 28, 2012; Lori Montgomery et al., "Origins of the Debt Showdown," www.washingtonpost.com, August 6, 2011; Peter Wallsten et al., "Obama's Evolution: Behind the Failed 'Grand Bargain' on the Debt," www.washingtonpost.com, March 19, 2012; Robert Woodward, *The Price of Politics* (New York: Simon and Schuster, 2012).

56. David Leonhardt, "The Gridlock Where Debts Meet Politics," www.nytimes.org, November 5, 2011; "No Thanks to Anyone," *Economist*, August 6, 2011, 25; Noah Feldman, "Debt-Deal Disaster Shows Genius of American Democracy," www.bloomberg.com, August 7, 2011.

57. Robert J. Samuelson, "The Welfare State Wins This Budget War," www.washingtonpost.com, August 7, 2011; Suskind, *Confidence Men*, 462–464.

58. "Another Doomed Exercise," *Economist*, February 25, 2012.

59. "Fixing the Tax Sieve," *Economist*, July 13, 2013, 27.

60. David Brooks, "The Structural Revolution," www.nytimes.com, May 8, 2012; Robert J. Samuelson, "Long-Term Understanding of the U.S. Economic Crisis," www.washingtonpost.com, May 4, 2012.

61. Jordan Weissmann, "Disability Insurance: America's $124 Billion Secret Welfare Program," www.theatlantic.com, March 27, 2013; Michael J. Boskin, "The 2016 Disability Insurance Time Bomb," *Wall Street Journal*, July 15, 2013, A13; Alan Bjerga, "Food-Stamp Use Climbs to Record, Reviving Campaign Issue," www.bloomberg.com, September 4, 2012; "Student Loans Outstanding Will Exceed $1 Trillion This Year," www.USATODAY.com, October 22, 2011.

62. "Eyes Wide Open," *Economist*, April 13, 2013, 34.

63. James Pethokoukis, "Let's Face It: The US Job Market Is Dead in the Water and Not Getting Better," www.net-ideas.org, September 6, 2013.

CHAPTER FIVE

1. Morton Keller, *Regulating A New Society* (Cambridge, MA: Harvard University Press, 1994), 125–148; Daniel Okrent, *Last Call: The Rise and Fall of Prohibition* (New York: Scribner, 2011); Salena Zito, "Obamacare Could Go Way of Prohibition," http://dyn.realclearpolitics.com, October 20, 2013.

2. Morton Keller, *The Unbearable Heaviness of Governing: The Obama Administration in Historical Perspective* (Stanford, CA: Hoover Institution Press, 2010), ch. 3; Ronald Suskind, *Confidence Men: Wall Street, Washington, and the Education of a President* (New York: Harper, 2011), 192, 195, 316–317, 322–326; John Cassidy, "Replay," www.newyorker.com, March 26, 2012; Carrie Budoff Brown and Glenn Thrush, "President Obama's Health Care Conversion," http://dyn.politico.com, September 22, 2013.

3. Catherine Rampell, "Academic Built Case for Mandate in Health Care Law," www.nytimes.com, March 28, 2012.

4. Suskind, *Confidence Men*, 261, 263.

5. Keller, *Unbearable Heaviness*, 84–85.

6. Suskind, *Confidence Men*, 345; Peter Baker, "Democrats Embrace Once Pejorative 'Obamacare' Tag," www.nytimes.com, August 3, 2012.

7. Suskind, *Confidence Men*, 345–346.

8. Frank Newport, "Americans on Health Care Reform: Top Ten Takeaways," www.gallup.com, July 31, 2009.

9. Keller, *Unbearable Heaviness*, 84–87.

10. http://bulletin.aarp.org, October 2009; Ezra Klein, "A Health Industry Expert on 'The Fundamental Problem with Obamacare,'" www.washingtonpost.com, January 9, 2014.

11. On the poll, see *Washington Examiner*, December 17, 2011; Sheryl Gay Stolberg, "Insurance Mandate May Be Health Care Bill's Undoing," www.nytimes.com, November 15, 2011.

12. Shikha Dalmia, "Americans Want More Control over Their Own Health Care," www.reason.com, April 3, 2012; "Obama and Democrats' Health Care Plan," www.realclearpolitics.com, March 24, 2013.

13. "A Not Very Happy Birthday," *Economist*, March 19, 2011, 37; David Boyer, "Obama Taunts Republicans, Touts Health Care Law," www.washingtontimes.com, September 26, 2013.

14. www.obamacarewatcher.org, February 29, 2012; Sally C. Pipes, *The Truth about Obamacare* (Washington, DC: Regnery, 2010).

15. Hal Scherz, "Meet the 'New' Donald Berwick," www.realclearpolitics .com, November 17, 2010; "Medicare Chief Steps Aside in Political Impasse," *Washington Times*, November 23, 2011.

16. Richard A. Epstein, "The Obamacare Quagmire," *Defining Ideas*, www.hoover.org., August 14, 2012.

17. Scott Spoerry, "Obama Drops Long-Term Health Care Program," www.cnn.com, October 17, 2011; "Piece by Piece, Will Obama's Health-Care Reform Law Be Dismantled?," www.csmonitor.com, November 1, 2011.

18. Steve Huntley, "More Bad News for ObamaCare," www.suntimes .com, June 10, 2011; David Brooks, "Buckle Up for Round 2," www.nytimes .com, January 6, 2011; Alyene Senger, "Obamacare's 2nd Birthday: Help for Those with Pre-Existing Conditions?," www.blog.heritage.org, March 21, 2012.

19. Richard Epstein, "Government by Waiver: The Breakdown of Public Administration," http://blogs.forbes.com, November 23, 2011; Caroline Baum, "McDonald's Get Taste of Obama Sausage-Making," www.bloomberg.com, October 7, 2010; "Waivers for Cronies," www.washingtontimes.com, March 27, 2012.

20. Sarah Cliff, "It's Official: The Feds Will Run Most Obamacare Exchanges," www.washingtonpost.com, February 18, 2013.

21. Sheryl Gay Stolberg, "Reaping Profit after Assisting in Health Care," www.nytimes.com, September 18, 2013.

22. Theodore Dalrymple, "Universal Mediocrity," www.city-journal .com, August 20, 2012.

23. Rachael Bade, "The 2014 Obamacare Tax Wave," htp://dyn.politico .com, January 6, 2014.

24. George Will, "Government by the 'Experts,'" www.washingtonpost .com, June 10, 2011; David Brooks, "Where Wisdom Lives," www.nytimes .com, June 6, 2011.

25. William A. Galston, "Old, Gray and Here to Stay," *American Interest*, September 1, 2011, 85–88; Charles Blahous, "Obamacare's Financial Unraveling: Predictable, and Predicted," www.realclearpolitics.com, October 9, 2014.

26. Daniel P. Kessler, "ObamaCare's Bogus Cost Savings," *Wall Street Journal*, March 14, 2012, A11.

27. Robert Pear, "Consumer Risks Feared as Health Law Spurs Mergers," www.nytimes.com, November 20, 2010; "Quality, Not Quantity," *Economist*, June 18, 2011, 75.

28. "Study: Despite Popular Theory, Medicaid Patients Visit ER Mostly for Emergencies," www.kaiserhealthnews.org, July 12, 2012; Julie Rovner, "Medicaid Expansion Boosted Emergency Room Visits in Oregon," www.npr.com, January 2, 2014.

29. Clayton Christensen et al., "The Coming Failure of 'Accountable Care,'" *Wall Street Journal*, February 19, 2013, A15; Jason Furman, "ObamaCare Is Slowing Health Inflation," *Wall Street Journal*, January 7, 2014, A15.

30. Charles Krauthammer, "Obamacare: The Reckoning," www.washingtonpost.com, March 22, 2012.

31. Noah Feldman, "How John Roberts Has Undermined Obamacare," www.bloomberg.com, October 8, 2013.

32. Joseph Rago, "The Forgotten History of Ryan's Medicare Reform," *Wall Street Journal*, August 14, 2012, A15; Robert Samuelson, "Why Ryan Might Be Right about Medicare," www.washingtonpost.com, August 19, 2012; Jay Cost, "Paul Ryan Spoke the Truth about Obamacare," www.weeklystandard.com, August 30, 2012.

33. Richard Epstein, "The Misplaced Emphasis on the Individual Mandate: Other ACA Features Are Far Worse," http://healthaffairs.org, June 11, 2012; Eduardo Porter, "Self-Interest Meets Mandate," www.nytimes.com, June 19, 2012; Joseph Antos and Michael R. Strain, "If You Don't Buy Insurance, Will You Really Pay the Tax?," www.american.com, July 17, 2012.

34. Peter Baker, "For Obama, a Signature Issue That the Public Never Embraced Looms Large," www.nytimes.com, June 29, 2012; "Poll: Support for Obamacare Repeal Is Plummeting," www.washingtonpost.com/blogs, November 13, 2012; "Will Americans Ever Love Obamacare?," http://dyn.politico.com, March 22, 2013; "Pew Poll: Health Care Law Faces Difficult Future," www.usatoday.com, September 16, 2013.

35. Grace-Marie Turner, "Obama's Strategy of Silence," www.spectator.org, September 12, 2011; "Swing States Poll: Health Care Law Hurts Obama in 2012," www.usatoday.com, February 27, 2012; Karen Tumulty, "Jim Webb: Health-Care Law Represents Failure for Obama," www.washingtonpost.com, April 18, 2012; Robert Samuelson, "Obama's Ego Trip," www.realclearpolitics.com, April 8, 2012; David Wiessel, "Litmus Tests for Health Law," *Wall Street Journal*, February 14, 2013, A2.

36. Michael O. Leavitt, "To Implement Obamacare, Look to Bush's Medicare Reform," www.washingtonpost.com, July 12, 2013; Ari Shapiro,

"Obama's Next Big Campaign: Selling Health Care to the Public," www.npr.org, May 28, 2013; Ezra Klein and Sarah Kliff, "Obama's Last Campaign: Inside the White House Plan to Sell Obamacare," www.washington post.com, July 17, 2013; Peter Suderman, "Selling Obamacare: Will It Ever Work?," http://reason.com, June 24, 2013.

37. Juliet Eilperin, "White House Ramps Up Effort to Sell Obamacare," www.washingtonpost.com, July 9, 2013; Sarah Kliff, "Budget Request Denied, Sebelius Turns to Health Executives to Finance Obamacare," www.washingtonpost.com, May 10, 2013; Robert Pear, "Potential Donors to Enroll America Grow Skittish," www.nytimes.com, May 19, 2013.

38. Bethany McLean, "Accounting for Obamacare: Inside the Company That Built Heathcare.gov," www.vanityfair.com, December 23, 2013.

39. Peter Suderman, "Obamacare's Failed State Exchanges," http://reason.com, Feb. 27, 2014.

40. "Analysis: Tens of Millions Could Be Forced Out of Health Insurance They Had," www.mcclatchydc.com, November 7, 2013; Ariana Eunjung Cha, "Second Wave of Health-Insurance Disruption Affects Small Businesses," www.washingtonpost.com, January 11, 2014.

41. Katie Thomas et al., "New Health Law Frustrates Many in Middle Class," www.nytimes.com, December 20, 2013; Anemona Hartocullis, "With Affordable Care Act, Canceled Policies for New York Professionals," www.nytimes.com, December 13, 2013.

42. Holman W. Jenkins Jr., "ObamaCare Questions Nobody Asked," http://online.wsj.com, November 12, 2013; Elizabeth Williamson and Louise Radnofsky, "Health Deadline Rattles Industry," *Wall Street Journal*, December 23, 2013, A1.

43. Jessica Meyers, "Tech Chief: Up to 40 Percent Obamacare Work Left," http://dyn.politico.com, November 19, 2013.

44. Jennifer Haberkorn and Carrie Budoff Brown, "Obamacare: One Blow After Another," http://dyn.politico.com, September 23, 2013.

45. Sarah Kliff, "In First Month, the Vast Majority of Obamacare Sign-Ups Are in Medicaid," www.washingtonpost.com, November 1, 2013; "Young, Fit and Uninterested," *Economist*, January 18, 2014, 29; Megan McArdle, "Where Have All the Uninsured Gone," www.bloomberg.com, January 21, 2014; "Health Insurance Enrollment by Hispanics Is Lagging in California," www.washingtonpost.com, December 14, 2013.

46. Robert Samuelson, "Obamacare's Next Hurdles," http://dyn.realclearpolitics.com, November 12, 2013; Klein, "A Health Industry Expert."

47. John Dickinson, "Error Message," www.slate.com, October 21, 2013; Ezra Klein, "Sorry Liberals, Obamacare's Problems Go Much Deeper than the Web Site," www.washingtonpost.com, October 25, 2013; Ronald Brownstein, "Obamacare's Problems Could Haunt Obama for Years," www.nationaljournal.com, November 15, 2013; Thomas B. Edsall, "The Obamacare Crisis," www.nytimes.com, November 20, 2013.

48. Jonathan Weisman, "With Health Law Cemented, G.O.P. Debates Next Move," www.nytimes.com, December 26, 2013; James C. Capretta and Yuvai Ldevin, "The Obamacare Opportunity," www.weeklystandard.com, May 5, 2014.

49. Michael Gerson, "Obamacare in Need of a Doctor," www.realclearpolitics.com, October 22, 2013.

50. Franklin Foer, "Obamacare's Threat to Liberalism," www.newrepublic.com, November 24, 2013; Michael Tackett, "Obamacare Fiasco Erodes Government as Problem-Solver Idea," www.bloomberg.com, November 25, 2013; Sean Trende, "No, Obamacare Isn't an Existential Threat to Liberalism," http://dyn.realclearpolitics.com, November 20, 2013; David Brooks, "The Legitimacy Problem," www.nytimes.com, December 23, 2013.

51. Erica Martinson, "Utterance of 2008 Still Haunting Obama," www.politico.com, April 6, 2012.

52. Jack Kelly, "Al Gore Goes on a Tirade," www.realclearpolitics.com, August 22, 2011.

53. Vauhini Vara, "Red Flags for Green Energy," *Wall Street Journal*, October 12, 2011, A3; Walter Russell Mead, "Global Green Agenda Continues to Fail," http://blogs.the-american-interest.com, May 28, 2012.

54. Andrew C. Revkin, "Obama's Next Steps on Energy and Climate," www.nytimes.com, November 7, 2012; Juliet Eilperin, "In Inaugural Address, Obama Makes Moral Case for Action on Climate Change," www.articles.washingtonpost.com, January 22, 2013; "Better Out than In," *Economist*, March 2, 2013, 13.

55. Steven Rattner, "The Great Corn Con," www.nytimes.com, June 24, 2011; Naftali Bendavid and Stephen Power, "Ethanol Suffers Rare Loss in Senate," *Wall Street Journal*, June 17, 2011, A4; "What Happened to Biofuels?," *Economist*, September 7, 2013, 18–19.

56. Charles Moore, "What the Green Movement Got Wrong," www.telegraph.co.uk, November 8, 2010.

57. Aaron Glantz, "Number of Green Jobs Fails to Live Up to Promises," www.nytimes.com, August 19, 2010; "Tangled Up in Green Tape," *Economist*, February 25, 2012.

58. "Wind Power in the United States" and "Solar Power in the United States," www.en.Wikipedia.org, are convenient summaries.

59. Eric Lipton and Clifford Krauss, "Rich Subsidies Powering Wind and Solar Projects," www.nytimes.com, November 12, 2011.

60. Carol D. Leonnig et al., "Obama's Focus on Visiting Clean-Tech Companies Raises Questions," www.washingtonpost.com, June 25, 2011; Leonnig and Joe Stephens, "Solyndra: Energy Dept. Pushed Firm to Keep Layoffs Quiet until after Midterms," www.washingtonpost.com, November 15, 2011; Leonnig and Joe Stephens, "Solar Projects Get Funding as Deadline Approaches," www.washingtonpost.com, September 30, 2011.

61. Stephens and Leonnig, "Solyndra: Politics Infused Obama Energy Programs," www.washingtonpost.com, December 26, 2011; Eric Lipton and Clifford Krauss, "A Gold Rush of Subsidies in the Search for Clean Energy," www.nytimes.com, November 11, 2011.

62. Daniel Yergin, *The Quest: Energy, Security, and the Reworking of the Modern World* (New York: Penguin, 2011); Charles R. Morris, *Comeback* (New York: Public Affairs, 2013) on Europe, see "Fracking Here, Fracking There," *Economist*, November 26, 2011, 75; "We Will Frack You," *Economist*, November 19, 2011.

63. "Gas Glut Transforms Industry," *Wall Street Journal*, April 11, 2012, A3.

64. "Sierra Club's Natural Gas," *Wall Street Journal*, May 30, 2012, A12; "America's Oil Bonanza," *Economist*, November 17, 2012, 16.

65. "EPA Backpedals on Fracking Contamination," *Wall Street Journal*, April 1, 2012, A3; Kimberley Strassel, "The 'Crucify Them' Presidency," *Wall Street Journal*, May 4, 2012, A11.

66. "Obama Abandons (Private) Labor," *Wall Street Journal*, November 17, 2011; "Obama Administration to Reject Controversial Keystone Pipeline," www.thehill.org, January 18, 2012; Abby W. Schachter, "Energy Independence and Its Enemies," *Commentary*, June, 2012, 24–29.

67. Brad Plumer, "How Democrats Have Shifted on Climate, Energy since 2008," www.washingtonpost.com, September 4, 2012; Eric Lipton and Clifford Krauss, "Fossil Fuel Industry Ads Dominate TV Campaign," www.nytimes.com, September 13, 2012.

68. "Europe's Energy Policy Delivers the Worst of All Possible Worlds, www.economist.com, January 5, 2013.

69. Benjamin Zycher, "'Carbon Pollution' and Wealth Redistribution," www.american.com, June 26, 2013; "Apocalypse Perhaps a Little Later," *Economist*, March 30, 2013; Robert H. Nelson, "The Fractured Left," www.weeklystandard.com, April 29, 2013.

70. Michael Grunwald, "Where Did the Transportation Stimulus Go?," *Time*, September 13, 2011.

71. George F. Will, "High Speed to Insolvency," www.newsweek.com, February 27, 2011.

72. Michael Barone, "Obama's Antique Vision of Technological Progress," www.realclearpolitics.com, February 3, 2011; "The Great Train Robbery," *Economist*, September 30, 2011, 16.

73. Alex Johnson, "Is Obama's Rail Initiative 'A Train to Nowhere?,'" www.msnbc.com, November 7, 2011.

74. Adam Nagourney, "California Bullet Train Project Advances Amid Cries of Boondoggle," www.nytimes.com, November 26, 2011; "Going Nowhere Fast," *Economist*, March 10, 2012, 42; Nagourney, "Lawmakers Vote to Move Ahead with California Rail Link," www.nytimes.com, July 6, 2012.

75. "Life in the Slow Lane," *Economist*, April 20, 2011, 29.

76. "Any State with the Right Reason," *Wall Street Journal*, May 30, 2012, A12; Joy Pullmann, "The Biggest Election Issue Washington Prefers to Ignore," http://thefederalist.com, November 25, 2013.

77. "The Floridian School of Thought," *Economist*, February 25, 2012, 42; "Extreme Couponing," *Economist*, August 18, 2012, 28.

78. Monica Langley, "U.S. Schools Chief Labors to Straddle Political Divide," *Wall Street Journal*, July 22, 2013, A1.

79. "Nope, Just Debt," *Economist*, October 29, 2011, 83; "The College-Cost Calamity," *Economist*, August 4, 2012, 57; Nathan Harden, "The End of the University as We Know It," www.the-american-interest.com, January-February 2013.

80. Peter Robinson, "The GOP's Immigration Fixation," *Wall Street Journal*, October 24, 2011; "Crying Wolf," *Economist*, November 19, 2011; "The Nativist Millstone," *Economist*, April 28, 2012, 31; Sean Trende, "Obama's Puzzling Immigration Decision," www.realclearpolitics.com, June 19, 2012.

81. "Jumping of the Fence," *Economist*, January 19, 2013, 34; "Immigration Reform; Washington Learns a New Language," www.economist.com, February 2, 2013; Sara Murray, "Red-State Democrats Wary on Immigration," *Wall Street Journal*, February 16–17, 2013, A4.

82. Sean Trende, "An Immigration 'Bonanza' for Democrats?," http://dyn.realclearpolitics.com, April 24, 2013.

83. "Mr. Geek Goes to Washington," *Economist*, August 24, 2013, 62.

CHAPTER SIX

1. George Kennan, *American Diplomacy, 1900–1950* (New York: New American Library, 1951); Robert Kagan, *Dangerous Nation* (New York: Knopf, 2006).

2. James Mann, *Rise of the Vulcans* (New York: Viking, 2004), on Bush; James Mann, *The Obamians: The Struggle Inside the White House to Redefine American Power* (New York: Viking, 2012).

3. Max Fisher, "American Isolationism Just Hit a 50-Year High: Why That Matters," www.washingtonpost.com, December 4, 2013.

4. Alan Dowd, "Three Centuries of American Declinism," http://www.realclearpolitics.com, August 27, 2007.

5. "After Bush," *Economist*, March 29, 2008, 4.

6. On liberalism and soft power, G. John Ikenberry, *Liberal Leviathan: The Origins, Crisis, and Transformation of the American World Order* (Princeton, NJ: Princeton University Press, 2012) and Joseph S. Nye Jr., *The Future of Power* (New York: Public Affairs Press, 2012); Colin Duyeck, *Hard Line: The Republican Party and U.S. Foreign Policy since World War II* (Princeton NJ: Princeton University Press, 2011).

7. Henry R. Nau, "The Jigsaw Puzzle and the Chess Board," *Commentary*, May 2012, 13–20.

8. Barack Obama, "Renewing American Leadership," *Foreign Affairs*, 86, no. 4 (2007): 2–15.

9. Ryan Lizza, "The Consequentialist," *New Yorker*, May 2, 2011, 4.

10. Lizza, "The Consequentialist," 10.

11. Mann, *The Obamians*, *passim*.

12. Lizza, "The Consequentialist," 5; "What Hillary Did Next," *Economist*, March 24, 2012, 31.

13. "Timetable Reflects Isolationist Surge," *Wall Street Journal*, December 4, 2009, A2.

14. Lizza, "The Consequentialist," 9.

15. Lizza, "The Consequentialist," 18; Charles Krauthammer, "The Obama Doctrine: Leading from Behind," www.washingtonpost.com, April 28, 2011; Douglas J. Feith and Seth Cropsey, "The Obama Doctrine Defined," *Commentary*, July–August 2011, 11–19.

16. "Napolitano Stands by Controversial Report," www.washingtontimes.com, April 15, 2009.

17. William Shawcross, "Terror on Trial," *Wall Street Journal*, January 7–8, 2012, C1; William Shawcross, *Justice and the Enemy: Nuremberg, 9/11 and the Trial of Khalid Sheik Mohamed* (New York: Public Affairs Press, 2012).

18. Peter Baker, "How Obama Came to Plan for 'Surge' in Afghanistan," www.nytimes.com, December 6, 2009; "To Kill an American," www.nytimes.com, February 5, 2013; Morton Keller, "Afghanistan and Other Small Wars," *Philadelphia Inquirer*, December 13, 2009.

19. Lizza, "The Consequentialist," 18.

20. Niall Ferguson, "Wanted: A Grand Strategy for America," www.newsweek.com, February 1, 2011; Leon Wieseltier, "Darkness Falls," www.tnr.com, March 11, 2011.

21. Scott Wilson, "Where Obama Failed on Forging Peace in the Middle East," www.washingtonpost.com, July 14, 2012.

22. Adam Garfinkle, "An Innocent Abroad," www.the-american-interest.com, November–December 2010; Mark Halperin, "Obama's Good News," www.thepage.time.com, November 7, 2011; Tony Blankley, "Mideast Communications Chaos," www.realclearpolitics.com, May 25, 2011.

23. "We're Back," *Economist*, November 19, 2011, 43; Walter Russell Mead, "America's Play for Pacific Prosperity," *Wall Street Journal*, December 30, 2011; Mark Lander, "Obama's Journey to Tougher Tack on a Rising China," www.nytimes.com, October 20, 2012; Isaac Stone Fish, "How Obama Tried and Failed to Make Friends with China," www .foreignpolicy.com, June 5, 2013; "Losing Its Rebalance," *Economist*, Feb. 14, 2014, 38.

24. Mann, *The Obamians*, 11; Ross Douthat, "It's Still the 9/11 Era," www.nytimes.com, October 4, 2011; Michael Barone, "Obama Succeeds Abroad When He Follows Bush, Clinton," www.realclearpolitics.com, December 26, 2011; Dick Cheney, "Giving the President His Due," *Wall Street Journal*, November 21, 2011, R15; David E. Sanger, *Confront and Conceal: Obama's Secret Wars and Surprising Use of American Power* (New York: Crown, 2012).

25. On Bush's foreign policy changes, see Peter Baker, *Days of Fire* (New York: Doubleday, 2013).

26. "Obama Job Approval-Foreign Policy," www.elections.huffingtonpost.com, January–February 2013.

27. Alex Koppelman, "Spinning Benghazi," www.newyorker.com, May 10, 2013.

28. Isaac Chotiner, "Syria Is Going to Become Al Qaedastan (and Three Other Myths About Obama's Syria Policy)," www.newrepublic.com, October 7, 2013; Julia Joffe, "The Syria Solution: Obama Got Played by Putin and Assad," www.newrepublic.com, Sept. 10, 2013; Michael Weiss, "The Unraveling," www.politico.com, Jan. 2, 2014.

29. Fouad Ajami, "Viewpoint: Echoes of Spanish Civil War in Syria," bbc.co.uk, Oct. 9, 2012; Barry Rubin, "Syria Is the Spanish Civil War of Our Time," rubinreports.blogspot.com, June 8, 2012; Daniel Larison, No, "Syria Is Not the 'Spanish Civil War of Our Time,'" www.theamericanconservative.com, June 8, 2012; Isaac Chotiner, "Syria is Going to Become AlQaedastan (and Three Other Myths About Obana's Syria Policy," www.newrepublic.com, Oct.6, 2013.

30. A. Wess Mitchell and Jakub Grygiel, "The Vulnerability of Peripheries," *American Interest*, Spring 2011, 5–16; "The Obama Doctrine," *Economist*, December 1, 2012, 40; "The Price of Detachment," *Economist*, March 23, 2013, 37. Robert Kagan, *The World America Made* (New York: Knopf, 2012), and Kagan, "Please Don't Go," *Economist*, March 28, 2012, 85, argue for continuing American leadership. Charles Kupchan, *No One's World: The West, the Rising Rest, and the Coming Global Turn* (New York: Oxford, 2012) argues against.

31. Walter A. McDougall, "The Unlikely History of American Exceptionalism," www.the-american-interest.com, March–April 2013.

32. Fareed Zakaria, "Obama's Syria Policy Is Full of Contradictions," www.washingtonpost.com, June 19, 2013; Robert W. Merry, "On Egypt, Obama Still Winging It," http://nationalinterest.org, July 5, 2013.

33. Bret Stephens, "The Kissinger Question," *Wall Street Journal*, May 14, 2013, A13.

34. "Action women," *Economist*, June 8, 2013, 14. On Syria, Michael Crowley, "Across the Red Line," http://content.time.com, August 30, 2013.

35. "Out of the Shadows," *Economist*, June 1, 2013, 25.

36. Vali Nasr, *The Dispensable Nation* (New York: Doubleday, 2013); David E. Sanger, "Obama's Evolving Doctrine," www.nytimes.com, October 25, 2013.

37. *Economist*, May 5, 2012, 54. On the European crisis, see Theodore Dalrymple, "The European Crack-Up," www.city-journal.org, Winter, 2012; Michael Lewis, *Boomerang: Travels in the New Third World* (New York: Norton, 2011).

38. "Tough Talk, No Strategy," *Economist*, March 3, 2012, 67; Gideon Rachman, "America and Europe Sinking Together," www.ft.com, July 4, 2011.

39. "After Austerity, What?," *Economist*, May 4, 2013, 57; "Europe's Tea Parties," *Economist*, January 4, 2014, 7.

40. Robert Kelley, *The Transatlantic Persuasion* (New York: Knopf, 1969); Morton Keller, "Anglo-American Politics, 1900–1930, in Anglo-American Perspective," *Comparative Studies in Society and History* 22 (July 1981): 458–477; "Grounded for Now," *Economist*, October 7, 2013, 60.

41. "Divided Kingdom," *Economist*, April 20, 2013, 25–27; "Unions, Inc.," *Economist*, April 6, 2013, 68.

42. "I Never Promised You a Rose Garden," *Economist*, May 12, 2012, 63; "A Growth Manifesto," www.economist.com, March 9, 2013.

43. Patrick Chamorel, "Specter of Decline," *Claremont Review of Books* 12, no. 1 (Winter 2011–2012): 40–42; "Which Way for Mr Hollande?," *Economist*, February 16, 2013, 53; "François Hollande, Liberal?," *Economist*, January 11, 2014, 43.

44. Paul Krugman, "Learning from Europe," www.nytimes.com, January 11, 2010; "Staring into the Abyss," *Economist*, November 12, 2011; "1789 and All That," *Economist*, February 11, 2012, 57.

45. Niall Ferguson, "How Europe Could Cost Obama the Election," www.thedailybeast.com, June 11, 2012; on the impact of Obama's campaign on English politics, "Baracking the Voters," *Economist*, December 22, 2012, 99.

CHAPTER SEVEN

1. Meyerson quoted in John Podhoretz, "An Obama Realignment?," www.commentarymagazine.com, December 2008; Thomas Edsall, "A Permanent Democratic Majority?," www.realclearpolitics.com, April 15, 2009.

2. Michael Barone, "The Depth & Breadth of GOP Victories," www.realclearpolitics.com, November 8, 2010.

3. Jonah Goldberg, "A Bear of a Problem for Obama," www.latimes.com, September 27, 2011; Victor Davis Hansen, "Our Year of Obama," www.nationalreview.com, December 30, 2009; Pär Jason Engle et al., "Where Are We in History? 2010 in the Longest Run," *The Forum* 8, no. 4 (2010), http://www.bepress.com/forum.

4. Thomas Geoghegan, "Ten Things Democrats Could Do to Win," www.thenation.com, September 9, 2010.

5. Kevin P. Phillips, *The Emerging Republican Majority* (Garden City, NY: Anchor, 1970); John B. Judis and Ruy Texeira, *The Emerging Democratic Majority* (New York: Scribner, 2004).

6. Sean Trende, *The Lost Majority: Why the Future of Government Is Up for Grabs—and Who Will Take It* (New York: Palgrave Macmillan, 2012).

7. Morton Keller, *America's Three Regimes* (New York: Oxford, 2007), part 4.

8. Jonathan Rauch, *Demosclerosis: The Silent Killer of American Government* (New York: Times Books, 1994) and *Government's End: Why Washington Stopped Working* (New York: PublicAffairs, 1999).

9. Ronald Brownstein, "Can Bipartisan Cooperation Save Us from Stalemate?," www.nationaljournal.com, May 9, 2013; "Knowing Best Is Not Enough," *Economist*, April 6, 2013, 42.

10. Jon Cohen and Dan Balz, "Independents Favor Cooperation, Are Dissatisfied with Political System," www.washingtonpost.com, August 21, 2012.

11. Scott Conroy, "Why the Third Party Dream Remains Just That," http://dyn.realclearpolitics.com, December 12, 2013.

12. Rachel Smolkin, "The Expanding Blogosphere," www.ajr.org, June–July 2004.

13. Gerald F. Seib, "Twin Forces Leading to Washington Gridlock," *Wall Street Journal*, July 26, 2011, A4; Keller, *America's Three Regimes*, ch. 12;

Morton Keller, *Affairs of State: Public Life in Late Nineteenth-Century America* (Cambridge: Harvard University Press, 1977).

14. "The party's (largely) over," *Economist*, October 23, 2010, 71; "Lonely at the Top," *Economist*, August 4, 2012, 55; "For the Birds," *Economist*, September 29, 2012, 64.

15. "The Bitter End," *Economist*, September 1, 2012, 30.

16. Michael Eisner, "The Big Fix?," www.latimes.com, March 20, 2012; Thomas L. Friedman, "Make Way for the Radical Center," www.nytimes.com, July 23, 2011; Alexis Simendinger, "Americans Elect Sputters in Effort to Field Nominee," www.realclearpolitics.com, May 8, 2012.

17. "Shindig Fatigue," www.economist.com, September 8, 2012; Sean Trende, "A Tale of Two Conventions," www.realclearpolitics.com, September 7, 2012.

18. Laura Meckler, "Obama Hits Hustings on His Own," www.online.wsj.com, August 31, 2012.

19. "Vicious or Virtuous?," *Economist*, April 16, 2011, 38; Charles Krauthammer, "The System Works," www.washingtonpost.com, August 11, 2011; "The Endless Campaign," *Economist*, August 27, 2011, 30.

20. Dan Balz and Jon Cohen, "Big Gulf between Political Parties, Divisions Within," www.washingtonpost.com, August 18, 2012.

21. Keller, *America's Three Regimes*, 271–274; Michael Scherer, "Inside Obama's Idea Factory," www.time.com, November 21, 2008.

22. Robert Samuelson, "Who Rules America?," www.washingtonpost.com, February 21, 2011; Frederick R. Lynch, *One Nation Under AARP: The Fight over Medicare, Social Security, and America's Future* (Berkeley: University of California Press, 2011).

23. "The Chamber of Secrets," *Economist*, April 21, 2012, 77.

24. Morton Keller, "An Election in History," *American Interest* 4 (January–February 2009): 88–93.

25. Keller, *Affairs of State*, ch. 14.

26. Glen Justice, "Even with Campaign Finance Law, Money Talks Louder Than Ever," *New York Times*, November 8, 2004, A16.

27. "The Money Behind the Elections," www.opensecrets.org; Nina Easton, "The Absurdity of Campaign Finance Reform," http://money.cnn.com, October 29, 2010.

28. Thomas B. Edsall, "Soros-Backed Activist Group Disbands as Interest Fades,"www.washingtonpost.com, August 3, 2005.

29. Kenneth P. Vogel, "The Left's Secret Club Plans for 2014, 2016," http://dyn.politico.com, April 24, 1914.

30. "The Hands That Prod, the Wallets That Feed," *Economist*, February 25, 2012, 35.

31. "Obama Tops Recent Presidents in Fundraising Attendance," www.usatoday.com, March 8, 2012; Jane Mayer, "Schmooze or Lose," www.thenewyorker.com, August 27, 2012.

32. Dan Eggen and T. W. Farnam, "Obama Fundraising Report Signals Juggernaut Campaign," www.washingtonpost.com, July 15, 2011; "The Money Primary," *Economist*, February 2, 2012, 30; Nicholas Confessore, "Liberals Steer Outside Money to Grass Roots Organizing," www.nytimes.org, May 7, 2012.

33. Jeremy W. Peters, "Americans for Prosperity Begins $25 Million Anti-Obama Ad Campaign," http://thecaucus.blogs.nytimes.com, August7, 2012; Nicholas Confessore, "Emanuel Takes on New Role as a 'Super Pac' Wrangler," www.nytimes.com, September 5, 2012; Mike Allen and Jim Vandehei, "GOP Groups Plan $1 Billion Blitz," http://dyn.politico.com, May 30, 2012.

34. Mark Lander, "Obama Rewarded '08 Fund-Raisers, Barring Some from Helping Now," www.nytimes.com, July 24, 2012; T. W. Farnham, "The Influence Industry: Obama Gives Administration Jobs to Some Big Fundraisers," www.washingtonpost.com, March 8, 2012; "Of Mud and Money," www.economist.com, September 8, 2012.

35. Matthew Continetti, "The California Captivity of the Democratic Party," http://freebeacon.com, May 31, 2013.

36. Matthew Continetti, "The Biggest Myth of 2012," http://freebeacon.com, August 24, 2012; "A Morning-After Constitutional?," *Economist*, November 24, 2012, 29; Continetti, "Obama Grows More Reliant on Big-Money Contributors," www.nytimes.com, September 12, 2012; Charles Gasparino, *Bought and Paid For: The Unholy Alliance between Barack Obama and Wall Street* (New York: Sentinel Press, 2010), ix–xi.

37. Eric Alterman, *What Liberal Media?* (New York: Basic Books, 2003); Tim Groseclose, *Left Turn: How Liberal Media Bias Distorts the American Mind* (New York: St. Martin's Press, 2011); Lymari Morales, "U.S. Distrust in Media Hits New High," www.gallup.com, September 21, 2012.

38. Morton Keller, "The Media: What They Arc Today, and How They Got That Way," *The Forum* 3, no. 1 (2005), http://www.bepress.com/forum;

William McGowan, *Gray Lady Down: What the Decline and Fall of the* New York Times *Means for America* (New York: Encounter Books, 2011); Mickey Kaus, "The NYT Gets More Like MSNBC Every Day," www.realclearpolitics.com, August 25, 2012.

39. Roger Simon, "Journolist Was an Offense Against Good Journalism," www.lexisnexis.com, July 26, 2010.

40. Jon Meacham, "The Mormon in Mitt," *Time*, October 8, 2012; Maureen Dowd, "Mitt's Big Love," www.nytimes.com, January 14, 2012, Maureen Dowd, "Hiding in Plain Sight," www.nytimes.com, July 24, 2012; Jodi Kantor, "Sharing Outsider Status and a Style of Coping," www.nytimes.com, May 25, 2012. Jason Horowitz, "The Genesis of a Church's Stand on Race," www.washingtonpost.com, February 29, 2012, is more balanced.

41. Jay Cost, "The Beltway Establishment Still Doesn't Get It," www.weeklystandard.com, May 21, 2012; William Galston, "Why Republicans Aren't the Only Ones to Blame for Polarization," www.tnr.com, May 18, 2012.

42. Peter Baker, "The Words Have Changed, but Have the Policies?," www.nytimes.com, April 2, 2009.

43. Trende, *Lost Majority*, 176–177.

44. "Are Polls Skewed Too Heavily Against Republicans?," www.theatlantic.com, September 25, 2012; Steven Shepard, "Obama Campaign Criticizes Gallup for Swing-State Poll," www.nationaljournal.com, October 15, 2012; Nate Silver, "Gallup vs. the World," http://fivethirtyeight.blogs.nytimes.com, October 18, 2012.

45. Jay Cost, "Inside the 'Poll-Ercoaster,'" www.nypost.com, September 23, 2012; Silver, *The Signal and the Noise: Why Most Predictions Fail—But Some Don't* (New York: Penguin, 2012).

46. Pew Research Center, "Beyond Red vs. Blue: The Political Typology," http://people-press.org, May 4, 2011.

47. Doug Mataconis, "Republicans Have Birthers, Democrats Have 9/11 Truthers," www.outsidethebeltway.com, April 25, 2011; Jonathan Kay, *Among the Truthers: A Journey Through America's Growing Conspiratorial Underground* (New York: Harper, 2011).

48. "Pat Robertson," "Tom Tancredo," en.wikipedia.org.

49. David K. Williams, *God's Own Party: The Making of the Christian Right* (New York: Oxford, 2010); Joel D. Aberbach and Gillian Peele, eds., *Crisis of Conservatism? The Republican Party, the Conservative Movement, and American Politics after Bush* (2011).

50. James Piereson, "The Mythical Mandate of 2008," www.real clearpolitics.com, December 20, 2010, dissents.

51. Theda Skocpol and Vanessa Williamson, *The Tea Party and the Remaking of Republican Conservatism* (New York: Oxford, 2012); Salena Zito, "Our New Jeffersonian Era," www.realclearpolitics.com, February 14, 2011; Charles Krauthammer, "Constitutionalism," www.washingtonpost .com, January 7, 2011; George F. Will, "An Anti-Authority Creed," www .washingtonpost.com, January 23, 2011.

52. Morton Keller, "The Anti-Progressive Era," http://www .advancingafreesociety.org, May 18, 2011; Nile Gardiner, "Barack Obama Is Facing an Anti-Big Government Revolution," http://blogs.telegraph.co.uk, November 9, 2011.

53. Brian Stelter, "CNBC Replays Its Reporter's Tirade," www .nytimes.com, February 23, 2009; Skocpol and Williamson, *Tea Party*, 45f.

54. Kate Zernicke, "A Young and Unlikely Activist Who Got to the Tea Party Early," www.nytimes.com, February 28, 2010; "Birth of a Movement," *Wall Street Journal*, October 29, 1920, A3.

55. Brian Stelter, "Reporter Says Outburst Was Spontaneous," www. nytimes.com, March 3, 2009; Skocpol and Williamson, *Tea Party*, ch. 5.

56. Liz Robbins, "Protesters Air Views on Government Spending at Tax Day Tea Parties across U.S.," www.nytimes.com, April 16, 2009; Ian Urbina, "Beyond Beltway, Health Debate Turns Hostile," www.nytimes .org, August 8, 2009; Joe Nocera, "Tea Party's War on America," www .nytimes.com, August 1, 2011; James Taranto, "Civility: The Denouement," www.wsjonline, August 2, 2011; Charles Lane, "Tea Party Terror?," www .washingtonpost.com/blogs, August 2, 2011.

57. Matt Bai, "Does Anyone Have a Grip on the G.O.P.?," www .nytimes.com, October 12, 2011; Michael Hirsh, "What Sparked the Tea Party," www.nationaljournal.com, November 13, 2010; David Brooks, "The Wal-Mart Hippies," www.nytimes.com, March 5, 2010.

58. Kate Zernike, "At Tea Party Movement, Looking to Forge a Full-Fledged Movement," www.nytimes.com, February 7, 2010; Kate Zernike, "Seeking a Big Tent, Tea Party Avoids Divisive Social Issues," www .nytimes.com, March 13, 2010.

59. "Lashing Out at the Capitol: Tens of Thousands Protest Obama Initiatives and Government Spending," www.washingtonpost.com, September 13, 2009; Peter Applebome, "In a Suburb, A Microcosm of the

Nation," www.nytimes.com, November 8, 2010; "The Good, the Bad and the Tea Parties," *Economist*, October 30, 2010, 34.

60. Michael Cooper, "Victories Suggest Wider Appeal of Tea Party," www.nytimes.com, November 3, 2010.

61. Paul Waldman, "What Happened to the Tea Party?," http://prospect.org, November 21, 2011.

62. Seth McLaughlin, "Tea Party Looks for Strength in Numbers," www.washingtontimes.com, December 29, 2011; Abby Rapoport, "Three New Facts about the Tea Party," http://prospect.org, April 29, 2013; Doyle McManus, "Is the Tea Party Over?," www.latimes.com, January 5, 2012.

63. "Another Moderate Shown the Door," *Economist*, May 12, 2012, 33; "IRS Scandal Fuels Tea Party Support," www.newsmax.com, August 28, 2013.

64. James Kurth, "The Foreign Policy of Plutocracies," *American Interest*, November–December 2011, 5–17; Jeffrey A. Winters, "Democracy and Oligarchy," *American Interest*, November–December 2011, 18–36; Jeffrey A. Winters, *Oligarchy* (Cambridge: Cambridge University Press, 2011); Jeff Madrick, *Age of Greed* (New York: Knopf, 2011).

65. E. J. Dionne, "Obama and the Case for Progressivism," www.realclearpolitics.com, December 8, 2011; Jonathan Cohn, "Obama Won a Mandate for Liberalism," www.realclearpolicy.com, November 7, 2012. For a conservative take, see Charles R. Kesler, *I Am the Change: Barack Obama and the Crisis of Liberalism* (New York: Brookside Press, 2012).

66. "Red Tape Rising," *Economist*, January 22, 2011, 35.

67. Joel Kotkin, "The Crisis of the 'Gentry Presidency,'" http://dyn.politico.com, September 14, 2011.

68. Dana Milbank, "Squawk Treatment: Progressives Voice Their Anger at Obama," www.washingtonpost.com, June 24, 2011; Drew Westen, "What Happened to Obama?," www.nytimes.com, August 6, 2011; Jonathan Chait, "What the Left Doesn't Understand about Obama," www.nytimes.com, September 2, 2011; Robert Tracinski, "The Peculiar Madness of Paul Krugman," www.realclearmarkets. com, August 6, 2011.

69. J. David Goodman, "From Canada to Meetup.com, the Journey of a Protest Meme," www.nytimes.com, October 13, 2011; Mattathias Schwartz, "Pre-Occupied: The Origins and Future of Occupy Wall Street," www.thenewyorker.com, November 28, 2011; Thomas Stackpole, "Meet the Ad Men Behind Occupy Wall Street," www.tnr.com, November 12, 2011; on

Graeber, Thomas Meaney, "Anarchist Anthropology," www.nytimes.com, December 11, 2011.

70. Bernard E. Harcourt, "Occupy Wall Street's 'Political Disobedience,'" www.nytimes.com, October 13, 2011.

71. Noonan, "The GOP Wins by Bruising," *Wall Street Journal*, October 22–23, 2011, A12; "Talking about a Revolution," *Economist*, April 7, 2012, 92; Kate Zernike, "Wall St. Protest Isn't like Ours, Tea Party Says," www.nytimes.com, October 22, 2011.

72. Erik Eckholm and Timothy Williams, "Anti-Wall Street Protests Spreading to Cities Large and Small," www.nytimes.com, October 4, 2011; Cara Buckley and Rachel Donadio, "Rallies across the Globe Protest Economic Policies," www.nytimes.com, October 16, 2011.

73. Brian Stelter, "Occupy Wall Street Occupies Headlines," www.nytimes.com, October 12, 2011; Arthur S. Brisbane, "Occupy Wall Street: How Should It Be Covered Now?," www.nytimes.com, November 4, 2011.

74. Ezra Klein, "The Four Habits of Highly Successful Social Movements," www.washingtonpost.com, October 5, 2011; Todd Gitlin, "The Left Declares Its Independence," www.nytimes.com, October 9, 2011.

75. Eric Lichtblau, "Democrats Try Wary Embrace of the Protests," www.nytimes.com, October 11, 2011; Steven Greenhouse and Cara Buckley, "Seeking Energy, Unions Join Wall Street Protest," www.nytimes.com, October 6, 2011; Marjorie Connolly, "Occupy Protesters Down on Obama, Survey Finds," www.nytimes.com, October 28, 2011.

76. James C. McKinley Jr., "At the Protests, the Message Lacks a Melody," www.nytimes.com, October 19, 2011; "Afterthoughts," *Economist*, September 22, 2012, 40; Todd Gitlin, *Occupy Nation: The Roots, the Spirit and the Promise of Occupy Wall Street* (New York: itbooks, 2011).

77. Rayhan Hrmanci, "Occupy San Francisco Is Nothing Like the Old Days," www.nytimes.com, October 14, 2011.

78. Alice Speri, "Occupy Wall Street Struggles to Make 'the 99%' Look Like Everybody," www.nytimes.com, October 28, 2011; Katherine Connell, "Study: OWS Was Disproportionately Rich, Overwhelmingly White," www.nationalreview.com, January 29, 2013.

79. John Heileman "2012 = 1968?," http://nymag.com, November 27, 2011; Nicholas Kristof, "The Bankers and the Revolutionaries," www.nytimes.com, October 1, 2011.

80. "Democracy in America," www.economist.com, October 11, 2011; Jeffrey Sachs, "The New Progressive Movement," www.nytimes.com, November 12, 2011; James Panero, "Commune Plus One," *New Criterion*, December 2011, 22–26.

81. Adam Nagourney, "Dissenting, or Seeking Shelter? Homeless Stake a Claim at Protests," www.nytimes.com, November 1, 2011; Matt Flegenheimer, "A Petri Dish of Activism, and Germs," www.nytimes.com, November 11, 2011; Cara Buckley, "When Occupying Becomes Irritating," www.nytimes.com, October 8, 2011; Malia Wollan and Steven Greenhouse, "With Port Actions, Occupy Oakland Tests Labor Leaders," www.nytimes.com, December 13, 2011.

82. Robert Mackey, "Occupy Movement Could Declare 'Victory' and Scale Back Camps, Founder Suggests," www.nytimes.com, November 15, 2011; Malia Wollan and Elizabeth A. Harris, "Occupy Protesters Shift Focus to Campuses," www.nytimes.com, November 14, 2011; Dana Milbank, "Occupy Wall Street Movement Has Hit a Wall," www.washingtonpost.com, June 18, 2012; "Occupy: A Movement That Didn't Satisfy," www.huffingtonpost.com, September 19, 2012; Jonathan Mahler, "Oakland, the Last Refuge of Radical America," www.nytimes.com, August 1, 2012.

CHAPTER EIGHT

1. Jonah Goldberg, "Sorting Out the GOP's 2012 Pack," www.realclearpolitics.com, December 22, 2010; "Who Dares Take Him On?," *Economist*, March 5, 2011, 33; David Brooks, "The Gingrich Tragedy," www.nytimes.com, December 9, 2011.

2. "How to Fix a Party," *Economist*, May 16, 2009, 41.

3. Peggy Noonan, "The GOP Wins by Bruising," *Wall Street Journal*, October 22–23, 2011, A17; Charles Kesler, "Debating the Debates," www.realclearpolitics.com, October 25, 2011.

4. David Brooks, "The Serious One," www.nytimes.com, November 8, 2011; Sean Trende, "So Far Stability Trumps Momentum," realclearpolitics.com, March 13, 2012; Lee Siegel, "Mitt Romney Is a Canny Politician Doing What's Necessary to Survive the Primaries," www.the dailybeast.com, February 26, 2012.

5. Jeff Zeleny and Jim Ruttenberg, "In Wisconsin, Romney Nears a Tipping Point in G.O.P. Race," www.nytimes.com, March 31, 2012.

6. "Open Goal, Useless Strikers," *Economist*, October 1, 2011, 36; Andrew Romano, "Can Mitt Close the Deal?" www.thedailybeast.com, September 25, 2011; Brooks, "The Gingrich Tragedy"; David Brooks, "In Defense of Romney," www.nytimes.com, October 3, 2011.

7. "Work in Progress," *Economist*, April 21, 2012, 39; Josh Kraushaar, "Romney Scaling the Blue Wall," www.nationaljournal.com, June 13, 2012; Morris P. Fiorina, "You're Likable Enough, Mitt," http://campaignstops.blogs.nytimes.com, June 7, 2012; "The Changing Man," *Economist*, August 25, 2012, 17; Mike Allen and Jim Vandehei, "The Un-McCain Campaign," http://dyn.politico.com, May 14, 2012.

8. "Moral Quandary," *Economist*, May 26, 2012, 36.

9. Steve Benen, "Real Romney: Real Scary," nydailynews.com, April 29, 2012; "The Silence of the Suits," *Economist*, October 13, 2012, 81.

10. Sean Trende, "To Move Polls, Romney Needs to Go Positive," www.realclearpolitics.com, July 25, 2012.

11. "Battle Stations," *Economist*, August 11, 2012; Charlie Cook, "It Shouldn't Be Close," http://nationaljournal.com, August 23, 2012; Peggy Noonan, "Time for an Intervention," *Wall Street Journal*, September 18, 2012.

12. Jay Cost, "The State of the Race," www.weeklystandard.com, September 3, 2012; "The Relaunch That Wasn't," *Economist*, September 22, 2012, 35.

13. Dan Balz, "Obama Did Not Change Washington: For Each Side, It's Clear Who's to Blame," www.washingtonpost.com, September 1, 2012; Laura Meckler, "Vow to Tame Partisan Rancor Eludes Obama Four Years In," *Wall Street Journal*, August 23, 2012, A1.

14. Douglas E. Schoen and Patrick H. Caddell, "One and Done: To Be a Great President, Obama Should Not Seek Reelection in 2012," www.washingtonpost.com, November 14, 2010; "Can Obama Keep Centrist Democrats in 2012?," www.realclearpolitics.com, August 5, 2012; Paul Krugman, "FDR, Reagan and Obama," www.nytimes.com, November 21, 2010; Robert Kuttner, "Saving Progressivism from Obama," www.huffingtonpost.com, November 21, 2010.

15. Christopher Santarelli, "Chris Matthews Doesn't Think Obama Actually Wants to Be President," www.businessinsider.com, November 21,

2011; Walter Russell Mead, "A President at Bay," http://blogs.the-american-interest.com, November 6, 2010; Peter Nicholas, "Obama's 'New Foundation' Gives Way—Maybe to a Catchier Catchphrase," www.latimes.com, February 9, 2011.

16. Peter Baker, "Obama Says Vote Turned on Economy," www.nytimes.com, November 7, 2010; Anne E. Kornblut, "'Soul-Searching' Obama Aides: Democrats' Midterm Election Losses a Wake-Up Call," www.washingtonpost.com, November 14, 2010; Ezra Klein, "With a Second Term Go Obama's Accomplishments," www.washingtonpost.com, February 20, 2012.

17. Charles Blow, "Inconvenient Income Inequality," www.nytimes.com, December 16, 2011.

18. Ross Douthat, "The Bully Populist," www.nytimes.com, January 25, 2012; Jim Vandehei, "The Political Transformation of Barack Obama," www.politico.com, February 9, 2012.

19. "Budget Plan Has Familiar Ring," *Wall Street Journal*, February 7, 2012.

20. Jonathan Easley and Amie Parnes, "President Obama to Hold First Press Conference of the Year on Super Tuesday," www.thehill.com, March 6, 2012; Frank Bruni, "Captain America?," www.nytimes.com, June 25, 2012.

21. "Obama Plays Voters' Psychiatrist-in-Chief on Trail," www.nytimes.com, October 26, 2010; Karen Tumulty, "Analysis: Obama's Private-Sector Comment Is Likely to Haunt Him," www.washingtonpost.com, June 8, 2012; Matthew Continetti, "Wreck-It Barack," http://freebeacon.com, July 27, 2012; Fred Barnes, "Barack Pinocchio Obama," www.weeklystandard.com, June 11, 2012.

22. Mike Allen and Jim Vandehei, "Obama Isolated Ahead of 2012," http://dyn.politico.com, November 8, 2010.

23. Mike Allen and Jim Vandehei, "Obama Stumbles Out of the Gate," http://dyn.politico.com, May 25, 2012; Ronald Brownstein, "Obama's Checklist," nationaljournal.com, May 24, 2012; Ezra Klein, "Why Obama Abandoned Audacity," www.washingtonpost.com, September 30, 2012; John Heileman, "Hope: The Sequel," http://nymag.com/, May 27, 2012. See also "Hope and Change, Four Years On," *Economist*, October 13, 2012, 43.

24. Karen Tumulty, "Obama Campaign's Rough Patch Concerns Some Democrats," www.washingtonpost.com, June 12, 2012; Julie Pace and

Jim Kuhnhenn, "Democrats Fear Obama May Lose," www.realclearpolitics.com, June 14, 2012; Matthew Continetti, "Obama's Pity Party," http://freebeacon.com, June 15, 2012.

25. "Four More Years?," *Economist*, September 1, 2012, 11; Peter Baker, "Obama Finds Campaigning Rules Clock," www.nytimes.com, May 28, 2012; Peter Baker and Eric Lipton, "In Tight Race, Obama Wields All Levers of Power in Reach," www.nytimes.com, September 19, 2012.

26. Jodi Kantor, "The Competitor in Chief," www.nytimes.com, September 2, 2012.

27. "Growing the Grassroots," *Economist*, April 14, 2012, 35; "Obama's Data Advantage," http://dyn.politico.com, June 9, 2012; Morton Keller, *Affairs of State* (Cambridge: Harvard University Press, 1977), 536; Douglas B. Sosnik et al., *Applebee's America: How Successful Political, Business, and Religious Leaders Connect with the New American Community* (New York: Simon and Schuster, 2006).

28. Lois Beckett, "Three Things We Don't Know about Obama's Massive Voter Database," www.propublica.org, March 28, 2012; "Deus ex Machina," *Economist*, November 3, 2012, 32; Jeff Zeleny, "On Sundays, Tight Obama Circle Sizes Up Election," www.nytimes.com, May 4, 2012; "The Ads Take Aim," *Economist*, October 27, 2012, 29. See also Sasha Issenberg, *The Victory Lab: The Secret Science of Winning Campaigns* (New York: Crown, 2012).

29. Sean Trende, "Obama Spending Blitz Brings Little Change in Race," www.realclearpolitics.com, July 23, 2012; Jim Ruttenberg and Marjorie Connolly, "Economic Fears Hurting Obama, Poll Indicates," www.nytimes.com, July 18, 2012; Susan Page, "Poll: Romney Preferred over Obama to Handle the Economy," www.usatoday.com, July 23, 2012; William Galston, "Treading Water: Why the Obama Campaign Is Doing Worse Than It Seems," www.tnr.com, July 13, 2012; Jeffrey M. Jones, "Young U.S. Voters' Turnout Intentions Lagging," www.gallup.com, July 13, 2012, Jeffrey M. Jones, "Democratic Voting Enthusiasm Down Sharply from 2004, 2008," www.gallup.com, July 25, 2012.

30. "The Class War over Class War," *Economist*, June 2, 2012.

31. Sean Trende, "Can Obama Resist the Forces of Gravity?," www.realclearpolitics.com, October 9, 2012.

32. Jim Rutenberg and Jeff Zeleny, "Campaign Moods Shift as Contest Tightens," www.nytimes.com, October 22, 2012.

33. Michael Barone, "Going Out on a Limb: Romney Beats Obama Handily," www.washingtonexaminer.com, November 2, 2012; Sean Trende, "A Close Race, with a High Degree of Uncertainty," http://dyn.realclearpolitics.com, November 6, 2012; Lou Cannon, "Parity Politics and the Ripple Election," http://dyn.realclearpoltiics.com, October 26, 2012.

34. Morton Keller, "An Election in History," *American Interest*, January–February 2008, 88–93.

35. Sean Trende, "How Likely Is an Electoral Vote/Popular Vote Split?," www.realclearpolitics.com, October 12, 2012.

36. Robert K. Kelner, "Early Voting Reform: A Ticking Time Bomb," www.weeklystandard.com, October 18, 2012; Rich Lowry, "Holder's Identity Problem," www.realclearpolitics.com, March 13, 2012; "Counting Voters, Counting Votes," *Economist*, October 27, 2012, 34.

37. "Election Results 2012: Voter Turnout Lower than 2008 and 2004, Report Says," www.abc15.com, November 8, 2012.

38. Peter Beinart, "Obama Victory Signals New Democratic Dominance in U.S. Politics," www.thedailybeast.com, November 7, 2012.

39. On Adams, Keller, *Affairs of State*, 250–251; Josh Kraushaar, "For Democrats, It's Not 2008 Any More," www.nationaljournal.com, October 18, 2012; Nate Silver, "House Divisions Sharpen as Swing Districts Decline," www.nytimes.com, December 27, 2012; Thomas F. Schaller, "Adapting to a politically divided nation," www.baltimoresun.com, March 18, 2014.

40. Monica Davey, "One-Party Control Opens States to Partisan Rush," www.nytimes.com, November 22, 2012; Michael Barone, "States Choose Own Paths with One-Party Governments," http://dyn.realclearpolitics.com, November 26, 1012; Glenn Thrush, "Obama's States of Despair: 2010 Losses Still Haunt," http://dyn.politico.com, July 26, 2013.

41. "Women in Congress," www.huffingtonpost.com, December 12, 2012.

42. Naftali Bendavid, "Southern White Democrats Face End of Era in Congress," *Wall Street Journal*, September 9, 2012, A1; "Faith on the Hill: The Religious Composition of the 113th Congress," www.pewresearchcenter.org, November 16, 2012; "Study: Kansas Congressional Delegation Is Most Conservative," www.mcclatchydc.com, May 7, 2012.

43. "Election 2012: A Milestone en Route to Becoming a Majority-Minority Nation," www.pewresearchcenter.org, November 7, 2011; Jeffrey

M. Jones, "Gender Gap in 2012 Vote Is Largest in Gallup's History," www.gallup.com, November 9, 2012.

44. Dante Chinn, "Women Are Not a Unified Voting Bloc," www.theatlantic.com, November 9, 2012; Joel Kotkin, "Sex, Singles and the Presidency," www.forbes.com, February 12, 2012.

45. Tom Kludt, "Young Voters Come Through for Obama Again," www.talkingpointsmemo.com, November 7, 2012; "Young Voters Supported Obama Less, but May Have Mattered More," www.pewresearchcenter.org, November 26, 2012.

46. "All Together Now," www.economist.com, December 15, 2012; David Brooks, "The Party of Work," www.nytimes.com, November 8, 2012.

47. Sean Trende, "The Case of the Missing White Voters," www.realclearpolitics.com, November 8, 2012.

48. "One Nation, Divisible," *Economist*, November 20, 2010, 33.

49. Robert Daltzell Jr., *The Good Rich and What They Cost Us* (New Haven, CT: Yale University Press, 2013).

50. Joel Kotkin, "The Unseen Class War That Could Decide the Presidential Election," www.newgeography.com, August 29, 2012; Robert J. Samuelson, "Big Labor's Big Decline," www.washingtonpost.com, February 28, 2011; Charles Murray, *Coming Apart: The State of White America, 1960–2010* (2012).

51. Michael Lind, "Behind the Red State-Blue State Divide," www.salon.com, March 15, 2012; Michael Barone, "In Terms of Geography, Obama Appeals to Academics and Clinton Appeals to Jacksonians," www.usnews.com, April 2, 2008.

52. Jodi Enda, "When Republicans Were Blue and Democrats Were Red," www.smithsonianmag.com, November 1, 2012.

53. Sean Trende, "Gerrymandering and the Republican House," http://dyn.realclearpolitics.com, July 1, 2013; Sean Trende, "Why Republicans Lost the Vote but Kept the House," http://dyn.realclearpolitics.com, May 16, 2013.

54. "Give Thanks for Suburbia," *Economist*, October 27, 2012, 36.

55. Bill Bishop, "Rural Democrats Stay Home in 2012," www.dailyyonder.com, November 16, 2012.

56. Jay Cost, "American Political Partisanship," www.weeklystandard.com, February 23, 2011.

57. "The Largest Political Machine," http://blogs.the-american-interest.com, July 13, 2012; Matt Bai, "How Much Has Citizens United Changed the Political Game?," www.nytimes.com, July 17, 2012; "Of Mud and Money," *Economist*, September 8, 2012, 61; Robert Samuelson, "The Super PAC Confusion," www.realclearpolitics.com, February 20, 2012; Neil King Jr., "SuperPAC Influence Falls Short of Aims," *Wall Street Journal*, September 24, 2012, A1.

58. Michael Barone, "Web and Debates Change Rules of Presidential Race," www.realclearpolitics.com, November 24, 2011; "How Social Media Elected an Unpopular President," www.socialable.co.uk, November 9, 2012.

59. Brownstein, "Towering Wave of Alienation Threatens Both GOP, Dems in 2012," www.nationaljournal.com, August 4, 2011; Sean Trende, "Gingrich and Romney Are 'Unelectable'? So Is Obama," www.realclearpolitics.com, January 31, 2012.

CHAPTER NINE

1. Ronald Brownstein, "Transformation vs. Restoration: Which Political Position Will Prevail?," www.nationaljournal.com, November 21, 2012; Sean Trende, "The Political Landscape after 2012," http://dyn.realclearpolitics.com, November 16, 2012.

2. Michael Scherer, "2012 Person of the Year: Barack Obama, the President," www.poy.time.com, December 19, 2012.

3. Jonathan Chait, "2012 or Never," www.nymag.com, February 26, 2012; Sean Trende, "Why 2012 Is Not the GOP's 'Last Chance,'" www.realclearpolitics.com, March 6, 2012; Sean Trende, *The Lost Majority* (New York: Palgrave Macmillan, 2012), conclusion; Morris Fiorina, "An Era of Electoral Instability," *American Interest*, March–April, 2013, 58–67; Ronald Brownstein, "A New Budget for a New Party," www.nationaljournal.com, April 11, 2013.

4. Ronald Brownstein, "How Millennials Have Already Reshaped Politics," www.nationaljournal.com, January 9, 2014.

5. "Above the Fray, but Part of It," *Economist*, June 29, 2013, 32; Gary Langer, "Record Support for Gay Marriage; Half See it as a Constitutional Right," http://abcnews.go.com, March 5, 2014.

6. John Avlon, "GOP's Surprising Edge on Diversity," www.cnn.com, January 18, 2013.

7. Trina Y. Vargo, "The Non-Existent Irish-American Vote," www.huffingtonpost.com, May 18, 2011; George J. Marlin, "The 2012 Catholic Vote: An Early Assessment," www.thecatholicthing.org, November 19, 2012; "A Contentious Flock," *Economist*, July 7, 2012, 33; Ben Shapiro, "The Death of American Religion," www.townhall.com, November 21, 2012.

8. On Asian-American diversity, see "All Together Now," *Economist*, December 15, 2012, 34.

9. Sean Trende, "The Case of the Missing White Voters Revisited," www.realclearpolitics.com, June 21, 2013; Sean Trende, "Does the GOP Have to Pass Immigration Reform?," www.realclearpolitics.com, June 25, 2014; Sean Trende, "The GOP and Hispanics: What the Future Holds," www.realclearpolitics.com, June 28, 2013.

10. Gerald F. Seib, "Key to Victory? Who Has the Best Ground Game," *Wall Street Journal*, October 9, 2012, A5; "Lift Every Voice," *Economist*, May 5, 2012, 29; "Mormon Faith to Take the Stage," *Wall Street Journal*, August 30, 2012, A5; Jonathan Merritt, "Election 2012 Marks the End of Evangelical Dominance in Politics," www.theatlantic.com, November 2012.

11. "One Nation, Divisible," *Economist*, November 20, 2010; Joel Kotkin, "How the South Will Rise to Power Again," www.forbes.com, January 31, 2013.

12. Joel Kotkin, "America's Last Politically Contested Territory: The Suburbs," www.thedailybeast.com, September 21, 2012; Joel Kotkin, "Demography vs. Geography," www.theamerican.com, December 8, 2010.

13. Josh Kraushaar, "Obama's Scant Democratic Bench," http://nationaljournal. com, September 4, 2012; Josh Kraushaar, "Democrats' Diversity Problem," http://nationaljournal.com, December 2, 2010. On Castro, see "The Waiting Is the Hardest Part," *Economist*, May 18, 2013, 30.

14. Jeff Zeleny, "G.O.P. Mulls a Strategy from Obama's Playbook," www.nytimes.com, January 24, 2013; Robert Draper, "Can the Republicans Be Saved from Obsolescence?," www.nytimes.com, February 14, 2013; "GOP Taps Tech Allies to Narrow Digital Gap," www.blogs.wsj.com, March 18, 2013.

15. Ross Douthat, *Bad Religion: How We Became a Nation of Heretics* (New York: Free Press, 2012), 268; Morton Keller, *America's Three Regimes: A New Political History* (New York: Oxford, 2007).

16. Ronald Brownstein, "States Are Diverging on Polarizing Social Issues," www.nationaljournal.com, August 1, 2013; Adam Nagourney and Jonathan Martin, "As Washington Keeps Sinking, Governors Rise," www.nytimes.com, November 10, 2013; Morton Keller, "Debt: The Shame of the Cities and States," *Policy Review* 161 (October–November 2011); Jonah Goldberg, "The Federalist Solution," www.realclearpolitics.com, March 21, 2012; Heather K. Gerken, "A New Progressive Federalism," *Democracy: A Journal of Ideas* 24 (Spring 2012). For a more skeptical view, see Mario Loyola, "The Federal-State Crack-up," *American Interest,* January–February 2013, 25–32.

17. Frank Newport, "Americans' Desire for Gov't Leaders to Compromise Increases," www.gallup.com, September 23, 2013.

18. A useful review essay is Morris P. Fiorina, "America's Polarized Politics: Causes and Solutions," *Perspectives on Politics* 11 (September 2013), 852–859. See also William Galston, "Why Republicans Aren't the Only Ones to Blame for Polarization," www.newrepublic.com, May 18, 2012.

19. John Dickerson, "Go For the Throat!," www.slate.com, January 18, 2013; Noam Scheiber, Obama Must Insist on Total Victory Over the GOP," www.newrepublic.com, August 28, 2013; Chris Mooney, *The Republican Brain* (Hoboken, NJ: Chichester Press, 2012); Sam Tanenhaus, "Why the GOP Is and Will Continue to Be the Party of White People," www.newrepublic.com, February 10, 2013; Jonathan Alter, *The Center Holds: Obama and His Enemies* (New York: Simon and Schuster, 2013). See also Paul Krugman, "From the Stupid Party to the Crazy Party," www.nytimes.com, September 20, 2013; Kim Messick, "The Conservative Crackup: How the Republican Party Lost Its Mind," www.salon.com, August 31, 2013.

20. Andrew Kohut, "Are the Democrats Getting Too Liberal?," www.washingtonpost.com, Feb. 28, 2014.

21. Harry J. Enten, "The Republican Party Is Not 'Electorally Damaged,'" www.guardian.co.uk, June 25, 2013; Sean Trende, "Why 2012 Post-mortems Overstate Republican Woes," http://dyn.realclearpolitics.com, April 4, 2013; Larry J. Sabato et al., "The Presidency's Political Price,

www.centerforpolitics.org, August 1, 2013. But see John B. Judis, "The Last Days of the GOP," www.newrepublic.com, October 10, 2013.

22. "Nostra Culpa," *Economist,* March 23, 2012, 36.

23. Tim Alberta, "The Cabal That Quietly Took Over the House," www.theatlantic.com, May 2013.

24. Tevi Troy, "Can Republicans Close the Pop Culture Gap?," http://dyn.realclearpolitic.com, March 21, 2013; Sean Trende, "Are Elections Decided by Chance?," http://dyn.realclearpolitics.com, August 13, 2013; Trende, "Are Republicans Really Out of Step?," http://dyn.realclearpolitics.com, August 14, 2013; "Path of least resistance," www.economist.com, Feb. 8, 2014; Doyle McManus, "The tea party grows up," http://articles.latimes.com, Feb. 16, 2014; Henry Olsen, "The Four Faces of the Republican Party," www.nationalinterest.org, March-April 2014.

25. Alex Roarty, "How Pat Toomey Became the Face of the Blue State GOP," www.nationaljournal.com, April 12, 2013; Joel Kotkin, "Class Warfare for Republicans," www.newgeography.com, April 29, 2013.

26. Karen Tumulty, "Libertarians Flex Their Muscle in the GOP," www.washingtonpost.com, August 1, 2013; Ross Douthat, "Good Populism, Bad Populism," www.nytimes.com, September 25, 2013; Ross Douthat, "Why Republicans Miss the Realists," http://douthat.blogs.nytimes.com, July 31, 2013.

27. Will Marshall, "What Progressives Must Do to End U.S. Malaise," www.realclearpolitics.com, April 13, 2013; Page Gardner and Celinda Lake, "Despite 'Autopsy,' GOP Could Have Revival in 2014," htt://dyn.politico.com, April 7, 2013; Joel Kotkin, "How Silicon Valley Could Destabilize the Democratic Party," www.forbes.com, January 9, 2014.

28. Sean Trende, "Fault Lines Loom for 'Dominant' Dem Majority," http://dyn.realclearpolitics.com, April 19, 2013.

29. Jay Cost, *Spoiled Rotten: How the Politics of Patronage Corrupted the Once Noble Democratic Party and Now Threatens the American Republic* (New York: Broadside Books, 2012); Thomas E. Mann and Norman J. Ornstein, *It's Even Worse Than It Looks: How the American Constitutional System Collided with the New Politics of Extremism* (New York: Basic Books, 2012); Adam Garfinkle, "Broken: A Primer on American Political Disorder," *American Interest,* January–February 2013, 6–24.

30. Sean Trende, "Congressional Elections and the Six-Year Myth," http://dyn.realclearpolitics.com, May 1, 2013.

31. Nolan McCarty et al., "Does Gerrymandering Cause Polarization?," *American Journal of Political Science* 53 (July 2009): 666–680; Nate Cohn, "Obama Is Wrong: Gerrymandering Isn't to Blame for the GOP Fever," www.newrepublic.com, February 14, 2013; Charlie Cook, "Death of the Swing State," www.nationaljournal.com, February 14, 2013; Joel Kotkin, "America's Red State Growth Corridors," *Wall Street Journal*, February 26, 2912, A15; John Harwood, "When a Second-Term President Nears the Midterm Shoals," www.nytimes.com, December 11, 2013.

32. Adam O'Neal, "More Voters Than Ever Identify as Independents," http://dyn.realclearpolitics.com, January 8, 2014; "Disapproval of Congress Hits All-Time High: Poll," www.washingtontimes.com, July 24, 2013.

33. Ryan Lizza, "The Second Term," www.newyorker.com, June 18, 2012.

34. Frank Luntz, "Why Republicans Should Watch Their Language," www.washingtonpost.com, January 11, 2012; Barack Obama, *The Audacity of Hope* (New York: Crown Publishing Group, 2006), 30.

35. "While Congress Sleeps," *Economist*, June 29, 2013, 31; Michael Scherer, "Obama's Second Inaugural: A New Term, a More Progressive Tone," http://swampland.time.com, January 21, 2013.

36. David Ignatius, "Out: Team of Rivals. In: Obama's Guys," www.washingtonpost.com, February 22, 2013; Robert Gates, *Duty: Memoirs of a Secretary at War* (New York: Knopf, 2014).

37. Nicholas Confessore, "Obama's Backers Seek Big Donors to Press Agenda," www.nytimes.com, February 22, 2013; Cameron Joseph, "Rebranded Obama Campaign Group Causes Frustration for DNC," http://thehill.com, January 22, 2013.

38. Jeff Zeleny, "Top Donors to Republicans Seek More Say in Senate Races," www.nytimes.com, February 2, 2013.

39. "Brigadoon Politics," *Economist*, May 11, 2013, 38; Ron Founier, "What If Obama Can't Lead?," www.nationaljournal.com, July 31, 2013.

40. "Cheer Up," *Economist*, March 16, 2013.

41. Josh Kraushaar, "Obama's Crisis of Competence," www.nationaljournal.com, July 3, 2013; Ezra Klein, "Is Obama's Biggest Problem Obama?," www.washingtonpost.com, July 12, 2013; Peter Baker and Jeremy W. Peters, "As Budget Fight Looms, Obama Sees Defiance in His Own Party," www.nytimes.com, September 18, 2013.

42. Ross Douthat, "The Great Disconnect," www.nytimes.com, June 22, 2013; Major Garrett, "For Democrats, It's Already Legacy Time," www.nationaljournal.com, June 25, 2013.

43. "W's Apprentice," *Economist,* May 18, 2013, 29.

44. George F. Will, "What Obama and the Tea Party Have in Common," www.washingtonpost.com, October 18, 2013.

45. David Shribman, "The Culprits Behind Today's Polarized Politics," www.realclearpolitics.com, November 20, 2011.

46. Ross Douthat, "The Kurtz Republicans," www.nytimes.com, October 13, 2013; Ross Douthat, "A Teachable Moment," http://douthat.blogs.nytimes.com, October 16, 2013; Avik Roy, "New Poll: Only One Third of Americans Support Repealing, Defunding or Delaying Obamacare," www.forbes.com, September 30, 2012; Sophie Novack and Clara Ritger, "Republican Alternative to Obamacare Relies on Repeal," www.nationaljournal.com, September 23, 2013.

47. Ron Fournier, "Why Obama Must Talk to the GOP," www.nationaljournal.com, October 7, 2013; Dan Balz, "Shutdown's Roots Lie in Deeply Embedded Divisions in America's Politics," www.washingtonpost.com, October 5, 2013.

48. Julie Hirschfield Davis, "Americans Reject by 61 percent Obama Demand for Clean Debt Vote," www.bloomberg.com, September 26, 2013.

49. Amy Goldstein and Juliet Eilperin, "HealthCare.gov: How Political Fear Was Pitted against Technical Needs," www.washingtonpost.com, November 2, 2013.

50. Joel Kotkin, "Bipartisan Distrust of the Beltway," www.ocregister.com, September 20, 2013; "No Way to Run a Country," *Economist,* October 5, 2013, 11.

51. Manu Raju and Anna Palmer, "GOP Seeks to Tamp Down Tea Party Clout," http://dyn.politico.com, November 7, 2013; Anna Palmer and Jake Sherman, "GOP and Conservative Groups: The Breakup Begins," http:/dyn.realclearpolitics.com, December 12, 2013.

52. Elise Vieback, "Right Shifts Fight Plan on ObamaCare," http://thehill.com, October 29, 2013; Siobhan Hughes, "GOP Gives Health Law Room to Stumble," *Wall Street Journal,* November 2–3, 2013, A4; Manu Raju, "Senate Democrats to White House: Fix Obamacare," www.politico.com, November 4, 2013.

53. On race, see "Waking Life," *Economist*, August 24, 2013, 24–26; on income inequality, see "Growing Apart," *Economist*, September 21, 2013; Charles Murray, *Coming Apart: The State of White America, 1960–2010* (New York: Crown Forum, 2012); Thomas Pigotty, *Capital in the Twenty-First Century* (Cambridge: Harvard University Press, 2014). See also Walter Russell Mead et al., *Plutocracy and Democracy: How Money Corrupts Our Politics and Culture* (Washington DC: American Interest Books, 2012). Nolan McCarty, "The Political Roots of Inequality," *American Interest*, May–June, 2013, 68–75, surveys the literature.

54. "Mobility, Measured," www.economist.com, Feb. 1, 2014.

55. "Body of Evidence," *Economist*, March 17, 2012, 87; "A Shrinking Slice," *Economist*, November 2, 2013, 12; "Not Always with Us," *Economist*, June 1, 2013, 22–24.

56. William Galston, "Why Obama's New Populism May Sink His Campaign," www.tnr.com, December 17, 2011.

57. James Bowman, "The Cycle Repeats," *New Criterion*, December 2012, 64–68.

58. Jackie Calmes, "In Talk of Economy, Obama Turns to 'Opportunity' Over 'Inequality,'" www.nytimes.com, Feb. 3, 2014.

59. Arthur C. Brooks, "America's New Culture War: Free Enterprise vs. Government Control," www.washingtonpost.com, May 23, 2010.

60. Jonathan Rauch, *Government's End: Why Washington Stopped Working* (New York: Public Affairs, 1994), 266.

61. Morton Keller, "The Rise and Stall of the Modern American State," www.the-american-interest.com, June-July 2014; Robert J. Samuelson, "The End of Government," www.washingtonpost.com, Feb. 9, 2014.

62. Jay Cost, "The Politics of Loss," www.nationalaffairs.com, June 20, 2012; Thomas B. Edsall, "The Politics of Austerity," http://campaignstops.blogs.nytimes.org, November 5, 2011; "Big Government and the Narcissism of Small Differences," www.economist.com, March 27, 2012; Bill Keller, "The Entitled Generation," www.nytimes.com, July 29, 2012.

63. Charles Lane, "Redefining American Government through Obamacare," www.washingtonpost.com, June 25, 2012; Lawrence Summers, "The Reality of Trying to Shrink Government," www.washingtonpost.com, August 19, 2012. See also Edward Glaeser, "Obama vs. Romney: The Battle of the Century," www.bloomberg.com, June 12, 2012: Matthew Continetti, "The End of the New Deal Order," www.weeklystandard.com,

September 5, 2011; Roger Kimball, ed., *The New Leviathan: the State versus the Individual in the 21st Century* (New York: Encounter Books, 2012).

64. "Taming Leviathan," *Economist,* March 17, 2011; Martin van Creveld, *The Rise and Decline of the State* (Cambridge: Cambridge University Press, 1999); Vito Tanzi, *Government versus Markets: The Changing Economic Role of the State* (New York: Cambridge University Press, 2011).

65. Joy Wilke, "Americans' Belief That Gov't Is Too Powerful at Record Level," www.gallup.com, September 23, 2013; "Rich Pickings," *Economist,* March 17, 2012, 69; Charles Lane, "Collective Action Is Overrated," www.washingtonpost.com, January 28, 2013; "The Voice of Public Choice," *Economist,* January 19, 2013, 76.

66. Walter Russell Mead, "The Once and Future Liberalism," www.the-american-interest.com, January 25, 2012; Walter Russell Mead, "Full Fathom Five: 5.0 Liberalism and the Future of the State," http://blogs.the-american-interest.com, January 20, 2013. See also Joel Kotkin, "Decentralize the Government," www.forbes.com, December 14, 2011; Niall Ferguson, *The Great Degeneration* (New York: Penguin, 2013).

67. "True Progressivism," *Economist,* October 13, 2012, 13–14.

68. Nathan Harden, "The End of the University as We Know It," www.the-american-interest.com, January–February 2013; "The Sharing Economy," www.economist.com, March 9, 2013.

69. "Northern Lights," *Economist,* February 2, 2013.

70. George E. Condon Jr., "Can Obama Dodge the Second-Term Trap?," www.nationaljournal.com, November 23, 2012.

71. Jane Harman, "Woodrow Wilson's Second Term May Be Model for Barack Obama's," http://dyn.politico.com, November 7, 2012.

72. David Rohde, "Obama's LBJ Moment: The War on Inequality is the New 'War on Poverty,'" www.theatlantic.com, February 2013; Cass Sunstein, "Obama, FDR and the Second Bill of Rights," www.bloomberg.com, January 28, 2013.

73. Ronald Brownstein, "Courting the Twenty-Somethings," www.nationaljournal.com, February 14, 2013.; Ross Douthat, "The Liberal Hour," http://douthat.blogs.nytimes.com, January 22, 2013; Paul Waldman, "The New Liberals," http://prospect.org, February 19, 2013; William Galston, "Obama Gives Little Ground to Republicans in State of the Union," http://dyn.realclearpolitics.com, February 13, 2013; Ronald Brownstein, "Why

Obama Is Giving Up on Right-Leaning Whites," www.nationaljournal .com, January 31, 2013.

74. Jim Vandehei and Mike Allen, "Obama, the Puppet Master," http://dyn.politico.com, February 18, 2013.

75. Kyle Russell, "The Obama Administration's Close Ties to the Media," www.russellbulletin.com, June 13, 2013.

76. "News of the World," *Economist*, March 17, 2012, 73.

77. Ronald Brownstein, "What United Obama's Coalition—and What Could Divide It," www.nationaljournal.com, February 21, 2013.

78. David Remnick, "Going the Distance," www.newyorker.com, January 27, 2014; James Oliphant, "Obama Begins to Say Good-Bye," www.nationaljournal.com, April 11, 2014.

Index

. . .

INDEX

INDEX